Approaches to Teaching the Works of Jack London

Approaches to Teaching World Literature

For a complete listing of titles, see the last pages of this book.

Approaches to Teaching the Works of Jack London

Edited by

Kenneth K. Brandt

and

Jeanne Campbell Reesman

The Modern Language Association of America

New York 2015

Library of Congress Cataloging-in-Publication Data

Approaches to teaching the works of Jack London / edited by Kenneth K. Brandt and Jeanne Campbell Reesman.
pages cm. — (Approaches to teaching world literature ; 132)
Includes bibliographical references and index.
ISBN 978-1-60329-142-2 (cloth : alk. paper) — ISBN 978-1-60329-143-9 (pbk. : alk. paper) — ISBN 978-1-60329-181-1 (EPUB) — ISBN 978-1-60329-182-8 (Kindle)
1. London, Jack, 1876–1916—Study and teaching. 2. London, Jack, 1876–1916—Criticism and interpretation. I. Brandt, Kenneth K., 1969– editor. II. Reesman, Jeanne Campbell, editor.
PS3523.O46Z54 2015
813′.52—dc23
2015002013

Approaches to Teaching World Literature
ISSN 1059-1133

Cover photo in the paperback and electronic editions: Jack London in cap and coat. Reproduced by permission of The Huntington Library, San Marino, California.

Published by The Modern Language Association of America
85 Broad Street, suite 500, New York, New York 10004–2434
www.mla.org

Dedicated to the memory of
the late Sam S. Baskett, Andrew J. Furer,
Debbie López, and Thomas R. Tietze

CONTENTS

PREFACE TO THE VOLUME

This volume is designed to provide innovative and informed strategies for teaching one of the most popular and complex writers of the twentieth century. The essays in this collection add a new, and much needed, dimension to Jack London studies by uniting innovative contributions to London scholarship, particularly over the past thirty years, with the tested pedagogical approaches of experienced teachers. Its critical essays offer more accurate accounts of the interrelatedness of London's life and his art than have generally been available in anthology headnotes and biographies; they also provide nuanced analyses of his diverse works and the cultural contexts in which his canon evolved. The selections reflect the racial, gender, and political issues in which the author engaged throughout his career and that have provided the impetus for much recent notable research on London and for a renewed interest in teaching his works.

The selection of essays is informed not only by the editors' long familiarity with London studies but also the wide-ranging responses to the pedagogical surveys we received from college and university faculty members who teach London. We sent our questionnaires to individuals active in London studies, including both emerging and eminent scholars in the field, as well as those who routinely teach London. The response to these surveys was substantial. As anticipated, we found that London's work was regularly taught around the world and at many instructional levels, from introductory courses to graduate courses. There was a strong desire for more pedagogical resources offering up-to-date critical and theoretical analysis as well as expanded contexts for teaching London.

The scope of this volume—which includes essays on the author's short fiction, novels, and nonfiction—strives to represent the range of both traditional and more recent critical and pedagogical approaches to London. London is in many ways an ideal choice for the classroom, since he appeals to undergraduate and graduate student readers and offers an eclectic range of subjects, settings, styles, and political orientations. As Charles N. Watson, Jr., expressed in response to our pedagogical survey:

> The multi-dimensional character of Jack London's writings has fruitfully adapted to changing modes of literary and cultural studies. London was a writer attuned to the complex and sometimes tangled strands of ideas, ideology, and aesthetics in his own time, and these have lent themselves equally well to conceptual frameworks and critical discourses that he himself could not have imagined. Perhaps that is the sign of a writer who will continue to engage teachers and students, albeit in radically different ways, for a long time to come.

Correspondingly, the essays in our volume are broadly representative of subjects, critical approaches, and pedagogies and in the types of institutions, students, and courses considered. The breadth of London's corpus is addressed, including both major and frequently taught texts such as *The Call of the Wild*, "To Build a Fire," "The Law of Life," *The Sea-Wolf*, and *Martin Eden*, but so too are his lesser-known works. The scope of the pedagogical practices presented here endeavors to offer educators the widest possible choice of original and exciting ways to enhance students' understanding and enjoyment of Jack London's works.

Part One

MATERIALS

Editions

Because Jack London has been such a popular writer for so long and because there has been a burst of scholarship on him in the last thirty years, there are numerous choices for teaching editions. The standard scholarly edition of London's short fiction is the Stanford University Press three-volume set *Complete Short Stories of Jack London*, edited by Earle Labor, Robert C. Leitz III, and I. Milo Shepard. This important collection presents London's 197 stories, some previously uncollected, in their order of composition, which is useful in charting London's development as a writer. However, it is too big and too expensive to assign as a textbook in undergraduate courses. Fortunately, since London's work is out of copyright, nearly all of his stories (and novels, as well as much of his nonfiction) are available online at *The Jack London Online Collection* Web site, maintained at Sonoma State University (http://london.sonoma.edu/Writings/).

The Library of America published two volumes of selections of London's work edited by Donald Pizer, *Jack London: Novels and Stories* and *Jack London: Novels and Social Writings*. Paperback anthologies of stories and excerpts from longer works are readily available. *The Portable Jack London*, edited by Earle Labor, reprints *The Call of the Wild* in full and offers a superb collection of London's short fiction, nonfiction, and letters. Its price and range of texts make it a popular and effective teaching edition. A. Grove Day's *Stories of Hawaii* is handy and inexpensive; it reprints *The House of Pride* and *On the Makaloa Mat*. Similarly, *Jack London's Tales of Cannibals and Headhunters: Nine South Seas Stories by America's Master of Adventure*, edited by Gary Riedl and Thomas R. Tietze, reprints the contents of *South Sea Tales* plus a few other Pacific stories and provides intriguing background to London's South Seas voyage. Riedl and Tietze also edited *A Son of the Sun: The Adventures of Captain David Grief*. In its series Bison Frontiers of the Imagination, the University of Nebraska has published *Fantastic Tales*, a collection of London's science fiction and fantasy stories, edited by Dale Walker. *The Asian Writings of Jack London: Essays, Letters, Newspaper Dispatches, and Short Fiction*, edited by Daniel A. Métraux, brings together an array of London's writings on Asia, and Métraux provides a perceptive historical analysis and insightful critical commentary that open up new dimensions to this underappreciated area of London studies.

For collections of the Klondike stories, instructors most often use the Oxford World's Classics edition The Call of the Wild, White Fang, *and Other Stories*; the Signet Classics The Sea-Wolf *and Selected Stories*; and the Penguin Twentieth-Century Classics edition of *Northland Stories* (with an excellent introduction by Jonathan Auerbach). Bantam's *"To Build a Fire" and Other Stories* is an inexpensive paperback that features a fine collection of London's northland, Pacific, and socialist stories selected by Pizer.

For London's most popular novels there is also a wide selection of teaching texts. Modern Library Classics has issued The Call of the Wild, White Fang, *and "To Build a Fire"*; *The Sea-Wolf* (2000); *John Barleycorn* (2001); *Klondike Tales* (2001); *Martin Eden* (2002); *South Sea Tales* (2002); and *The Star Rover* (2003). The best edition of *The Call of the Wild* is edited by Daniel Dyer (1995) and features illustrations; it is not only an attractive hardback but also furnishes an extremely detailed set of annotations—Dyer personally retraced much of London's trail in the Klondike and provides information on the settings of the novella. It is also offered in a lower-priced paperback edition suitable for classroom use. Earl and Elizabeth Wilcox's 2003 Riverside edition of *The Call of the Wild* provides an excellent selection of germane cultural documents along with a solid collection of critical essays, but it is out of print. Also available is the Broadview edition of *The Call of the Wild*, edited by Nicholas Ruddick (2010). This volume includes appendixes of letters, reviews, and relevant historical and philosophical documents that comprehensively contextualize the novella.

In addition to the Modern Library Classics and Oxford World's Classics series' editions that combine *The Call of the Wild* and *White Fang*, the Library of America edition of *The Call of the Wild* (2009) in the Paperback Classics series is an affordable classroom text. *The Sea-Wolf* is available in a number of editions; in addition to the Signet version, other frequently used editions are The Sea-Wolf *and Other Stories* from Penguin Twentieth-Century Classics and the 1992 Oxford World's Classics paperback. The 1993 Penguin edition of *Martin Eden* remains in print.

We recommend, however, that teachers consider ordering the version in *Jack London: Novels and Social Writings*, since they will also get *The Iron Heel*, *The People of the Abyss*, and *The Road*.

The Road is also available from Nabu Press (2011); a good edition that includes *The Road* but that is now out of print is Richard Etulain's collection of London's tramp writings (*Jack London on the Road*). In addition, Rutgers University Press published an edition of *The Road* in its Subterranean Lives series, edited by Todd DePastino (2006). *The Iron Heel* is available in a 2006 edition from Penguin. *Burning Daylight*, *The Valley of the Moon*, and *A Daughter of the Snows* are not as readily available, but all can be ordered in inexpensive print-on-demand versions: Tutis Digital Publishing in India reprints *A Daughter of the Snows*; Echo Books, *Burning Daylight*; Aegypan, *The Valley of the Moon*. *The Abysmal Brute*, *The Game*, and *Before Adam* have all been republished by the University of Nebraska Press. Matthew Asprey has also edited a collection of London's writings set in the San Francisco Bay Area, *Jack London: San Francisco Stories*.

There are a couple of works that are seldom taught but that would be interesting additions to the syllabus: *The Scarlet Plague* and *The Star Rover*. *The Scarlet Plague*, available from Nuvision, is the futuristic tale in which only a few human beings survive after a germ experiment at Berkeley fails and spreads a terrible plague around the world. The 2014 *Star Rover* edition available from Createspace includes the stories "The Minions of Midas," "The Eternity of Forms," and "The Man with the Gash." This novel is at once an indictment of the California prison system and a fantastic tale of a man who is able to leave his body through "astral projection" and visit various reincarnations of himself.

Among London's nonfiction, the most often taught are his socialist essays from *War of the Classes* and *"Revolution" and Other Essays*, as well as *The People of the Abyss*, *The Cruise of the* Snark, *John Barleycorn*, and *The Road*. There is a good selection of the socialist essays and excerpts from *The People of the Abyss* in *The Portable Jack London*; a facsimile of the first edition of *Abyss* is also available from Lawrence Hill Books and several other reprint houses. Jonah Raskin's *The Radical Jack London* reprints a collection of London's politically charged essays, speeches, journalism, short stories, and novel excerpts. Daniel J. Wichlan's *Jack London: The Unpublished and Uncollected Articles and Essays* offers a selection of some of London's lesser-known but important nonfiction, and his *The Complete Poetry of Jack London* brings together London's published and unpublished poetry.

John Barleycorn is included in the Oxford World's Classics series (1989) and in the Modern Library Classics series (2001). *The Cruise of the* Snark is available in a handsome paperback edition from National Geographic (2003), which, unlike all the other editions, uses images from London's photo albums to illustrate the book. Another usable teaching edition has been published by Penguin (2004), which includes appendixes that reprint excerpts from Charmian London's *The Log of the* Snark and from *Snark* crew member Martin Johnson's *Through the South Seas with Jack London*, as well as reprints of London's nautical-themed essays "That Dead Men Rise Up Never" and "The Joy of Small Boat Sailing." *The Cruise of the* Snark is also available from several reprint houses such as Narrative Press.

A useful resource for London's other nonfiction is King Hendricks and Irving Shepard's collection of London's war correspondence and sports writing, *Jack London Reports*, but unfortunately it is out of print. This collection includes the Jack Johnson world heavyweight match coverage and the Mexican revolution correspondence. For studying London's thoughts about writing, a useful resource is Dale Walker and Jeanne Reesman's *No Mentor But Myself: A Collection of Articles, Essays, Reviews, and Letters by Jack London, on Writing and Writers*, published by Stanford University Press.

The standard edition of London's letters is the Stanford three-volume *Letters of Jack London*, edited by Earle Labor, Robert C. Leitz III, and I. Milo Shepard. This superbly edited edition is a broad selection of the thousands of letters London wrote.

Biography

Despite the intensity of interest in London's life, only recently has there been an authoritative biography. Earle Labor's recent *Jack London: An American Life* is the most authoritative biography to date. Before it, the best choice was

Russ Kingman's *Pictorial Life of Jack London*, accompanied by his *Jack London: A Definitive Chronology*. If Kingman seems unduly admiring of his subject, he at least gets his facts right. Nearly all of London's biographies are plagued by exaggeration and distortion, such as the biography by Alex Kershaw. Certain distortions picked up by biographers such as Kershaw may have started with Irving Stone's *Sailor on Horseback*, a fictionalized biography that helped revive London's career when it appeared in 1938. In it, Stone concocts the idea that London killed himself with morphine, despite evidence to the contrary. (London most likely died of kidney failure, which brought on a stroke—his kidneys were irreparably damaged by the large doses of corrosive sublimate of mercury he applied to his Solomon Island sores, or "yaws," toward the end of the *Snark* voyage.) Stone tried to portray London as an artist doomed by his excesses—and this does have some basis—but Stone went so far in sensationalizing London that subsequent biographers were inappropriately influenced, as were dozens of headnotes in anthologies, to claim London's death was a suicide. Labor's masterpiece solves all of these problems at last.

Some valuable biographies include those by Dyer (designed for high school students) and Charmian Kittredge London's two-volume biography of her husband, which, though imbalanced and lacking any account of William Chaney's being London's probable biological father, nevertheless offers a unique perspective on London and incorporates key primary materials. Her *The Log of the* Snark recounts the couple's 1907–09 Pacific voyage. London's daughter Joan's *Jack London and His Times*, Richard O'Connor's *Jack London: A Biography*, Andrew Sinclair's *Jack: A Biography of Jack London*, Clarice Stasz's *American Dreamers* and *Jack London's Women*, and Franklin Walker's excellent *Jack London and the Klondike* are also noteworthy. Though compromised by inaccuracies and lack of documentation, *Jack London's Women* gives needed attention to some of the female subnarratives in London's life story, especially that of his mother, Flora Wellman; his half sister, Eliza London Shepard; his first wife, Bess Maddern London; his daughters, Joan and Becky London; and Charmian. Also significant is Joan Hedrick's *Solitary Comrade*. James M. Haley's 2010 biography, *Wolf: The Lives of Jack London*, provides a fairly comprehensive and readable account of the author's life but offers little that has not been covered by previous biographers. Haley's notion that London was gay is far-fetched.

In the *Jack London Journal*, Stasz ("Charmian") and Jacqueline Tavernier-Courbin ("Bessie") contributed important essays on the women in London's life. Douglas Robillard published Anna Strunsky's personal narrative of her relationship with London, based on her unpublished manuscript, which is held at Yale's Beinecke Library. Strunsky was London's collaborator on *The Kempton-Wace Letters* and a lively intellectual and socialist. Their love affair ended abruptly when she hesitated to answer his proposal of marriage, after which he precipitously married Bessie Maddern. When that marriage became sour, London and Strunsky began their love affair once again; however, when Anna found out Bessie was pregnant with London's second daughter, she broke things off. She gives a moving personal account both of London the man and of London the committed socialist.

London's biography received an important and sensitive, if not scholarly, source in Eugene Lasartemay and Mary Rudge's study of London's relationship with his loving African American "mother," Virginia Prentiss, *For Love of Jack London: His Life with Jennie Prentiss—A True Love Story*; it is regrettable that the authors do not provide sources and other documentation.

Reference Works

The most thorough and comprehensive reference work on London is the *Critical Companion to Jack London: A Literary Reference to His Life and Work*, by Jeanne Campbell Reesman. It offers a critical introduction; a chronology; annotations of most of his works, including synopsis, commentary, and notes on characters; and a "People, Places, and Ideas" section. David Mike Hamilton's *"The Tools of My Trade": The Annotated Books in Jack London's Library* is a fascinating guide to London's reading. Homer Haughey and Connie Kale Johnson compiled the *Jack London Homes Album* and *Jack London Ranch Album*, which are heavily illustrated. Gregory W. Hayes and Matt Atkinson provide a thorough history of the construction and burning of London's Wolf House in their *Jack London's Wolf House*. Joan Sherman's *Jack London: A Reference Guide* and Dale L. Walker and James E. Sisson III's bibliography, which used to be updated in the now defunct *Jack London Newsletter*, are sadly out of date. Excellent summaries of scholarship on London are to be found in the yearly volumes of *American Literary Scholarship*. In addition, Reesman's "Prospects for the Study of Jack London," published originally in *Resources for American Literary Study* and later revised, summarize scholarship and editions. Her Oxford online bibliography ("Jack London") is comprehensive.

Literary Criticism

Although some significant critical articles and dissertations appeared in the years following London's death in 1916, and although he was written about by such early-twentieth-century figures as Joseph Conrad, George Orwell, Theodore Roosevelt ("'Nature Fakers'"), H. L. Mencken, and Carl Sandburg, London did not gain serious, sustained critical recognition or a place on college and university syllabi until four decades after his death. As Paul Lauter has made clear, before the 1960s American critics tended to concur with Granville Hicks that London placed himself within his characters as "the superman in red," his books conceived merely "on the egoistic level" (Lauter 11); these early critics also agreed with Oscar Cargill and Arthur H. Quinn that London was a purveyor of violence for the sake of violence (Sherman 132, 136, 150). But the real problem lay squarely in London's socialism, especially during the Cold War. These stereotypes began to be challenged by a few new voices, beginning with Sam S. Baskett's 1956 Rinehart edition of *Martin Eden* and his essays, published in leading journals, and then work from Maxwell Geismar, Kenneth Lynn, and Charles Child Walcutt ("Jack London"). The later 1960s brought Franklin Walker's book on London in the Klondike (*Jack London*), Philip Foner's collection and study of London's socialist writings, a reissue of Joan London's biography, and numerous other books and articles. In 1967 Hensley C. Woodbridge inaugurated the *Jack London Newsletter*, the first London journal. Earle Labor emerged as one of London's most influential scholars, especially in using mythological and Jungian approaches and emphasizing the overall symbolic dimensions of London's work. His 1974 volume on London in the Twayne United States Author Series became a key critical reference for London scholars. It was followed by James McClintock's study of London's short fiction, *White Logic*, the first book devoted to the short stories. (Unfortunately, McClintock dismisses everything London wrote after 1910.) Stasz published a pioneering essay on London's androgynous characters ("Social Darwinism"); Susan Ward and Tavernier-Courbin ("Bessie"; "Jack London and Anna Strunsky") published essays on London's women; and the first essay collection appeared in 1978 (Ownbey).

Critical work on London continued to move ahead in the 1980s. *The Novels of Jack London: A Reappraisal*, by Charles N. Watson, Jr., provided an invaluable study of London's major novels. Carolyn Johnston published *Jack London—An American Radical?*, a study of London's socialism; Tavernier-Courbin edited *Critical Essays*. Stoddard Martin included London in his study of modern California fiction, and Donald Pizer gave London extended treatment in his authoritative study of American literary naturalism. Dennis Hensley's essay on London's use of King James English is an especially useful article. In *Labor of Words*, Christopher P. Wilson includes a chapter on *Martin Eden* that examines the role of the professional writer in the literary marketplace of the late nineteenth and early twentieth centuries.

The 1990s saw less emphasis on London's life and more on analyzing his writings, including new theoretical and critical approaches from race, gender, feminist, and cultural studies, as reflected in Leonard Cassuto and Jeanne Campbell Reesman's collection *Rereading Jack London*. Susan Nuernberg's collection, *The Critical Response to Jack London*, helpfully traces London's influence on various audiences, including those abroad. Critical books multiplied: Tony Williams's *Jack London: The Movies* is the first book-length study on films adapted from London's works; Jonathan Auerbach's *Male Call* provides a study of London's celebrity image; Christopher Gair's *Complicity and Resistance in Jack London's Novels* added a cultural studies monograph on London's fiction; Tavernier-Courbin's The Call of the Wild*: A Naturalistic Romance* offers an extended study of London's most famous work; Labor's critical introduction was expanded and retitled *Jack London: Revised Edition*, written with Reesman;

and Reesman's *Jack London: A Study of the Short Fiction* traces the themes of justice, community, and imagination through London's stories to demonstrate stylistic and thematic interconnections.

From the 1990s and in to the 2000s, the pace of London scholarship increased greatly, with the publication of dozens of new editions, journal issues, books, and articles on London in print, as well as a proliferation of Web sites. A number of significant book-length studies appeared: *Jack London: One Hundred Years a Writer* is a collection of original critical essays edited by Sara S. Hodson and Reesman. In its essays, London's relationship with Strunsky (Tavernier-Courbin, "Jack London and Anna Strunsky"), father and son issues in London's work (Riedl and Tietze, "Introduction"), the mature strengths of the late short fiction (Berkove, "Jack London's 'Second Thoughts'"), *Martin Eden* (Baskett, "Jack London 'in the Midst of It All'"; DeGuzmán and López; McElrath), and *The Little Lady of the Big House* (D. Campbell, "'The (American) Muse's Tragedy'") are analyzed. Bert Bender (*Descent*; *Evolution*; "Jack London") and Lawrence I. Berkove ("*Before*") also added insightful perspectives on the Darwinian and evolutionary dimensions of London's works.

Instructors will also find the essays in *The Oxford Handbook of American Literary Naturalism*, edited by Keith Newlin, extremely useful to explore the ways London's work fits into naturalist tradition and to assess how the various critical characterizations of the genre have shifted and expanded over time—especially during the last three decades—to incorporate issues such as race, class, and gender. *Critical Insights: Jack London*, edited by Berkove, offers a valuable assemblage of London scholarship. This volume reprints a selection of seminal contributions to the field by critics including Baskett ("Jack London's Heart"), Earl Wilcox ("Kipling"), McClintock ("Jack London's Use"), Nuernberg ("New York City"), Reesman ("Jack London, Jack Johnson"), Stasz ("Androgyny"), Tavernier-Courbin ("Romantic Novel"), Walcutt ("Jack London"), and Jay Williams ("Cell"). It also features new contributions, starting with an essay by Berkove ("On Jack London") that traces the influence of evolutionary theory on London's work and contributions from Labor ("Biography"; "From 'All Gold Canyon'") and Robert Roper ("*Paris Review*") that provide succinct biographical accounts of the author. Next, Kenneth K. Brandt offers an original Darwinian analysis of *Martin Eden* ("Love"); Reesman explores the parallels and differences between the literary careers of Twain and London ("Literary Careers"); Donna M. Campbell astutely surveys the critical reception of London over the decades ("Critical Reception"); and Tavernier-Courbin examines how London's intimate personal experiences and broader cultural struggles converged to fuel some of the major conflicts in his life and in his writing ("Jack London in Context").

Increasingly, critics situate London in relation to other writers: Edith Wharton, Edgar Allan Poe, Herman Melville, Henry James, William James, Kate Douglas Wiggin, Charles Warren Stoddard, and others (Renza; D. Campbell, "'(American) Muse's Tragedy'"; Dooley; Sorrentino). London also makes interesting appearances in recent critical surveys, including Joseph McLaughlin's

Writing the Urban Jungle: Reading Empire in London from Doyle to Eliot; Mary Lawlor's *Recalling the Wild: Naturalism and the Closing of the American West*, a reframing of the conflict between realism and romanticism in *The Call of the Wild* and *Martin Eden*; and Michael Szalay's *New Deal Modernism: American Literature and the Invention of the Welfare State*, which sees *Martin Eden* as a representation of literary professionalism in which writers are paid for their process—"work performed"—rather than their products. London's radical socialism is analyzed (Homberger), and London is situated among other naturalists (Howard) for his documentary eye. Rod Edmond's *Representing the South Pacific: Colonial Discourse from Cook to Gauguin* devotes chapter 7, "Skin and Bones: Jack London's Diseased Pacific," to London's portrayals of leprosy in *The Cruise of the* Snark, "Good-By, Jack," "The Sheriff of Kona," "Koolau the Leper," as well as *South Sea Tales* and *The House of Pride* and identifies Kristevan abjection in the racialized body in "The Red One." Of special interest to readers of "Koolau the Leper" was the publication of Frances Frazier's translation of Piilani Kaluaikoolau's *The True Story of Kaluaikoolau: As Told by His Wife, Piilani*.

Cultural studies approaches continue to focus on race, class, and gender, now central to critical discourse on London. A good example is Marsha Orgeron's investigation of his relation to the dawning motion picture industry, particularly his interest in writing works suitable for film and how it influenced his style, which, Orgeron correctly observes, became more cinematic. She focuses on the "transitional" moment when print and visual culture coevolved with London's writings, using the example of *Hearts of Three* (1920), an unusual creation masterminded by London's editor at *Cosmopolitan*, Edward Grant Sisson. The novel was written after the screenplay.

As the decade went on, the centrality of questions about race in London's life and career continued to inspire debate and interpretation; in response, Reesman's *Jack London's Racial Lives* comprehensively examines the central and troubling aspect of race in his writing and provides a critical biography of London that focuses on his experiences with people of different races. More recently, Jay Williams's *Author Under Sail: The Imagination of Jack London, 1893–1902* is the first installment of a two-volume biography that situates the author's creative process within the context of the publishing industry. Williams draws extensively on archival material and London's business dealings as a professional writer to develop innovative readings of many lesser-known early works and offers an expanded appraisal of London's authorial identity in relation to bohemianism, the imagination, photography, socialism, theatricality, and spiritualism.

London's Photography

Few today realize that London was an artist with his camera as well as his pen. As a war correspondent and travel writer, London made about twelve thousand photographs, mostly pasted in the Londons' albums, which are held at the Huntington Library. He also left negatives for approximately one-third of the photographs. The book *Jack London, Photographer*, by Reesman, Hodson, and Philip Adam, is a handsome art book of nearly two hundred of London's photographs that includes a general and chapter introductions linking the photographs to the rest of his career, and especially to his writing.

Periodicals

The *Jack London Newsletter* contributed greatly to London studies from 1967 to 1989, though some of the publication's articles lacked scholarly rigor. Yet many a Jack London scholar today got her or his start there and still quotes from its articles. The *Jack London Journal* was an annual that offered in-depth scholarly essays and publication of primary materials, founded by Jay Williams. It published seven issues from 1994 through 2000 and then stopped production. *The Call: Magazine of the Jack London Society* has been published twice yearly by the Jack London Society since 1989 and prints short articles about London on many topics. The journal *American Literary Realism* and *Studies in American Naturalism* have published a great deal of London criticism.

Pedagogical Studies

Dyer's *Jack London's* Call of the Wild *for Teachers* is a comprehensive guide to teaching the novella to precollege students. The Enriched Classics edition of *The Call of the Wild* and "Bâtard" includes basic but usable critical excerpts, textual notes, discussion questions, and commentary on the text's historical context. In 2004 *Eureka Studies in Teaching Short Fiction* published a special issue titled *Jack London*, which included pedagogically oriented essays on "The Law of Life," "To Build a Fire," "The Mexican," "A Piece of Steak," "Koolau the Leper," "Mauki" "The House of Pride," "The Inevitable White Man," "The League of Old Men," and *Martin Eden*.

Audiovisual and Electronic Resources

London has always been a presence in the media; the last few years have seen special programs on him produced by the History Channel, the Outdoor Channel, A&E's *Biography*, National Public Radio, and BBC Radio 1, among others. *The Internet Movie Database* lists at least 120 films about or based on the works of London. Among films available for showing in class are Peter Svatek's made-for-television *The Call of the Wild* (1997), starring Rutger Hauer and narrated by Richard Dreyfuss; Randal Kleiser's *White Fang* (1991), starring Klaus Maria Brandauer and Ethan Hawke; David Cobham and Claude Fournier's television films of *Tales of the Klondike* (1981), narrated by Orson Welles; Peter Carter's

Klondike Fever (1980), starring Jeff East, Rod Steiger, Angie Dickinson, and Lorne Greene; Michael Curtiz's *The Sea-Wolf* (1941), starring Edward G. Robinson, Ida Lupino, and John Garfield; Alfred Santell's *Jack London* (1943), starring Michael O'Shea and Susan Hayward; and William Wellman's *The Call of the Wild* (1935), starring Clark Gable and Loretta Young.

Topics Entertainment's compact disc set *Best of Jack London: Short Stories* provides exceptional readings of several London stories, including "The House of Pride, "To Build a Fire," and "In a Far Country."

Although it contains a few factual errors, the Kultur Films documentary *Great Writers: Jack London* showcases a number of engaging images of London and his various milieus that can enhance students' appreciation of his work. Both the A&E Network and the French filmmaker Michel Viotte have presented engaging documentaries about London's life.

The most important electronic resource is the *Jack London Online Collection* (http://london.sonoma.edu/), maintained by Roy Tennant and Stasz at Sonoma State University. It is an invaluable source for obtaining London's works and some photographs. It includes biography, bibliography, frequently asked questions, audio recordings, letters, digitized versions of his writings, images of friends and family, images of London and his world, some of London's photographs, research aids, resources for students and teachers, organizations, links, publications, and announcements. Also of great value is the *World of Jack London* Web site (http://www.jacklondons.net/). It too offers digitized versions of London's works, interviews with scholars and teachers, a great deal of biographical information, London's uncollected journalism, several book-length works on London, and more.

A London LISTSERV (jack_london@listhost.uchicago.edu), managed by Jay Williams, connects scholars, students, and fans with one another and with important ongoing issues in studying London. Other notable Web resources include the Web site of the Jack London State Historic Park in Glen Ellen, California (http://www.parks.sonoma.net/JLPark.html), *Jack-London.fr* (http://www.jack-london.fr/), the untitled Web site at http://www.jacklondon.com/, the Web site of the Jack London Research Center at Centenary College (http://www.centenary.edu/english/events/London), and *Jack London International* (http://www.jack-london.org/).

Organizations and Conferences

The Jack London Foundation is a philanthropic organization that publishes the *Jack London Foundation Newsletter*, begun by Russ Kingman and Winnie Kingman (http://jacklondonfdn.org/). It supports the Jack London Research Center in Glen Ellen, which holds items collected by the late Russ Kingman. The foundation aids in the development of curricular materials for K–12 classrooms and sponsors an annual writing contest for students. The Jack London Society also hosts a Web site with current author news, back issues of the *Call*, symposium announcements, and membership information (jacklondonsociety.org). The Jack London Collection at the Huntington Library holds approximately fifty thousand items and is the largest London archive in the world. It maintains a very useful Web site well suited to investigating backgrounds for teaching London (http://www.huntington.org). Another major collection of London materials, the Jack London Collection, is housed at the Merrill Library at Utah State University (https://library.usu.edu/specol/digitalexhibits/jacklondon/index.htm). The Jack London Collection at Sonoma State University Library (http://library.sonoma.edu/regional/special/london.php) was founded in 2000 by the collector and enthusiast Waring Jones, who donated items he collected and those collected by Carl J. Bernatovech. The collection is especially strong in movie memorabilia, first editions, and magazine first appearances, along with materials written about London.

Part Two

APPROACHES

Introduction

London seemingly had to be "rescued" by a half century of scholars: there were many simplistic ideas about him in literary studies, first and foremost that he was merely a "popular author." Now that so much has been unearthed for scholars to consider, Jack London stands on his own critically. Yet critics or no critics, Jack London has never wanted for readers around the world—his popularity has wavered with academics, not with "the common reader." London was a prolific, popular, and influential author, and future scholars and teachers will find there is still much to discover and understand. In this introduction, we have been able to mention only some of the critical work on London, though compelling examples abound in almost every area of London studies. London is an ideal choice for the emerging scholar of American literatures who focuses on comparative and multicultural study, since there remain many opportunities for investigating this non-quite-canonical writer whose works explore topics of class, race, and gender. London certainly suggests himself as an apt subject for border and postcolonial studies. As perspectives on key social and artistic issues change, scholars, teachers, and students find something in London to address understandings of literatures and societies past and present, as well as some of humanity's most archetypal questions, especially as embodied in his perspectives from the "other's" point of view—cannibals in New Hebrides, Japanese foot soldiers in Korea, Native women in the Northwest. Interestingly, his work, set on such an international stage, works well in classrooms from the sixth grade to graduate school. London is a household name—at times an icon of Americanness—around the world. He is one of America's best claims to a world author, and in some important ways one of the most representative of American writers. He continues to attract new generations of teachers and critics just as he remains a hardy staple on the bookshelves of the world.

The essays that follow encompass a broad selection of Jack London's writings and explore crucial issues and conflicts that have captivated, provoked, and edified readers, teachers, and students of the author's work for over a century. Our range of approaches is suitable for teaching graduate seminars and upper- and lower-division undergraduate courses, as well as two-year college courses—and more. Overall, the collection registers the significance London's work has held and continues to hold for a diverse selection of educational environments, students, and courses.

The general structure of the book reflects the primary concerns of recent London scholarship, the major themes and conflicts in the London canon, and the varied pedagogical opportunities London's work offers instructors. The opening section, "Intellectual and Cultural Contexts," provides essays that help contextualize London's identity as author, celebrity, and thinker, with a particular focus on how London incorporated Darwinism and other philosophical viewpoints into his writing. The essays in the second section, "Class, Politics, and

Ideology," explore London's commitment to socialism and class politics, highlighting approaches to teaching some of his most important political fiction such as *The Iron Heel* and "South of the Slot." Essays in the next section, "Intersections of Race and Gender," concentrate on London's depiction of racial "others" in settings ranging from California to the Yukon to the Pacific islands or focus on the wide range of gender representations in London's work, from familiar works such as *The Sea-Wolf* to lesser-known texts such as "Samuel," *A Daughter of the Snows*, and *The Valley of the Moon*. The essays in the final section, "Classroom Contexts," detail course designs that focus more extensively—or exclusively—on London. This section also offers an assortment of approaches based in ecocriticism, animal studies, legal theory, and regional history that cover key works such as "To Build a Fire," *The Call of the Wild*, and "Koolau the Leper." For instructors seeking to design special topics courses that incorporate London's writings, the approaches offered by Andrew Furer and Jeanne Campbell Reesman present inventive possibilities. Others interested in designing single-author courses on London will find models for organizing their syllabi in the essays by Earle Labor (an undergraduate seminar) and Shannon Cotrell (a composition course).

London's life of physical adventure, intellectual intensity, and personal achievement is a central and challenging subject of much scholarship on the author. As intriguing and inspiring as the life of this cultural icon has been for generations of readers and scholars, his biography has been frequently corrupted through exaggeration and misinformation and has at times overshadowed his artistic efforts and literary contributions. Some critics and scholars have found it easy to succumb to naturalistic and romantic stereotypes of London. One of our key concerns has been to ensure that the volume's essays accurately inform teachers about London's biography and its complicated relationship to his writings. Instructors less familiar with London's work and biography will likely find the essays by Sara S. Hodson, Sam S. Baskett, Jay Williams, and Labor exceptionally helpful in gaining a greater understanding of the key features and recurring conflicts in the author's life and work. These approaches help elucidate the ways London's personal experiences, political views, and cultural contexts shaped his work and continue to provide pedagogical strategies for understanding his efforts to construct his identity as a literary artist and as a public figure.

London was one of the very first celebrities, in the modern sense of the word, and readers have always been attracted to his exciting life and the many hurdles he overcame; but today's readers must also remember that London's sales depended to some extent on his image in newspapers and magazines and that he was quite conscious of manipulating that image. How did he deploy his public image in his writings? How are students to understand such autobiographical frameworks? How has the perception of London as a "popular writer" who wrote adventure yarns and dog stories impeded or enhanced his standing as a serious "literary writer"? Hodson's "Jack London, Celebrity," reveals how the author's performances as an adventurer, public intellectual, and social crusader have both enhanced and distorted his identity as an American writer. Drawing on her experiences as a lecturer, exhibition coordinator, and curator of literary manuscripts at the Huntington Library—whose 594-box Jack London archive is the world's largest—Hodson recounts dealing with the legacy of Jack London's celebrity image. In particular, she focuses on the semi-autobiographical novel *Martin Eden* and the memoir *John Barleycorn* to illuminate how London aggressively self-promoted his image as a personal celebrity as well as his books to become one of the twentieth century's first megastars. Even today, Hodson observes, "everyone knows a little bit about London, and a few people know quite a bit, but audiences are usually stunned when I tell them about the full extent of London's many careers, as adventurer, sailor, journalist, photojournalist, and more. Clearly, what the general public knows about London originates in large part from his highly successful self-promotion" (Hodson). Hodson not only provides a lucid account of the development of London's celebrity image but also clarifies the enduring legends and persistent misconceptions about the autobiographical elements of his work, his heavy drinking, and the manner of his death. In terms of literary context, Barry Menikoff's essay offers an approach to *Martin Eden* that positions students to understand London as a writer caught between a waning Victorian culture and the dislocating ethos of an emergent modernism. Though London is usually classified as a naturalist, many of his themes, particularly in *Martin Eden*, anticipate modernism's concerns with consciousness, alienation, and disillusionment. As Menikoff points out, it is not difficult to find affinities between London and modernists like Fitzgerald and Hemingway and Conrad—even as he also draws inspiration from earlier writers such as Kipling, Stevenson, and Browning. Menikoff also makes the case that London's combination of accessibility and seriousness is a deliberate and effective literary strategy that should be celebrated.

Focused less on London's public persona and more directly on his literary output, the approaches presented by the pioneering scholars Labor and Baskett can be read effectively alongside Hodson's. The collection's concluding essay by Baskett, full of the wisdom of his sixty-year-long career teaching Jack London internationally, is attentive to the popular/serious writer duality in London's career and argues for balance between what Morris Dickstein calls a scholarly detached "hermeneutics of suspicion" in employing literary analysis and the ordinary reader's more spontaneous reactions of "wonder and surprise," both important factors in London's continuing appeal to scholars, teachers, and students around the world (qtd. in Baskett, in this volume). Along with discerning discussions of "To Build a Fire" and *The Call of the Wild*, Labor details his method of teaching the short story "The Night-Born" using the psychoanalytic theories of Jungian psychology. Labor also provides a descriptive rationale for the organization of his single-author undergraduate seminar on Jack London.

Using the selections in *The Portable Jack London*, edited by Labor, Cotrell shares his own design and teaching strategies for his London-based composition course. Drawing on ideas from the ecocritical theorists Lawrence Buell, Yi Fu Tuan, and Harold Fromm, Cotrell describes how he positions first-year students to read stories such as "Love of Life" and "All Gold Canyon" in a way that helps them "focus on the mental and physical challenges of adapting to their new surroundings." He also has students read "The Apostate" and selections from *People of the Abyss* to develop research paper topics on man-made environments such as cities and factories.

Although, London is still known today by most as the author of *The Call of the Wild* and "To Build a Fire," many of his other writings have enjoyed a resurgence of critical attention over the last three decades. As Aaron Shaheen remarks in his response to our pedagogical survey,

> I show [students] how London's more political works have been marginalized. Those students familiar with *White Fang* and *The Call of the Wild* are surprised to learn of London's proletarian sympathies and are interested to know why/how this part of London is muted. This initial surprise makes for a great introduction to his controversial social views.

Several of the essays address London's complex relation to the socialist movement and clarify the socialist views he practiced and wrote about in his essays and speeches, as well as his fiction. They characterize the distinguishing features of his literary socialism and investigate how London's personal politics finds outlets for expression in his creative writings. It is a fitting irony that one of the things that formerly kept critics away from London, his radical social thought and critique of capitalism in the United States, is now what attracts many new scholars and teachers to his works. A number of essays attest to the continuing relevance of the political aspects of London's life and work. Respondents to our pedagogical survey revealed a strong sense that presenting London's political radicalism along with his socialist ideology enriched their teaching experiences and roused the intellectual curiosity of students who previously perceived the author as a mere "adventure" writer. Although he was a member of the Socialist Party for twenty years, his political views often deviated from party lines. London reveals his passionate commitment to socialism most directly in his essays and speeches, and, as Jeanne C. Reesman has remarked, while little of his fiction is overtly political, "there is scarcely a story that does not demonstrate the author's devotion to a sense of justice and identification with the common man and woman" ("Prospects" 148).

Jay Williams's "Jack London and Socialism" provides a comprehensive view of London's involvement with socialism and its influence on his writing. Its political focus adds another dimension to Hodson's, Labor's, and Baskett's essays and also can be read as an effective overture to other essays that focus on related political issues, such as those by Paul Lauter, Robert M. Dowling, and Shaheen. Williams maintains that "London was a consistent advocate for a particular ideology of American socialism. He was neither a propagandist (in the modern sense of the word) nor a theorist. He both advocated and practiced socialism, and what he practiced coincided with what he wrote." Williams examines several of the author's early socialist essays and, drawing on Marx and Engel's figure of the specter, explores how London fuses spiritualism and politics. Socialism for London, Williams claims, "was a specter, but not because it was created by the bourgeoisie to scare the people away from revolutionary change; it was a specter because it was a very real power, a power invested in the working class that would violently change American society." As Williams's essay and the work by other contributors make clear, London's radical views on class conflict and his commitment to socialist ideals were abiding influences on the content and themes of his writings, and they highlight the author's struggle to resolve his competing ideological attractions to such opposite poles as individualism and egalitarianism. Lauter's "Teaching *The Iron Heel*," for instance, closely examines the compound narrative frames that structure the novel. He also provides a close reading of the novel's first nine expository chapters, which differ from the decidedly more action-driven last sixteen chapters. For Lauter, the first nine chapters "represent London's efforts to bring the ideas of scientific socialism to as wide an audience as he could reach." Taking a different tack, Shaheen's essay on *The Iron Heel* describes specific classroom procedures for instructors to introduce students to the dialectic structure of rationality and myth as exposited by Max Horkheimer and Theodor Adorno in *Dialectic of Enlightenment*. This pedagogical process increases their understanding of Western history and prompts them to reconsider the often indefinite distinctions between twentieth-century leftist and rightist totalitarian regimes. Dowling, in his essay, notes that London "wrote 'South of the Slot' as a satiric treatment of middle-class progressives' naive and self-serving attempts to engage in the notorious class struggle that in many ways defines turn-of-the-twentieth-century America." Dowling's approach illustrates how instructors can use the framework of Antonio Gramsci's concepts of hegemony and counterhegemony and contradictory consciousness to enhance students' understanding of the class divisions London depicts in the story.

Many instructors will also find valuable connections among essays from different sections in the book. Essays focusing on *The Call of the Wild*, for example, demonstrate that this novel is unusually amenable to a variety of approaches. Kenneth K. Brandt's essay addresses the novel's relation to social Darwinism and to Thomas Henry Huxley's ideas of ethical adaptation using the seemingly incongruous popular culture icons Gordon Gekko, from Oliver Stone's 1987 film *Wall Street*, and Rudolph the Red-Nosed Reindeer. Michael Lundblad further widens the biological frame for reading *The Call of the Wild* by drawing on recent scholarship in animal and animality studies. He explores the moral and philosophical distinctions between human and nonhuman animals and the representation of animality and, through a provocative examination of Buck and his human counterparts, shows how London's supposed evolutionary discourse covertly discloses larger cultural anxieties regarding homoerotic desire. Drawing on a different set of cultural resources in her Law and Literature course, Alicia Mischa Renfroe uses *The Call of the Wild*, along with *The People of the Abyss*, to explore contending definitions of legal selfhood as proposed by Enlightenment "natural law." She offers a pedagogical approach that compares the positions of Hobbes, Locke, and Rousseau with London's naturalist views of poverty and Upton Sinclair's industrial nightmare in *The Jungle*. Read alongside each other, these essays provide insights on London's most famous novel that can be readily integrated into an array of classroom settings.

Keith Newlin explores *The Sea-Wolf* as primarily a novel of ideas. Asking students to consider contemporary cinematic superhero melodramas that feature a good guys versus bad guys scheme, he demonstrates how the novel can be taught as "a melodramatic battle between [the] opposing philosophies" of socialist ideals and Herbert Spencer's social Darwinist individualism. Jeff Jaeckle also makes use of film in his essay, which describes an approach to teaching *The Sea-Wolf* by using Michael Curtiz's 1941 film adaptation of the novel to highlight London's blurring of gender roles and complicated depictions of sex, homoeroticism, and androgyny. Anita Duneer also explores gender and androgyny in the novel through a method that encourages students to interrogate the dichotomies that structure the narrative—such as romance/realism, idealism/materialism, leisure class / working class, civilization/savagery. Duneer posits that London's "interest in androgyny—and what it signifies as an incorporation of opposing sexual or gendered attributes—implies, in a broader sense, his search for a philosophical middle ground that resists the various polarizations that he dramatizes throughout the novel." Turning to one of London's most unusual stories, "Samuel," which teems with lush understories of meaning, Donna M. Campbell examines how cultural and anthropological elements of this story—including superstition, dialect, naming, archetypes, myths and fairy tales—can be presented effectively in the classroom.

As Duneer's and other approaches in the collection reveal, much of London's work unfolds as an interplay of dichotomous political or philosophical positions, and throughout his fiction in particular London tends to juxtapose the major intellectual movements and conflicts of his day to fuel thematic tensions in his novels and stories. As Susan Nuernberg has noted, the view that London was intellectually and philosophically "confused" has been a prominent issue in London studies. Early scholars were inclined to see him as a "mess of contradictions" (xxiii). Yet London's later critical readers have attended to the complex ways his weltanschauung accommodated thinkers such as Darwin, Marx, Nietzsche, and Jung and how London might oppose competing discourses of colonizers and colonized in many of his stories, such as "Mauki," "The Chinago," "When Alice Told Her Soul" or "The Water Baby."

When the Klondike gold rush occurred in 1897, the nation's collective mindset defined gold as the new test of character. Although London was unsuccessful at gold mining, he claimed to have gained his perspective in the Klondike and emerged from the snowfields to pursue the craft of writing, not so much to portray individual heroics (especially white, Kipling-esque zone conquerors) as subjects but more to show how conflicts within communities—especially racial and class conflicts—shape individual character. He would go on to explore such conflicts in many settings, following a lifelong pattern of attempting to describe an "alien" community from the inside out—to belong imaginatively to that community. This curiosity about diverse peoples and places, building on his unstable childhood psychological formations of class and race and complicated by what he thought of as the scientific authority of race theory or racialism, resulted in a pattern of identifying with nonwhite characters in a short story even as he might foment his social Darwinist theories of racial superiority in a newspaper column. Several of the essays offer innovative approaches to teaching lesser-known but important works as part of a project to describe the author's nontraditional treatments of race. In stories such as "Mauki" and "The House of Pride," London unambiguously demonstrates the moral bankruptcy of white dominance. In stories such as "The Inevitable White Man," he satirizes racist, capitalist, and imperialist values. Many of his best tales tell of the failures of different races to communicate with one another. And yet whenever he is weakest in his writing, the cause is usually to be found in his racialist beliefs.

Concerning gender in his fiction, London experimented with gender roles, sexuality, and androgyny. Many critics, such as Jaeckle and Duneer explore the gender-bending, androgyny, homosexual, and Darwinian sexual competition of *The Sea-Wolf*, and that London drew many young but independent Indian women as heroines in the Klondike stories and modeled characters upon his adventurous, athletic, and sexually liberated wife, Charmian Kittredge London. María DeGuzmán and Debbie López analyze race and gender in *Martin Eden*, while Andrew J. Furer examines London's bewildering but powerful portrayal of "new womanhood" in *A Daughter of the Snows*.

London employs a largely feminist narrative perspective in *Burning Daylight*, *The Valley of the Moon*, and *The Little Lady of the Big House*, even while he supports a certain mobility for the part of white male "pioneers" of California, Gina Rossetti's essay on *The Valley of the Moon* addresses this dynamic in examining how racial identity is often linked to American identity. Rossetti situates *The Valley of the Moon* within the ideological context of the era to demonstrate how instructors can effectively reveal to students how notions of nativism and pastoral romance create a "kind of nostalgia—a backward glance to an era that never was." Her approach also usefully details how teacher-scholars can cultivate students' awareness of their own cultural frames of reference, which helps to avoid "short-circuiting" class discussions about race and American identity. As a counterpoint, Terry Reilly's essay offers a fascinating mix of cultural interpretations from his multicultural student population of Alaskan Natives, military personnel, and students from the lower 48 and from foreign countries to show how students can best understand their differing ideas of the function(s) of literature.

The volume's essays provide recommendations on teaching London in classrooms from the undergraduate to doctoral level (see, e.g., Reesman's essay on teaching Literatures of the South Pacific to students in a cross-cultural, transnational PhD in English program). Thus London's presence in the college or university classroom is one that presents an exciting diversity of settings, subjects, and styles, a presence certain to stimulate critical reading, writing, and discussion—and one that also imparts more than a little taste of adventure. Similarly, the pedagogical expeditions in this volume offer an enlivening array of original theoretical insights into London's work that will deepen the teacher-scholar's understanding of the complexity of his canon as well as the political-historical contexts that shaped his writings.

Jack London, Celebrity

Sara S. Hodson

> Now I don't know anything about magazine affairs, but as a tyro, it seems to me that certain advantages ought to accrue to *The Pacific Monthly* through publishing this stuff. You did the Jack London advertising while you were bringing out *Martin Eden*. This advertising, to a certain extent represents so much ploughed ground. I should imagine that the simplest sort of announcement to the effect that you had practically a year's supply of further matter from Jack London would be sufficient seed for the aforesaid ploughed ground. (London, *Letters* 2: 824)

When Jack London wrote this letter in 1909 to Lucius C. Pease, the editor of the *Pacific Monthly*, pressing his case for a higher rate of authorial pay based on his considerable fame, he was an established, celebrated writer whose renown stretched throughout the United States and beyond. His novel *Martin Eden* was nearly at the end of its serial publication in the *Pacific Monthly* and would appear in book form from Macmillan in another month. With his customary brash self-confidence and in the full assurance of his reputation and popularity, London knew he could demand and receive the highest pay rates for his stories and essays.

In the decade leading up to the publication of *Martin Eden*, the young author had burst on the public scene and captured readers' imaginations with his robust tales of adventure and headline-grabbing exploits. In 1899, the year after London returned from a gold-seeking sojourn in the Klondike, his tales of the opportunities and hardships of life in the northland began to appear in such periodicals as the *Atlantic Monthly*, *McClure's*, *Overland Monthly*, the *Youth's Companion*, and *Harper's Bazaar*. These stories, with their vivid, muscular prose and strong themes of survival and peril, stood in stark contrast to the gentler magazine fare hitherto familiar to readers. The reading public embraced London, and by 1900 his first book, a volume of Klondike short stories entitled *The Son of the Wolf*, appeared from Houghton Mifflin. More books followed in the next two years, and then, in 1903, the publication of three important, disparate books secured London's status as one of the most popular and famous writers of his time: the classic novel *The Call of the Wild*; *The People of the Abyss*, his account of poverty in the East End of the city of London; and *The Kempton-Wace Letters*, a treatise on love, written with Anna Strunsky. Each volume drew scores of reviews and critical analyses, keeping London's name prominently in the media for much of the year. Publication of his major titles *The Sea-Wolf* in 1904 and *White Fang* two years later, together with a steady outpouring of other books as well as stories in periodicals, further burnished London's already considerable celebrity status. After publication of *Martin Eden* in 1909, London continued to issue novels, collections of short stories, and nonfiction works, including *The House of Pride* (1912), *The Valley of the Moon* (1913), and *The Star Rover* (1915). By his death in 1916 at the age of forty, Jack London had published an astonishing fifty books.

The American public watched eagerly, not only for the latest titles from London's pen but also for the latest accounts of his adventures, all of which made headlines. Following his Klondike exploits in 1897–98, London lived for seven weeks in 1902 among the poor and homeless in the East End of London, served as a war correspondent and photojournalist for the Russo-Japanese War in 1904, and filed the first eyewitness account of the 1906 San Francisco earthquake and fire ("Story of an Eyewitness"). In 1907 London launched the grandest of his adventures when he sailed with his wife, Charmian, and a small crew on a projected round-the-world voyage on the *Snark* (the boat whose construction he oversaw), writing tales and photographing the islands and their people, following in the paths of such writers as Herman Melville and Robert Louis Stevenson. On returning to his California ranch, London embarked on a project to farm the land according to ecological principles designed to preserve and renew the soil. In 1912, he returned to the sea for a five-month voyage with Charmian around Cape Horn aboard the *Dirigo*. Two years later, he reported for *Collier's* magazine on the United States occupation of Vera Cruz ("Mexico's Army").

By virtue of both his writings and exploits, Jack London was larger than life, a celebrity before the concept was widely known. As a product of the American West in the latter half of the nineteenth century, London was perfectly situated to invent himself as a writer and celebrity. The young nation offered seemingly endless opportunities for achieving fame, for several reasons. Its society looked to the future, not to the past; it was the land of opportunity; and it presented the chance for ambitious, enterprising individuals to invent themselves. London, like others of his time and before him, took hold of his own life and parlayed his talents and charisma into international celebrity. Leo Braudy, in *The Frenzy of Renown*, has described American democracy as the successor to eighteenth-century Europe; under America's democracy, the new industrial society toppled the strict social demarcations that had prevailed for centuries (7, 14). In the past, fame was achieved by virtue of one's lofty station in life, a station into which one was born. But the social changes that began in the eighteenth century meant that people could define themselves beyond the limitations of class and family. Fame came within reach of anyone. Humble beginnings no longer dictated the heights to which one could climb.

Born into this climate of opportunity, London also was likely motivated by forces both in himself and surrounding his birth and early life. David Giles, in his essay "The Quest for Fame," cites D. Keith Simonton's identification of factors contributing to greatness (475). One factor is adversity in early life, leading to a strong determination to succeed. London surely qualifies as overcoming adversity, given his illegitimate birth to a mother who tried to abort him and his childhood of such abject poverty that he was forced to leave school at an early age and embark on years of menial wage earning as a "work beast" (London, *John Barleycorn* 965). His writings, both early and late, contain abundant references to his miserable childhood and youth and to his determination to escape stultifying poverty. A second factor noted by Giles that may have contributed to London's drive for success and fame is early mental stimulation. London's discovery of the Oakland Public Library and the worlds it opened for his young mind is a well-known feature of his formative years. This awakening of his love of books and reading, coupled with his drive to escape poverty and adversity, surely contributed to his pursuit of fame and success as a writer.

To Giles's motivating factors of early adversity and mental stimulation we may add single-mindedness, a factor also identified by Braudy (19). London, like many famous figures, was possessed by a single goal in his path to fame. From the moment he decided to become a writer, he hewed to this goal, no matter what obstacles threatened to deflect him from his path. Every time he had to pawn his typewriter and return to the life of a work beast, he did so with the firm conviction that the situation was only temporary and that he would soon resume his course toward full-time writing. When he was strongly pressured by family to take a post office job for its steady income and job security, he steadfastly refused, insisting that he would become a writer.

With his single-minded ambition to write and his recognition of American opportunity, London strode confidently toward the fame that would set him apart and ensure that his books would be best sellers. To attain this goal, he had to become what Braudy calls a "socially acceptable individualist" (8). That is, he needed to be unusual enough to fascinate but sufficiently familiar not to threaten. London seems to fulfill both parts of this paradox. He embodies the American duality of "conformity" and "individualism," in Braudy's words (8, 10). Throughout his life, he repeatedly emphasized that he was not an individualist. In support of this claim, he espoused socialist views that allied him to the common man and woman, and he wrote extensively on behalf of socialism. He also wrote stories, novels, and a nonfiction work (*The People of the Abyss*) that passionately advocated a better life for the downtrodden and poor. In this, he clearly identified with them by virtue of his humble origins.

His individuality, however, is evident, denials notwithstanding. He was a self-made man and was fiercely proud of being so, and he set himself apart from his contemporaries by never missing the opportunity to remind his readers and the general public of his accomplishments. He also stood apart by virtue of his status as a best-selling author, outstripping all but a very few other writers in sales figures and earning headlines for it; moreover, as a famous author, he could ignore the bleating of those who would criticize him, secure in his conviction that they misunderstood him. On 5 November 1915, he wrote his fellow writer Mary

Austin a letter of vigorous advice in response to her complaint that the world misunderstood her. After noting that his own books have repeatedly failed to "get across," London insists that this never bothers him, that he is above any concern about the public boxing his works into the confines of his image:

> I am telling you all the foregoing merely to show that it is a very bone-head world indeed, and, also, that I never bother my head when my own books miss fire. And the point I am making to you is: why worry? Let the best effort of your heart and head miss fire. The best effort of my heart and head has missed fire with you, as it has missed fire with practically everybody else in the world who reads, and I do not worry about it. I go ahead content to be admired for my red-blood brutality and for a number of other nice little things like that which are not true of my work at all. (*Letters* 3: 1513–14)

London goes on in this letter to make an astonishing assertion of his own singularity: "Those who sit alone must sit alone. They must continue to sit alone. As I remember it, the prophets and seers of all times have been compelled to sit alone except at such times when they were stoned or burned at the stake. . . . The world feeds you, the world feeds me, but the world knows damn little of either of us" (1514).

While single-mindedly driven to write, London would not give up the adventuring life he loved, and, of course, his high-profile adventures attracted the public's attention, admiration, and envy, further setting him apart. As he pursued his goals to write and achieve fame, he also lusted for adventure and for the chance to try out his theories about scientific farming and about such projects as housing the poor. To follow these other ambitions, he needed to make money. As he wrote to his friend Cloudesley Johns on 1 March 1900, "I am writing for money; if I can procure fame, that means more money. More money means life to me" (*Letters* 1: 164). Even if we suspect London of protesting too much in his frequent insistence on writing only or primarily for money, his ambition for wealth is evident throughout his writing career. He strove always to earn top dollar from publishers and magazines, and he argued his case strenuously (as in the quotation that begins this essay). This open desire for money could be seen as unseemly. As Braudy has pointed out, the preoccupation with money was viewed as entrepreneurial, a goal at odds with the desire for fame based on literary excellence (464). Fame could also be deemed unbecoming, for in London's time, as in our own, fame was equated with best-seller status rather than with literary quality.

Thus, to finance his adventures with the rewards from his writing, London learned early on how to promote and market himself and his works. He aggressively pressed his editors and publishers for higher pay. He also knew that notoriety would sell books, so he became adept at promoting himself through the media. He made himself available and was the ideal interviewee, offering up frank opinions in perfect sound bites.

Jack London shrewdly and effectively marketed himself, as Jonathan Auerbach demonstrates in *Male Call: Becoming Jack London*. Auerbach notes that

> more than any other American writer of his time, London entered the profession of letters completely lacking cultural capital—education, social connections, and access to the centers of publishing; more than any of his contemporaries, he also understood how success in twentieth-century magazine and book production so depended on symbolic capital—mass marketing, self-promotion, and the projection of an exciting name. (2)

Auerbach traces London's view of the craft of writing and publishing through a series of London's early essays that offer advice to other writers eager to enter the writing game. In pieces like "On the Author's Philosophy of Life," "First Aid to Rising Authors," and "The Question of a Name," London gives advice about how to go about selling one's work rather than recommendations for creating the actual content (Auerbach 21–36) Noting the importance of a trademark to a writer and his reputation, London recommended that writers put a "stamp of 'self'" on their work, a "stamp of personality of individual view" that would imbue all an author's works with his "self," in contrast to individual copyrighting of each work. In this way, London elevated the author to preeminence over his or her actual writings. Auerbach remarks: "Embodying publication itself, the person of the author would carry far more weight than his or her specific written work: a unifying trademark, applied to various products across the board" (25).

Following his own advice, London early on adopted the wolf as his trademark, using it repeatedly to represent himself and his qualities in his writings, from *The Sea-Wolf* to northland tales featuring wolf packs, and also in such items as his wolf-head bookplate. He named the dream home he was designing Wolf House, and his friend George Sterling called him Wolf. The wolf thus became an authorial logo for London, a trademark by which he was known and that he could use to market himself, and he was wildly successful in this marketing.

As Auerbach points out, in the early years of his career, London astutely timed the publication of his stories and novels to the best advantage for sales and publicity. London's extensive, detailed notes of magazine sales, for example, reveal that, in submitting his stories to magazine editors, there was more method than random chance operating. When he submitted "An Odyssey of the North" to the *Atlantic Monthly*, London, in a shrewd move, simultaneously wrote to the magazine's parent company, Houghton Mifflin, to pitch a volume of his Klondike stories. Both proposals were accepted, by the same editor, and London achieved his breakthrough in a magazine with national circulation as well as his first volume of collected stories (Auerbach 38).

London's success at self-promotion is borne out by the numerous clippings, reviews, advertisements, and the like that populate the extensive scrapbooks in the archive of his papers at the Huntington Library. Everything he did, and everything he was rumored to be doing, made headlines. For example, as a journalist in Korea for the Russo-Japanese War, he filed stories for the Hearst newspaper syndicate. Typically, his newspaper stories were accompanied not by a war photograph from the front but by a portrait of London. This was caused partly by the slow pace of getting photographs back to the States from the front, but even more by the fact that, for the American public, the reporting by the famous Jack London was of more interest than the war itself. When London's camera was confiscated and he was imprisoned by the Japanese authorities, the news sped around the world and people waited anxiously for information about his fate. Nearly a decade later, in the run-up to the Mexican War, London's notoriety again served to stoke the rumor and publicity mill. Known to be sympathetic to the Mexican revolutionaries' resistance, London began to be mentioned in news stories as a participant and indeed a leader in various actions of the revolution. A headline in the *Chicago Daily Drovers Journal* proclaimed, "Jack London an Insurrecto. Well-Known Author Said to Be at Head of Mexican Rebels" (Reesman, *Jack London's Racial Lives* 272). London denied all the rumors, but the headlines continued until newspapers finally began to publish corrections, including one that asserted that an impostor was posing as the famous author. The question of London impostors loomed even larger, for an impressive number of Jack London impersonators dotted the landscape throughout his life, lending even more hyperbole to the lore of London and further fascinating the public.

London's self-promotion also led him to embrace product development and new technologies that could serve to spread his fame. For example, exploiting his image as a hard drinker, he launched the Jack London Grape Juice Company with two partners, only to see it fail a year later. This is a wonderful example of London taking a negative feature of his reputation and turning it to his advantage. He was a self-professed heavy drinker, referring to his drinking frequently and focusing on it in his memoir *John Barleycorn: Alcoholic Memoirs*. In the book, he asserts that he didn't enjoy drinking but that, beginning in his days on the Oakland waterfront, he drank to be one of the guys, and he boasts that he could out-drink all comers. Whether he was an alcoholic is subject to debate among London scholars and fans, but it is a fact that he drank heavily. He frankly exploited this image to promote his comradeship with the common man and to assert his manly toughness. The alcoholic reputation continues to this day, so that London's hard drinking is one of several facts about his life that is well known to a wide portion of the general public.[1] The recognition of London as a drunk contributes to the current thriving of Heinold's First and Last Chance Saloon on Jack London Square in Oakland. This is the bar where London spent many an hour imbibing with his mates, and it survives today, in the original building with its grievously tilting floor and venerable stained wood that seems to exude the aromas of all the beers quaffed over the years. The saloon is a favorite tourist destination, and it reeks not only of beer but also of London's storied drinking history.

In a more savvy enterprise than his grape juice company, London recognized the potential of the new film industry and worked tirelessly to see his stories made into feature films. His energetic salesmanship paid off, and, on 5 October 1913, he and Charmian attended the premiere of Bosworth, Inc.'s *The Sea-Wolf*, the first feature-length film produced in the United States. Despite this success, London suffered many of the setbacks so common to the film industry. A surprisingly high percentage of his exhaustive daily correspondence focused on film rights, production companies, profit margins, and the other issues surrounding the creation and marketing of feature films.

Jack London's literary works, adventures, ranching, and other enterprises like film development and grape-juice marketing—all the features of his persona that promoted his celebrity—are found at the Huntington Library, the largest archive of his papers, which has been under my administration for more than thirty years. From the press clippings contained in enormous scrapbooks (actually, six-inch-thick ledgers) to London's extensive correspondence, the collection is rich in documentation of London's renown. The collection includes photographs, some that are formal portraits of the handsome author and others that capture informal activities, and there is an ephemera section that yields scores of little publications that tell the author's story to an eager world of readers. All this and more invite research and help make the London archive the most heavily used of all literary personal-paper collections in the library.

Readers everywhere are devoted to London and hold him and his writings in high esteem. They read and reread his books and stories, and they feel an extraordinary kinship with him in a very personal way that one doesn't often see. This perception was strengthened when I curated a major exhibition on London in 1998. The show was an overview of London's life and works and treated his journalism and adventures, as well as his major books. The exhibition proved to be extremely popular, and the curator's tours I conducted demonstrated yet again how people view London and respond to him. For graphic evidence of this response, we have in the Huntington's archives a large volume in which exhibition visitors recorded their comments about London, filling more than three hundred pages. The personal notes proved to be utterly astonishing, bespeaking people's deep feeling of connection to London. For example, one English teacher noted that London, more than any other writer, succeeds in getting students interested in literature. Another visitor remarked that seeing London's manuscripts put his strength, caring, and boundary testing on display, offering a complete picture of the man and his work. Beyond the scores of comments like these, it was stunning to see that nearly two-thirds of the comments in the volume began "Dear Jack" and went on to address the visitors' feelings directly to London.

The general public knows a fair amount about London, much of it based directly on the celebrated bits of publicity that he promoted about himself.

Thus, people tend to know that he wrote dog stories, embarked on exciting adventures, and died under unusual circumstances. No matter what they do or do not know, though, there are specific aspects of London's life and works about which there is nearly universal awareness. Nearly everyone has at least heard of *The Call of the Wild*. The title is, in fact, so well known as a catchphrase that it would be hard to find anyone who isn't familiar with it, even among those who have never read the book and may not even know where the phrase originated. It is used in advertisements, cartoons, jokes, and news headlines, to name just a few, attesting to London's successful self-promotion, as well as to the classic status of his most famous novel.

We can assume that London, given his lifelong effort to promote his own status as a celebrity, would be delighted to know that the title of his most famous book occupies a prominent and seemingly permanent place in popular parlance. Where *The Call of the Wild* exemplifies the fruits of London's cultivation of fame, other books and writings deal with the nature and attainment of notoriety.

One of London's novels in particular speaks directly to the matter of fame and authorship. *Martin Eden* deals specifically with this theme, telling the story of a young author who achieves fame and success only to be disillusioned by it, ultimately taking his own life. Now acknowledged to be one of London's finest, the novel is at least partly autobiographical, although scholars differ about the extent to which it reflects London's actual life. Classroom study of the book will enable students to follow several approaches to the novel and to the question of how it might afford insight into London's life. The protagonist, Martin Eden, like London, is a poor, rough-hewn young man who has dropped out of school and signed on as a seaman in an effort to make a life. He meets the well-to-do Morse family, whose refined ways and easy knowledge of literature and the arts charm him and whose daughter Ruth does the same, just as her real-life counterpart, Mabel Applegarth, captivated the young Jack London. Longing to be like the Morses and to become a writer, Martin Eden pursues both goals with an inexhaustible fervor. He eventually attains literary fame just as spectacular as London's own renown, only to become disillusioned and take his own life.

The book's obvious parallels to the arc of London's life have led to the prevailing view that it is heavily autobiographical, down to the last detail, including Eden's disillusionment and suicide. This view was reinforced by London's own writings, which closely mirrored the feelings he infused into his protagonist. Toward the end of the novel, when Eden has reached the nadir of his depression, he comments about the emptiness of his notoriety, "You see I have not changed, though my sudden apparent appreciation in value compels me constantly to reassure myself on that point. . . . I am personally of the same value that I was when nobody wanted me. And what is puzzling me is why they want me now. Surely they don't want me for myself, for myself is the same old self they did not want" (913).[2]

Similar disillusionment flares in London's novel-memoir *John Barleycorn*: "The things I had fought for and burned my midnight oil for had failed me. Success—I despised it. Recognition—it was dead ashes" (1065).[3] London, however, makes clear on many occasions that he does not suffer the empty disillusionment expressed in his memoir and embodied in Martin Eden. Unlike Martin, who has no sense of the "collective human need" that could enable him to find fulfillment (Braudy 534), London feels a strong kinship with his fellow man and woman. As he wrote in a letter to the *San Francisco Bulletin* on 7 January 1910, in explanation of his novel, "Martin Eden killed himself; I am still alive. Why am I alive? Because of my faith in man, a faith which Martin Eden never achieved . . . I retain my belief in the nobility and excellence of the human. I believe that spiritual sweetness and unselfishness will conquer class" (*Letters* 2: 865–66). Years later, at a time when London was chronically ill and when his death was just fourteen months away, he still expressed his optimism and faith in life and humanity: "while I have suffered much, I have lived much, seen much, and felt much that has been denied to the average man. Yes, indeed, the game is worth the candle" (*Letters* 3: 1503). Clearly, London holds to dreams and ambitions that bring fame but that also connect him to humanity, while Martin possesses only the desire for fame, unleavened by deeper, more fulfilling forces.

Braudy takes this further, arguing that London uses Martin Eden as a tool to control and purge his own excesses in the quest for fame (534). Similarly, as Auerbach points out, London makes celebrity a driving force in other works, sometimes in subtle or unexpected ways. That is, he uses his writing to explore his thinking about his own celebrity, using his fame to craft his characters and plot (*Male Call* 232–37). In *The Valley of the Moon*, for example, London writes himself into the novel, not only as the wealthy and famous landowner and then as a poet encountered by the main characters Saxon and Billy but also as the young boy Jack, who encourages Saxon to leave the city and the harm it is causing her marriage. In doing so, London recognizes, tweaks, and exploits his own fame as key plot elements in the novel. Meanwhile, in *Little Lady of the Big House*, as Auerbach observes, London makes the woman, Paula, carry the mantle of "celebrity." It is she, not the London-based character, who is superhuman, bigger than life, and who has had to do nothing more than to "be herself." Noting that celebrity is examined throughout the novel, Auerbach points out that "London's characters are still plagued with the fatal facility of self-advertisement, but now they know it and act to expose it in each other" (237). In Auerbach's view, London began his career aspiring to fame and renown, and, always looking forward, he crafted his career to achieve that goal. Once he attained celebrity, all he could do was look back and reexamine it.

There are broad benefits to studying London's reputation that go beyond close readings of his works. Looking at London's reputation, we can trace the influence he exerted on other authors. As Jeanne Campbell Reesman points out in *Jack London's Racial Lives*, London's influence may be seen not only in the works of writers like Stephen Crane, Frank Norris, and Theodore Dreiser but also in the writings of Ernest Hemingway, a link that was noted by Braudy too and that merits further study. She goes on to observe that London's influence on writers of color has been completely overlooked. Reesman prepares the ground for this analysis by tracing London's influence in the works of the black writers Richard Wright and Oscar Micheaux (302–03).

Students will be able to examine London as an example of the self-made man, a product of the young American democracy, who invented himself and seized his opportunities to succeed and to establish his fame worldwide. Viewing him in this context, and in the context of celebrities who came before him, students will be able to analyze the characteristics and qualities that contribute to celebrity. They will be able to place him in a line of American celebrities who created themselves and their images in a climate of openness and opportunity. From Benjamin Franklin, who dressed in animal skins to play the primitive before the European courts, it is a direct line to Jack London, who dressed in boots, flowing shirts, and a Baden Powell hat to play the gentleman rancher, a role the public adored.

By viewing Jack London as a celebrity, students will be able to compare and contrast him and his literary output with contemporary authors and their writings. As we have seen, London stands apart from his contemporaries in the way he exploited the media to promote himself and the sale of his books. Where other authors of his time followed the long tradition of simply writing books and hoping silently that publication and book sales would follow, London was ahead of his time in aggressively promoting his works to the book-buying public. Like authors today, he knew that he needed to be a savvy marketer to secure both fame and book sales. Students will be able to see from London's life that he would thrive and fit perfectly in today's marketing-heavy world. Having grown up in a media age, they will understand London's enterprise and find him a fascinating example of the marketing and promotion that are such a familiar and integral part of everyday life today. Using London as a basis, students may also investigate the entire phenomenon of literary celebrity—for example, how attaining fame might change an author, how the pursuit of notoriety could affect a writer's craft, and whether writing for the market corrupts an author's creativity.

Jack London is an excellent choice for discussing and studying celebrity. He cultivated fame as a writer, exploiting his adventures to enhance his reputation as a writer and promoting his name with editors and publishers in order to gain the maximum income and exposure from his works. A success story in his attainment of the American dream, he embodied the traits of the seeker of success, rising out of his lower-class roots by sheer force of his single-minded ambition and determination. Recognizing that fame would bring more success to him, he shrewdly set about making his name known far and wide. In doing so, he exploited the media, and he danced on the line between asserting his individuality and feeling a kinship with humanity. His individuality enabled him to embrace his celebrity, while his fellow feeling for others provided him with the grounding that gave his life meaning and fulfillment. He produced essays about the craft of writing, and, tellingly, they deal at least as much with how to achieve fame and monetary success as they do with the actual techniques of writing. Were he alive today, London would have his own Web site, and he would be an energetic tweeter and blogger. He would embrace *Facebook* and other social-networking platforms. Like the writers of today, he would be in constant communication with his fans, encouraging them to read his books, offering insight into his creative process, and entering into dialogue with them. London loved to argue and debate with friends, especially over the dining table, and he would, were he alive today, pursue this love through every form of social-networking technology available to him. In studying London as a celebrity, students will discover that he is not so alien from their own time and way of life. Just as famous in his own day as Stephen King and J. K. Rowling are today, he stands as an early achiever in the now familiar arena of literary success and celebrity on the grand scale.

NOTES

[1] This was brought home to me recently, when a news article about my Huntington exhibition on the poet and legendary boozer Charles Bukowski included the humorous observation that he is not the only sex-obsessed, alcoholic author whose papers I look after—a reference to Jack London.

[2] Citations to *Martin Eden* are from the version in *Jack London: Novels and Social Writings*.

[3] Citations to *John Barleycorn* are from the version in *Jack London: Novels and Social Writings*.

Teaching the Ideas in *The Sea-Wolf*

Keith Newlin

Jack London was interested in ideas above all: while his writing is sometimes dull and his plots contrived, the issues that captivated his generation—the lure of the Nietzschean individualist, the vogue of Herbert Spencer, the attraction of socialism—continue to live and still capture the attention of students. *The Sea-Wolf* (1904) provides an ideal opportunity to understand the appeal of philosophical issues that most students are themselves facing, for in this novel London shapes these ideas into a melodramatic battle between opposing philosophies. While critics typically castigate the novel's melodrama and reliance on popular magazine conventions, London was an astute student of popular literature and recognized that melodrama is an ideal form in which to convey the ideas that most mattered to him, for melodrama's Manichaean polarities exhibit the issues and their contexts clearly, and indeed melodrama is part of the generic form of naturalism. In short, critics who complain that London sacrificed art by caving in to commercial narrative strategies misunderstand an essential generic component of naturalism and therefore also misunderstand London's intent in the novel: to convince readers, by appealing to their emotions, that success and prosperity are achieved through cooperation, not through capitalist individualism, which is a false lure.

Teachers might begin discussion of *The Sea-Wolf* by pointing out that London was keenly aware of the paradox that faces any novice writer with artistic ambitions. "[A]n aspirant," he wrote in 1902,

> is conclusively a man who has not arrived, and a man who has not arrived has no pull on popularity. Being a man, and empty-pursed, he must eat. Being an artist, possessing the true artist-soul, his delight is to pour out in printed speech the joy of his heart. And this is the paradox he faces and must compass: *How and in what fashion must he sing the joy of his heart that the printed speech thereof may bring him bread?*
>
> ("Again the Literary Aspirant" 48)

But London also fully recognized that the literary marketplace demanded that a writer attract and retain a steady audience for his work; what's more, he applauded this commercial relation between writer and audience:

> And why should it not be frankly commercial in a commercial age? The deepest values of life are today expressed in terms of cash. . . . This being so—the making of money the most vital fact in life today—it is only fair that literature be expressed in terms of cash. And it is not only fair but it is good business sense for an editor to print in the pages of his magazine that which a large number of people want to read. (49)

The trick, as London saw it, was to discover how to be true to one's artistic ambitions and yet still earn a living from one's labors. One solution was to satisfy the reader's demand for adventurous plots, thrilling sensation, and comforting sentiment but to smuggle within the tale the ideas that most interested the writer—an application of the sugar-coated-pill principle. In an oft-quoted letter to George Brett, his editor at Macmillan, London sketched this approach to a novel that would become *The Sea-Wolf*:

> I am on the track of a sea story, however, which shall have adventure, storm, struggle, tragedy, and love. The love-element will run throughout, as the man & woman will occupy the center of the stage pretty much of all the time. Also it will end happily. The *motif*, however, the human motif underlying it all, will be what I may call *mastery*. . . .
>
> Of course, this underlying motif, will be *underlying*; it will be subordinated to the love motif. The superficial reader will get the love story & the adventure; while the deeper reader will get all this, plus the bigger thing lying underneath. (*Letters* 1: 337–38; 20 Jan. 1903)

London's adroit assessment of his own role in the increasing commodification of literature determined not only the content but also the structure of *The Sea-Wolf*. To suggest "the bigger thing lying underneath," London was drawn to melodrama because its focus on the event, its polarization of conflict, and its didactic expression of thesis provided him with an effective medium through which to express his vision of human beings subject to the law of evolution. Since students have only a hazy idea of what melodrama is, I usually begin discussion by asking them to outline the structure of popular movies featuring "superheroes"—James Bond, Spiderman, Batman, the Terminator—that is, those that pit the good guys against the bad guys. Students then easily comprehend the inevitable plots and unambiguous characterizations that typify melodrama, though I have to tease out the ethical implications. I then invite them to consider the melodrama of London's characterization of human struggle, which he explained in "Wanted: A New Law of Development":

> In this struggle, which is for food and shelter, the weak individuals must obviously win less food and shelter than the strong. Because of this, their hold on life relaxes and they are eliminated. And for the same reason that they may not win for themselves adequate food and shelter, the weak cannot give to their progeny the chance for survival that the strong give. And thus, since the weak are prone to beget weakness, the species is constantly purged of its inefficient members. (174)

In planning *The Sea-Wolf*, London intended to contrast two dominant ideas then current: the attraction of capitalist materialism, in which might makes right and the philosophies of Herbert Spencer and Friedrich Nietzsche are enlisted to support a vision of society that rewards competition and strength of will as the inevitable consequence of evolution, and the appeal of socialist idealism, in which society is evolving to a higher plane where people work to propagate a moral society founded on sympathy, service, altruism, and cooperation.

To enable students to understand London's portrayal of Wolf Larsen and the purpose of the Maud Brewster section, I begin with a summary of Spencer's theories, which I give them as a brief handout summarizing portions of *First Principles* (1864), *Principles of Biology* (1871), and *Principles of Sociology* (1876–97). Spencer's basic move is to posit the "persistence of force"—that which causes things to change—as a fundamental (or first) cause. Evolution is the action of force on matter, and whenever force acts on a stable mass of something (i.e., protoplasm), changes occur: unified masses become diverse (i.e., individuals). Evolution is an increase in diversity accompanied by integration, or the interdependence of parts. Spencer believes that the homogeneous is inherently unstable, since the persistence of force upon its parts must cause differences to occur. The homogenous must inevitably develop into the heterogeneous. The eventual result is a state of equilibrium because evolutionary forces can't go on forever in the direction of increasing heterogeneity.

Because diversity is more complex than unity, evolution is thus a progression from the simple to the complex. Spencer gives the evolutionary process moral weight by terming this process a progression from the primitive to the advanced. When Spencer applies this basic theory to biology, the resulting observations are that the lowest organisms are the simplest and that the higher are the more complex because they show a greater degree of integration—or interdependence of parts. As Ronald Martin summarizes, "a particular individual of a species survives because its inner, adaptive forces can accommodate the various outer forces and changes of force and sustain the moving equilibrium that is life" (48). This adaptation takes place first through functional changes (a person becomes a blacksmith), which produce structural changes (increased muscularity). The acquired characteristics pass to the next generation through heredity, Spencer believed. Spencer concluded that those organisms survive and prosper whose functions are most in sync with the environment (in equilibrium); those die who are out of sync.

When Spencer applies the theory of natural selection to society, it becomes a theory of social selection, couched in terms of the mental evolution of man. Like Jean-Baptiste Lamarck, Spencer believed that mental characteristics could be inherited. Spencer combined Lamarckian theory with natural selection; the result is a theory of evolutionary idealism: the intellect of the race will become cumulatively better, eventually resulting in the "ideal man"—the altruistic man. Spencer saw a direct correspondence between an organism and society; that is, he thought that both were organic in structure and function. Spencer admits the differences (like individual consciousness) and tries to minimize them. But he believes that the similarity holds: like an organism, society evolves.

Social man is a product of society, who, to maintain equilibrium, must conform his actions to the welfare of the whole. Society thus acts to restrain and control the aggressive egoist impulses of primitive man and to foster altruism, which is the final product of man's evolution. Evil, in Spencer's system, is simply the "non-adaptation of constitution to conditions" (qtd. in Hofstadter, *Social Darwinism* [1955] 40); because everything is in a process of adaptation, evil tends to disappear. To show that altruism will result from evolutionary pressures, Spencer attempts to base the development of ethics on evolutionary principles, as he argues in *Principles of Sociology*: "primitive" societies, he argues, govern through fear and group pressures, which combine to deselect man's egoism. To survive in the group, one must eradicate selfishness. Man learns that obeying rules enables him to survive; he therefore recognizes the utility of rules and the "intrinsic authority" of them (2: 228). Man thus gradually conforms to the group voluntarily, for he recognizes that it is good to do so; when he does, it is no longer necessary for society to compel him to conform.

Nations will eventually learn the value of mutual cooperation (the "interdependence of parts") for the benefit of all, and war will cease. Eventually, the need for governmental control diminishes (except for basic services); the resulting society is an industrial society, based on contract—one that respects the individual and minimizes state involvement and emphasizes laissez-faire economics. Spencer therefore opposes state intervention into the evolutionary process, for such intervention only retards the "natural progression" of man toward perfection. The poor, Spencer says, are unfit (they haven't adapted) and should be eliminated: "The whole effort of nature is to get rid of such, to clear the world of them, and make room for better." Those who die because of stupidity, vice, or idleness are the same as those who physically aren't fit to live: "If they [people] are sufficiently complete to live, they *do* live, and it is well they should live. If they are not sufficiently complete to live, they die, and it is best they should die" (qtd. in Hofstadter, *Social Darwinism* [1955] 41). Spencer argues against aid to the poor, state-supported education, regulation of housing, even licensing of doctors, tariffs, state banking, and so forth, because this is state intervention into the evolutionary process. Spencer, however, supports *voluntary* aid to the poor because it has an elevating effect on donors and leads to an increased development of altruism. But compulsory measures prevent the operation of natural selection and are a return to militarism.

With this summary as a guide, I invite students to see the *Ghost* as a microcosm of the Spencerian universe and to find examples of London's literary treatment of Spencer's ideas. Students typically see that Humphrey Van Weyden is, at the beginning, an instance of figurative "protoplasm" that, acted on by Wolf's "force"—his directive to find one's own legs to stand on—adapts into a more developed individual. Propelled by Wolf's brutality, Hump must adapt to his environment or cease to exist. And he does: his muscles develop; his inclination to passive acceptance evolves into a ferocity that enables him to survive, which is adroitly illustrated in the scene where Hump swaggers about, sharpening his knife to intimidate Thomas Mugridge, the ship's cook. Hump takes his place in the heterogeneous environment of the *Ghost*, with its clear division of labor—hunters, pullers, steersmen, cook, and mate—all at an equilibrium, with Wolf's brutality holding at bay the desire of the men to disrupt the stable order of this primitive society.

But what of Wolf's materialism, his selfishness and cruelty? London also was attracted to the cult of the strong, in particular Arthur Schopenhauer's "will to live" and Nietzsche's "will to power," and much of the appeal of the first part of the novel stems from London's combination of the philosophies. Schopenhauer believed that the desire to live was fundamental to all life, and only through the act of living does life attain meaning. Nietzsche argued that the will to live was more properly the will to power—that man is by nature selfish, cunning, avaricious, and amoral. "Since pleasure comes from the fullest and most satisfying use of one's faculties," Charles C. Walcutt explains, "it follows that the main concern of the superman is to perfect his instincts, to develop himself into the highest conceivable type of human kind. Those ethical ideals which teach man to deny himself, to sacrifice himself for the weak, to restrain his impulses as fundamentally evil are the doctrines preached by weaklings in their efforts to protect themselves from the strong" (*American Literary Naturalism* 93). Students easily see that this philosophy informs the famed "yeast" passage, where Wolf reduces life to "a mess. . . . It is like yeast, a ferment, a thing that moves and may move for a minute, an hour, a year, or a hundred years, but that in the end will cease to move. The big eat the little that they may continue to move, the strong eat the weak that they may retain their strength. The lucky eat the most and move the longest, that is all" (520).[1] All life is "piggishness," and Wolf is the strongest yeast.

Much of the appeal of the *Ghost* section of *The Sea-Wolf* stems from Hump's resistance to Wolf's materialism, and students typically excel in identifying examples of the conflict of philosophies. In one pivotal scene, for example, Hump complains of the injustice of Mugridge's theft of his money. Wolf's reply combines Nietzsche's doctrine that the strong must inevitably prevail and acting altruistically is a betrayal of the self with Spencer's premise that those who are fittest ultimately prevail. Wolf tells Hump:

> Might is right, and that is all there is to it. Weakness is wrong. Which is a very poor way of saying that it is good for oneself to be strong, and evil for oneself to be weak—or better yet, it is pleasurable to be strong, because of the profits; painful to be weak, because of the penalties. Just now the possession of this money is a pleasurable thing. It is good for one to possess it. Being able to possess it, I wrong myself and the life that is in me if I give it to you and forego the pleasure of possessing it. (543)

To Hump's claim that Wolf wrongs him by withholding the money, Wolf replies, "I do wrong always when I consider the interests of others" (543). In the world of the *Ghost*, altruism has no place, and the ensuing debate over the place of altruism, including an explicit reference to Spencer's position, concludes with Hump crying, "Then you are an individualist, a materialist, and, logically, a hedonist" (545). At this point, the Nietzschean position has triumphed in this battle of ideas.

London has stacked the deck in the shipboard scenes—Hump's idealism never has a chance in the face of Wolf's assertive will, backed up by his physical strength and his relentless focus on considering foremost his own desire and dealing summarily with any opposition. But this is the way it goes with melodrama, with its simplicity of characterization, its reliance on a force or two to propel its plots, the repeated employment of coincidence in and the polarized arrangement of its action, its reliance on sensation and sentiment to appeal to readers' emotions, and the frequency of romantic subplots and stilted dialogue.

London's intent in this first half of his melodrama was to point to the appeal of the Nietzschean *Übermensch* but also to reveal the limitations of the figure, which he would develop in the Maud Brewster section. During his time on the *Ghost*, Hump learns three lessons (which I direct students to observe by pointing them to key scenes):

The law of the Darwinian world. In the struggle for existence, the strong prevail in the competition to survive. Hump first resists but is eventually drawn in to become part of the competition for survival and even takes pleasure in some aspects of it—chiefly by marveling at his newfound strength and by dominating Mugridge and discovering therein the joy of mastery. "My reason dictated that the beating Thomas Mugridge had received was an ill thing," he reflects, "and yet for the life of me I could not prevent my soul joying in it" (576).

The limitations of capitalism. Hump observes how the strong exploit the weak, the rich exploit the poor. After a storm separates the sealing boats from the *Ghost*, Wolf steals the boats of the *Macedonia* for his own gain; the *Macedonia*'s hunters readily switch allegiance when paid off in increased "lay" or in whiskey.

The limitations of materialism. Early on, Hump observes that Wolf is "very lonely. . . . His tremendous virility and mental strength wall him apart" (540). As he comes to accept Wolf's lessons, Hump feels his isolation and becomes increasingly melancholy and suicidal—which suggests that without idealism, life loses value. At one point Hump reflects, "I found myself afflicted with Wolf Larsen's repulsive ideas. What was it all about? Where was the grandeur of life that it should permit such wanton destruction of human souls? It was a cheap and sordid thing after all, this life, and the sooner over the better. Over and done with! I, too, leaned upon the rail and gazed longingly into the sea, with the certainty that sooner or later I should be sinking down, down, through the cool green depths of its oblivion" (602).

When London had half completed the novel in September 1903, he sent it to Brett and enclosed a synopsis, which I share with students, that indicated he planned to divide the novel into two sections, with each illustrating an opposing philosophy: "In fact, brutality and the triumph of materialism will be the dominant note of the first half of the book, and of the second half the dominant note will be love and the triumph of idealism" ("Synopsis of Sea Novel"). London worried that the brutality of the first half would offend readers, and he noted in an "Amplification of Synopsis of the Last Half of Sea Novel" that it "may be liberally blue-penciled. The thing I wish to emphasize," he continued, "is that the second half will be written in a different key (style of course, remaining unchanged), the key will be that of the song a man sings of himself and his love, and the man, in turn, clever of phrase, deep of insight, and, in the last analysis, romantic and idealistic." Distributing the full synopses to students also has the salutary effect of enabling students to see that writing is usually planned and carefully considered by an author, and not the result of some mystical inspiration, as many often believe.

London parted company with Spencer over the end result of the evolutionary process. Spencer believed that in a complex industrial society, competition ultimately meant the elimination of the poor and the weak, and, indeed, the state should not intervene to enable the weak to survive. But London saw in the play of economic forces the eventual emergence of a socialist state, as he explained in "Wanted: A New Law of Development":

> The cardinal tenet of Socialism is that forbidding doctrine, the materialistic conception of history. Men are not the masters of their souls. They are the puppets of great, blind forces. The lives they live and the deaths they die are compulsory. All social codes are but the reflexes of existing economic conditions, plus certain survivals of past economic conditions. The institutions men build they are compelled to build. Economic laws determine at any given time what these institutions shall be, how long they shall operate, and by what they shall be replaced. And so, through the economic process, the Socialist preaches the ripening of the capitalistic society and the coming of the new co-operative society. . . .
>
> When the common man's day shall have arrived, the new social institutions of that day will prevent the weeding out of weakness and inefficiency. All, the weak and the strong, will have an equal chance for procreation. And the progeny of all, of the weak as well as the strong, will have an equal chance for survival. (192–93; 207)

As every melodramatist knows, good melodrama requires the opposing forces of heroism and villainy to be nearly equal, for audiences must entertain some doubt about which will prevail. With a working definition of melodrama's narrative strategies, students find examples of Wolf's callous brutality, of Hump's quailing before Wolf's greater strength, and especially of titillating scenes of sensation designed to appeal to readers' emotions, such as the incident where Mugridge becomes a bit of shark bait, losing his foot in the process, whereupon the shark is punished by being thrown into the sea with its jaws pried open, doomed to lingering starvation.

While critics have typically castigated the final section of the novel, in which Hump and Maud play house on Endeavor Island, I find that when students understand the purpose of melodrama, they don't share the critics' condemnation. I summarize the critics' response and remind them of the battle of philosophies London has set forth. Students usually argue that, in writing *The Sea-Wolf*, London devoted the Maud Brewster section to show the ultimate triumph of socialism over materialism, which London illustrates in two parallel but opposing scenes. In the *Ghost* section, the law of the survival of the fittest prevails: because each man acts according to self-interest, the men never successfully combine individual strengths to overcome Wolf's greater strength—which London illustrates superbly in the forecastle scene, where the men try to kill Wolf. While the men gang up on Wolf, they don't coordinate their actions: Leach calls several times for a knife; no one lights a lamp; all is confusion. But on Endeavor Island, Hump and Maud form a social compact where effort is for the common good—which London illustrates magnificently in the mast-raising scene. Individually, Hump and Maud are too weak to raise the mast, but united by a common goal, they are able to overcome individual weakness and raise the mast. London devotes so much space to the protracted process to illustrate, not the sexual metaphor so dear to recent criticism, but "the coming of the new cooperative society."

Like others of the naturalists, London was immensely attracted to Spencer's evolutionary synthesis, which encouraged a melodramatic perception of the world. Spencer's paradigm tends to polarize the subjects of inquiry—into the knowable and the unknowable, stability and instability, homogeneity and heterogeneity, evolution and dissolution, reflecting the late nineteenth century's preoccupation with either-or abstractions: the rich and the poor, supply and demand, science and faith, progress and poverty. Just as melodrama insists on the ultimate vanquishment of misfortune, Spencer's evolutionary synthesis assured people that the conflict of forces tended toward a harmonious equilibrium in which conflicting forces achieved a balance that benefited society. In *The Sea-Wolf*, and in particular the Endeavor Island section, we see London's evolutionary optimism in perhaps its clearest form.

NOTE

[1] Citations to *The Sea-Wolf* are from *Jack London: Novels and Stories*.

An Evolutionary Approach to *The Call of the Wild* and *White Fang*

Kenneth K. Brandt

Charles Darwin's theory of evolution was the most abiding influence on Jack London's work, and *The Call of the Wild* and *White Fang* offer excellent opportunities for introducing undergraduates to key evolutionary principles and controversies. Two of Darwinism's most influential theorizers, Herbert Spencer and Thomas Henry Huxley, propagated contrasting responses to the evolutionary paradigm—a dramatic ideological clash particularly suited to the structuring devices of both novels. Here I describe how I teach *The Call of the Wild* by alerting students to the specifics of the Spencer-Huxley divide. Then, more briefly, I outline how students can organize a group report on *White Fang*.

To structure class discussion I often use short, open-book quizzes that ask students to select and comment on two significant passages from the assigned reading. Their task is to provide a paragraph of interpretive commentary on passages that they feel embody thematic high points in the text's themes, characterizations, or conflicts. One by one, students then share their individual responses, which provide the foundation for class discussion and interchange. This process elicits student input and exchange and, at the same time, permits the instructor opportunities to integrate compact, specific "lecture" commentary into a discussion-based format. Teaching in a computer-equipped classroom with a projector, I either use sources drawn directly from the Internet or present the secondary excerpts quoted below using a combination of *PowerPoint* slides and *Word* documents. Students can later access these sources, documents, and links on *Blackboard*. Below are some essential evolutionary points that I integrate into the class exchange as we discuss student-chosen passages from *The Call of the Wild*.

Adaptation: Social Darwinism, Spencer, and Huxley

Buck's movement from the principled, bucolic Southland to the amoral, primal Northland offers numerous opportunities to make thematic connections with evolutionary themes and conflicts. One of the most effective ways of introducing social Darwinism is through the logical fallacy *argumentum ad naturam*, the "appeal to nature." The Web site *Fallacy Files* is an expedient source to begin a discussion centered on the differentiations that can be made between what may be defined as natural or unnatural and what may be judged moral, immoral, or amoral (Curtis). To elaborate on this fallacy and to direct the discussion toward some more specific aspects of social Darwinism, I use Gordon Gekko's "greed is good" speech from Oliver Stone's film *Wall Street* to provide a vivid example of how social Darwinists typically emphasize self-interest, brutish struggle, and laissez-faire economics. As his name implies, Gekko is something of a reptile, but to encourage some debate I ask students if he makes any valid points or if his speech is in any way compelling. As the debate progresses, I introduce a few key concepts from Spencer to guide the discussion toward explaining some of Spencer's basic concepts. First, to convey the basic process of adaptation, I present students with Spencer's definition of life from *First Principles*: "Life is definable as the continuous adjustment of internal relations to external relations" (70). I then focus students' attention on a passage from Spencer's *Social Statistics* that articulates a core tenet of social Darwinism:

> [Imperfect Beings] are nature's failures, and are recalled by her laws when found to be such. Along with the rest they are put on trial. If they are sufficiently complete to live, they *do* live, and it is well they should live. If they are not sufficiently complete to live, they die, and it is best they should die. (415)

For Spencer, *Homo sapiens* is merely another "organism," inescapably subject to the same fundamental evolutionary laws as all other life-forms. For social Darwinists, the "survival of the fittest," as Daniel C. Dennett puts it in *Darwin's Dangerous Idea*, "is not just Mother Nature's way, but *ought* to be *our* way" (461). It should be our way, the social Darwinian argument goes, because if nature is permitted to take its course, the ensuing adaptations will result in social progress and the collective elevation of humankind. For now, then, it is best to overlook the misery many must experience as we advance, for all that suffering is just evolution's way of working out the kinks as we ascend toward ever greater perfection. Students generally understand that Spencer's views are ethically untenable, but a spirited class discussion can be initiated by asking the class to share versions of social Darwinism from their own social, athletic, education, and employment experiences. Students may consider, for instance, how the discourse of academic achievement at times co-opts the rhetoric or ideology of social Darwinism.

To help illuminate the ethical problems that arise in student commentary and debate following a discussion of these questions, I introduce the distinction that Thomas Henry Huxley makes between cosmic evolution and ethical evolution in "Evolution and Ethics." One of Huxley's central points is that evolution is not synonymous with progress or improvement. Evolution is a process that is arbitrary rather than progressive since organisms that happen to fit into a given environmental niche survive, reproduce, and are, therefore, deemed fit. I present students with a somewhat lengthy but absolutely essential passage where Huxley describes the amoral effect of "conditions" on the evolutionary process:

> "Fittest" has a connotation of "best"; and about "best" there hangs a moral flavour. In cosmic nature, however, what is "fittest" depends upon the

> conditions. Long since I ventured to point out that if our hemisphere were to cool again, the survival of the fittest might bring about, in the vegetable kingdom, a population of more and more stunted and humbler and humbler organisms, until the "fittest" that survived might be nothing but lichens, diatoms, and such microscopic organisms as those which give red snow its colour; while, if it became hotter, the pleasant valleys of the Thames and Isis might be uninhabitable by any animated beings save those that flourish in a tropical jungle. They, as the fittest, the best adapted to the changed conditions, would survive. (501)

Here Huxley dismantles the notion that ethical integrity should be automatically bestowed on the well-adapted organism or individual. To resuscitate students from Huxley's Victorian prose and to make this point more memorable, I provide students with a reading of the song "Rudolph the Red-Nosed Reindeer" as a Huxleyan evolutionary fable: Rudolph's shiny red nose (a mutation) makes him a social pariah (no reindeer games—that is, no sex, no offspring). This initially maladaptive variation, however, becomes an adaptive characteristic because of a change in environmental conditions (the foggy Christmas Eve). As lead reindeer, he pulls Santa's sleigh through the fog successfully and ascends to an especially high social status. Loved by all reindeer, he becomes a historical icon, and, it can be inferred, the much adored Rudolph has frequent reproductive opportunities and many progeny—a Darwinian success story. The point to impress upon students is that Rudolph himself does not become a more robust or ethically better reindeer. His fitness gains, rather, come about only because of a fortuitous environmental change. This provides an example of how, as Lawrence I. Berkove observes, "'fitness' is always relative to variable and random external conditions" ("Jack London and Evolution" 252). Huxley is not comfortable with the capricious nature of this "cosmic" evolutionary process, and he proposes the alternative of "ethical evolution":

> [T]he strongest, the most self-assertive, tend to tread down the weaker. But the influence of the cosmic process on the evolution of society is the greater the more rudimentary its civilization. Social progress means a checking of the cosmic process at every step and the substitution for it of another, which may be called the ethical process, the end of which is not the survival of those who may happen to be the fittest, in respect of the whole of the conditions which obtain, but of those who are ethically the best. (502)

Directly countering Spencer's view of the evolutionary process as salutary and intrinsically progressive, Huxley goes on to contend "that the practice of that which is ethically best—what we call goodness or virtue—involves a course of conduct which in all respects is opposed to that which leads to success in the cosmic struggle for existence. . . . It repudiates the gladiatorial theory of existence" (502). To track the nature of Buck's adaptations, I ask students to be on the lookout for instances in which Buck's actions resemble a Spencerian gladiator, a Huxleyan ethicist, or a fusion of both.

The Struggle for Supremacy

One passage, for example, that students respond to is from the section in chapter 2 where Buck steals a chunk of bacon, including the following: "This first theft marked Buck as fit to survive in the hostile Northland environment. It marked his capacity to adjust himself to changing conditions, the lack of which would have meant swift and terrible death."[1] Students are quick to make the connection between London's language and Spencer's claim that life is a "continuous adjustment of internal relations to external relations." Students should consider how Buck's adaptation can simultaneously constitute a developmental progression and an ethical compromise. This theft, London writes, marks the "decay or going to pieces of his moral nature, a vain thing and a handicap in the ruthless struggle for existence" (21). This observation seems to affirm Huxley's view that the "influence of the cosmic process on the evolution of society is the greater the more rudimentary its civilization." A few sentences later, London sounds a decidedly ambivalent note on Buck's adaptation, stating that "[Buck's] development (or retrogression) was rapid" (22). Students also often cite the famous paragraph that begins, "There is an ecstasy that marks the summit of life" (33–34) as the first complete, amoral correspondence between Buck ("internal relations") and the primordial Northland ("external relations"). Discussion can center on how Buck must become more "gladiatorial" in the Northland—a situation most college students can identify with as they prepare to enter what they commonly refer to as "the real world"—that is, the social Darwinian world. Buck is clearly in the "gladiatorial" mode in chapter 2, but what other options are available for him? Few, if any, students judge Buck negatively for having to do what he has to do in this dog-eat-dog world. In relation to Buck's predicament, students are often willing to discuss the ways they have had to compromise (or have refused to compromise) their ethical principles or their political ideals to comply with the status quo.

Students also tend to select passages focusing on the rivalry between Buck and Spitz, noting how Buck's efficient adaptation to conditions brings him into direct conflict with the lead dog. Evolutionary psychologists often observe that high-status males have more control over resources and more opportunities for reproduction than lower-status males. London's depiction of the hierarchical dynamics of the dog team offers a stark rendering of male status competition and conflict. The forensic evolutionary psychologists Joshua D. Duntley and Todd K. Shackelford maintain that "an individual in a group cannot ascend a status hierarchy without displacing someone above, bumping that person to a lower position and inflicting costs associated with status loss." They go on to note that "the potential for large fitness gains associated with increases in status would have created selection pressure for specialized cognitive adaptations that lead to hierarchy ascension and other cognitive mechanisms to prevent large status falls" (5). Most disturbingly, they contend that "death by homicide often has cascading deleterious effects on a victim's inclusive fitness. . . . A murder victim's fitness losses can potentially be translated into rival's fitness gains" (10). In other words, the most complete way to get rid of your rival is to kill him or her, which is exactly what Buck and Spitz want to do to each other. We witness various attempts by Buck and Spitz to undermine each other, and students often comment on the incident when Spitz deviously attacks Buck when the team is overrun by starving huskies: "[Buck] flung himself upon another, and at the same time felt teeth sink into his throat. It was Spitz, treacherously attacking from the side" (26). Instructors can shape the discussion of this and related passages by initiating a character analysis that compares and contrasts Buck and Spitz. Students should not overlook that Buck—who garners so much reader sympathy— engages in a prolonged "insidious revolt [that] destroy[s] the solidarity of the team" and that there is no greater delight to him than to "precipitate a fight amongst his mates and tangle the traces" (33, 36). Plainly, the objective of these machinations is to displace Spitz so that Buck can ascend to lead dog. The instructor should be sure to point out the eventual Darwinian confirmation of Buck's fitness in the description of his progeny at the end of the novella, which is evidenced in the "change in the breed of timber wolves . . . [some seen] with splashes of brown on head and muzzle, and with a rift of white centering down the chest" (85). To what degree, I ask students, is Buck's success dependent on the same kind of devious and bullying behavior that enabled Spitz's dominance? What, precisely, if anything, makes Buck a "better" dog than Spitz? Is he merely the more conniving bully? Buck, not Spitz, initiates the fight in which he defeats his rival, and as the other dogs converge to rip the wounded Spitz to shreds, "Buck stood and looked on, the successful champion, the dominant primordial beast who had made his kill and found it good" (375). At this point, is there any connection between ethical integrity and the capacity to survive?

Most students readily recognize the flexibility of London's allegory in *The Call of the Wild*: Buck's actions are believable as actual dog behavior, but it is also clear that certain behaviors are applicable to and reflections of human tendencies. Many students remark that the "goodness" of the kill at the end of chapter 3 is less problematic ethically because, at this point, London is not anthropomorphizing Buck as much as he does later. A number of students, though, do voice strong criticisms about the pervasiveness of animal cruelty and animal violence in the novella. I have found this complaint is the leading reason why students form a dislike for the book, and the instructor should be prepared to handle these concerns in a sensitive and serious manner. One way to partially allay student concerns about the prevalence of animal brutality is to discuss how Buck's relationship with John Thornton offers a more altruistic alternative to the viciousness of the Buck-Spitz rivalry.

John Thornton and Reciprocal Altruism

Ordinarily, the Thornton-Buck interspecies relationship would be defined as "symbiotic," but the intensity of their bond and the scope of London's allegory strongly suggest a reading that blurs traditional species boundaries. With the entrance of John Thornton a more romantic narrative strand emerges that differs from the previous discourse of brutish struggle. London uses this emotionally charged language to delineate the bond that develops between Thornton and Buck. Thornton, for example, arouses in Buck "a love that was feverish and burning, that was adoration, that was madness" (60). Although some critics have chided London for a seeming sentimental lapse in this section of the novel, students are—mainly because of personal dog-ownership experiences—drawn to passages that describe Thornton and Buck's special rapport. Furthermore, instead of signifying a stylistic slump, London's expressive prose here is particularly well suited to depict some key dynamics of reciprocal altruism, a crucial concept for evolutionary psychologists. E. O. Wilson provides a good working definition of reciprocal altruism as "[t]he trading of altruistic acts by individuals at different times. For example, one person [the donor] saves a drowning person [the recipient] in exchange for the promise (or at least the reasonable expectation) that the altruistic act will be repaid if circumstances are ever reversed" (229–30). It is critical here to make a distinction with "kin selection," in which altruistic acts favor genetically related individuals and, hence, one's own genetic interests, since recipient relatives carry a percentage of the donor's genes. In London's work, reciprocal altruism reveals itself through various depictions of group solidarity, mutual cooperation, and unspoken codes of "fair play." His fiction frequently highlights heroic individual acts that enhance the survival capacity of the group and, therefore, each of its members. Alex Rosenberg clarifies the cooperative calculus of reciprocal altruism, noting that

> at first glance . . . reciprocal altruism looks like an evolutionary impossibility. More precisely, natural selection relentlessly shapes organisms for individual fitness maximization. An act is deemed altruistic if it results in an increase in the fitness of another organism and a decrease in the fitness of the actor. For persistent cooperation among organisms to emerge, therefore, there need to be acts of reciprocated altruism, *such that the net pay-offs to mutual cooperators are greater than the rewards of mutual non-cooperation*. (321; emphasis added)

The ideal character in London's work is most often one who is self-reliant *and* cooperative. Individuals who work together and avoid the ills of petty self-interest tend to flourish ethically and genetically. Notably, Thornton himself is a rugged individualist who is also the recipient of altruistic acts: after he freezes his feet on the trail, his partners "[make] him comfortable and [leave] him to get well" and later return with a raft to regroup (59). Thornton performs a similar altruistic act when he saves Buck's life from the cheechako trio of Hal, Charles, and Mercedes, who showcase a fatally nonadaptive disregard of reciprocal altruism in their abusive overworking of the sled dogs. Enthralled by his new "ideal master" (60), Buck demonstrates reciprocity by his willingness to obey Thornton's command to jump off a cliff (63), by defending Thornton against "Black" Burton (63–64), by saving Thornton from drowning in the rapids (64–66), and by winning the sled-pulling contest (66–70). To varying degrees, these potentially self-destructive reciprocal donations imperil Buck's fitness, but he performs them in response not only to Thornton's heroic rescue but also to his sustained affection. Thornton's love and care are generous but unconfining. "Love, genuine passionate love were [Buck's] for the first time," yet his "kindliness and largeness" allow Buck wider access to his instinctual self (59). At the same time, Buck's altruistic acts safeguard Thornton and enable the gold-mining expedition to the "weird lake country" (72). When Thornton and his party are killed by the Yeehats, Buck "reciprocates" by slaughtering the assailants. Brutal as this episode is, Buck's carnage functions to restore the reciprocal balance with Thornton. This decisive unbinding reciprocal donation allows him to fully unite with his primal wolf-self: "He had killed man, the noblest game of all. . . . And as never before, he was ready to obey [the call of the wild]. John Thornton was dead. The last tie was broken. Man and the claims of man no longer bound him" (84). Thus begins Buck's distinctly amoral Darwinian existence as he becomes a demonic alpha predator. It seems like Gordon Gekko is back on the rampage, slicker than ever. The final paragraphs detailing Buck's wolf identity open up a variety of possibilities for class discussion: Should we be concerned that this is not the most socially responsible way to end Buck's story? To what extent are "conditions" to blame (or to exalt) for Buck's fate? What sort of political agenda does the novel end up advocating? And yet again, To what extent do having a dog as protagonist and Buck's integration into the pack at the end of the novella mollify the text's harsher Darwinian implications?

Organizing a Group Presentation on White Fang

We revisit the implications of *The Call of the Wild's* conclusion in a twenty-minute group presentation on *White Fang* at the end of the term. At the conclusion of *The Call of the Wild*, Buck is wild, free, and dominant; at the end of *White Fang*, the hero is tame, subservient, and domesticated. The novel ends as the newly christened "Blessed Wolf" acquiesces to Dolly and their new litter of puppies—this married-with-children status is a far howl from Buck's apotheosis as the "Ghost Dog." Imagine Gordon Gekko repudiating Wall Street for the modest life of a devoted suburban husband-father working as a home security agent. In effect, London's two works offer contrasting versions of the American dream—one of the frontier and another of the hearth. In *The Call of the Wild*, the escape from the society and the return to nature foster a regeneration of a primal, more authentic, and, finally, a transcendent self. In *White Fang*, the establishment of stable domesticity, self-restraint, and a nuclear family allows a socialized and secure identity to emerge.

Presenters should consider such oppositions as they approach the main task of their report, which is to share with the rest of the class some of *White Fang*'s main thematic features while keeping in mind the evolutionary ideas covered earlier in the course. To facilitate this process I have students analyze the ways White Fang adapts to the four major environments he encounters: his early experiences discovering the world in the wild, the time he spends with Gray Beaver and the Indians, his trials with Beauty Smith, and his more compassionate experiences when Weedon Scott becomes his owner. This arrangement works best if each student presents an analysis of one of the environments. Group participants usually find that London's depiction of environmental determinism is suitably detailed and generally credible throughout the novel. They also note that, ethically, White Fang becomes the "better" dog, but Buck's story, for the most part, remains more compelling. *The Call of the Wild* seems more concerned with internal longing and release, while *White Fang* is about external forces and compliance. Group members are inclined to focus on White Fang's rehabilitation and retraining under the influence of Weedon Scott, and most see it as idealistic but plausible given White Fang's intelligence and his devotion to Scott. Still, most reporters agree that White Fang's onerous "rehab" is less engrossing than Buck's reprimitivization.

To broaden the discussion on White Fang's protean capacity to adapt, the instructor can prompt students to make comparisons and contrasts with other realist and naturalist texts that feature characters who have had to cope with variations in their social and physical environments. In *Daisy Miller*, for instance, the urbane Frederick Winterbourne lives on, while Daisy dies, but he remains emotionally stunted by his social conditioning. Students might go on to consider why Mark Twain's wily Huck Finn survives while Stephen Crane's seemingly adept Billie ("the oiler") in "The Open Boat" dies. Another comparison can be made with Lily Bart in *The House of Mirth*: from an ethical perspective, how does Wharton position the reader to evaluate Lily's social "maladaption"? These and other comparisons allow students to revisit and review a wide range of texts covered in the course and make the *White Fang* presentation an excellent one to schedule as the final group report.

NOTE

[1] Citations to *Call of the Wild* are from *Jack London: Novels and Stories*.

Martin Eden: Portrait of the Artist, American Style

Barry Menikoff

All the world loves a lover, so who could not love Jack London and his alter ego, Martin Eden? And who could be indifferent to F. Scott Fitzgerald and his chorus line of sad young men or Ernest Hemingway and his broken if unbowed expatriates in Paris and Italy? With movie-star good looks before movies became the rage—muscular, athletic, and sporting a smile that could charm the *wahines* from the beach—London, like Eden, emerged as a literary colossus moments before modernism swept away the physical and intellectual ruins of the Great War and planted itself firmly in the twentieth century. But in one of those ironies of history, or fate, London got caught, like the narrator in Matthew Arnold's poem, between two worlds, one dying and the other not quite born. He was of the new century, yet not new enough for the modernists, and so his dazzling success and impressive achievement—some fifty volumes in a career that barely spanned twenty years—came to be regarded as something of a curiosity, the work of a man driven by an old American idea: that one could make oneself whatever one wanted in this, the great land of freedom and liberty. London, like Eden, was an autodidact, and if he posed no threat to Benjamin Franklin, his singular success as a writer was viewed as nothing more than a fluke of popular culture, a by-product of the profusion of magazines and newspapers in the early years of the century, a world of print that craved reams of copy. It was a rough equivalent of our own world of blogs, except that the printers paid for the copy, and the writers entertained high expectations. Martin, scribbling away in the squalid, grubby room he rented from the desperately poor but kindhearted Maria, depicts Grub Street, American-style, as a place that chewed up hacks and artists alike, a picture that London tacitly counterpoints to the even darker English one in George Gissing's *New Grub Street*. If London's tableau of pen and inkers was written from the bottom up, it was part of a storied tradition that goes back to Jonathan Swift and that has carved its own place in American literature.

Edgar Allan Poe tried to keep himself afloat by juggling editing and writing. Herman Melville was the undisputed genius writer defeated by the marketplace, ending his days anonymously with an unpublished masterpiece at home. Closer in time to London was Henry James, whom Eden mentions in his panoply of authors; James notably composed a series of stories about the writing life. Unlike London's novel, these stories were written as far away from Grub Street as Mayfair was from the East End. Nonetheless, James shared with his compatriot a conviction that the reading public was at best indifferent to serious writing and contemptuous of it at worst. Stories like "The Next Time," "The Middle Years," and "The Real Thing" serve as useful comparisons with *Martin*

Eden because they dramatize, in a lower pitch and a more figured manner, the common problem faced by all serious writers of fiction. If, as Freud said, what drives an artist is the ambition for fame, fortune, and the love of a beautiful woman (i.e., sexual desire), then a wonderful comparison could be explored between Martin Eden and the young novelist in James's "The Lesson of the Master." The differences in style and execution between James and London are prominent, but the underlying view of the creative process and the idea that art is the sublimation of instinctual drives will bring these two craftsmen closer and suggest projects that are original as well as exciting.

London was an adventurer as well as a lover, and like Eden he loved the sea almost as much as he loved women, which is not surprising for a man born in the city of the Golden Gate. The sea figures throughout his work, in major books like *The Sea-Wolf*, in stories set in the Hawaiian archipelago, and in *Martin Eden*, wherein the hero is a sailor whose "rolling gait" makes him feel like a bull in a china shop when he enters the Morse home.[1] London's great sea adventure was the building of the *Snark*, a vessel that would carry him and Charmian and their small crew around the world for upward of half a dozen years. Whether he was emulating Robert Louis Stevenson, whose travels in the Pacific were by this time the stuff of legend, or whether he simply wanted time away from civilization, to sail, write, soak up the sun, and take some leisure, the voyage and the dream were aborted in under two years. It was a major disappointment. But the sheer audacity of the episode—like his time in the Alaskan Klondike or the road travels that led to a jail stint at the other end of the continent—highlights a man genuinely set apart from other writers. Clearly he was not the artist in an ivory tower, as James is often thought of, or even Thomas Hardy, who mined gold from his quiet home in Dorset. London was a city boy, once a street tough, and the survival skills he learned growing up in the Bay Area, on the sea, in the Arctic, and on the road were not the ordinary equipment of a writer to be. It is true that hard times often make for good fiction, but that template for becoming a writer would not become fashionable until a quarter of a century after London's death. It was figured in the career of a writer like Richard Wright, whose autobiography *Black Boy* offers an instructive parallel to *Martin Eden*. Wright describes conning the public library to check out books, a service available only to whites but essential for him to transform himself from an ignorant country boy into a literate and knowledgeable man. London, like Eden, had access to the Oakland Free Library and was taken under the wing of the library's venerable Ina Coolbrith. If books and learning were matters to live for in both London and Wright, they are themes that stretch back in American writing to Melville, who "swam" through libraries, and forward to a contemporary like Richard Rodriguez, who in *Brown* trumpeted the breadth of his reading, diverse enough so that he, a California son of Mexican immigrants, could travel in his imagination to the Depression-era tenement of a Brooklyn Jew like Alfred Kazin.

Thus, *Martin Eden* is a cornucopia of books—Algernon Conrad Swinburne, Robert Browning, George Bernard Shaw, William Ernest Henley, James, and

Joseph Conrad, citing just the literary types—and their purpose is not merely to chart Martin's intellectual development but to reverence the process of reading and learning that is embodied in books. This strong connection with other books makes teaching London much deeper—especially for English majors.

One of London's and Eden's idols, Stevenson, exemplified the idea of writing as a hard and disciplined job of reading, thinking, and putting pen to paper until thought and expression were one. It is as if both London and Eden, following Stevenson, replicated in their histories Francis Bacon's famous remark: "Reading maketh a full man; conference a ready man; and writing an exact man." Another writer mentioned more than once in the novel, Rudyard Kipling, also exhibits the pattern of the artist as reader and disciplined worker. Kipling also serves as a case study of an artist who is suddenly taken up by the public and then spit out after he has served their interest and no longer slakes their thirst. London refers to Kipling's meteoric success with *The Light That Failed* and has Eden make reference to it, although not by title, after he himself has become the lion of the day. In our own time, when celebrity culture absorbs such attention, it would be instructive to read these writers in the context of London's (and Eden's) career. What precisely is the relation of the writer to the audience? Another way of putting it for students to discuss is, For whom is the artist writing? And what should be the subject matter of the work? These are classic questions of aesthetics, and it would be appropriate for a class reading *Martin Eden* to explore them in depth.

Eden repeatedly states his philosophical bias in the novel—he is a realist and he can only write about the world as it is, or the world as he knows it ("I must have the real or nothing"). Is this an Aristotelian injunction? Is it a plea for verisimilitude? Compare Eden's position to that of his close friend Russ Brissenden, who has such contempt for the public that he would rather his poetry remain mute than be submitted to a great beast that will mutilate it with misreading, which is exactly what happens. This too is a question that would excite controversy among students. Who does not have an opinion about J. D. Salinger and what he was doing in his final years? And if a class learns that Franz Kafka gave orders to his close friend to burn his manuscripts, what does that say about a writer's relation to his own work? The classicists believed that art was made for others to enjoy and learn from; the Romantics preferred to see themselves as their own subject and their own best audience. In *Martin Eden* these ideas compete in the persons of Eden and Brissenden. And yet the two are not so far apart as they might seem, for Brissenden is astonished at Martin's blindness to Ruth's real being, while Martin believes that Brissenden's work exists on a level beyond the material. These issues of art and artist and audience can be teased out of the questions raised here. For a class in American literature, London would slip into a set piece on naturalism along with Stephen Crane, Frank Norris, Theodore Dreiser, and perhaps Edith Wharton. A more telling question might ask whether Martin Eden is as much of a realist as he believes. For the central fact of the novel is that he misconstrues the driving force of his ambition—he is impelled by his profound love for Ruth to achieve fame and fortune, but he is deluded by her personality. Brissenden, like Will Olney before him, knows that Ruth is nothing but a simple bourgeois, and when he realizes how besotted Martin is with her he foretells the tragic future of his friend. Since students never tire of riffing on why men and women cannot make it (in fiction), there could be no more intriguing puzzle than to place *Martin Eden* alongside James's *The Portrait of a Lady*, where Isabel Archer, a beautiful woman beguiled by love, acts with her eyes wide open and marries one of the most sinister men in James's canon. And James too was a realist, so the textbooks tell us, which leads one to wonder what use the word has when two such gifted persons as Martin Eden and Isabel Archer cannot see that which is right before their eyes.

Serious or modernist fiction in the years before the zenith of the Jazz Age purposefully stood apart from its popular cousin in a variety of ways, not the least by snubbing its nose at the sale of modernist books. This is not to say that all those serious writers were indifferent to money. Looking back again to the fin de siècle, James had already picked up the sobriquet "the Master," but his books sold so poorly that he turned to writing plays, which were then disdained while audiences lined up around the block to see Oscar Wilde. Conrad, among the first of the new modernists, chafed at the dismal sales of his books. D. H. Lawrence had some early modest success. Virginia Woolf as good as published herself with the Hogarth Press. James Joyce, whose portrait of the young Stephen Dedalus is the *Mona Lisa* of the art novel, depended for his livelihood on the kindness of friends. With the exception of James and Conrad, each of whom Eden tips his hat to, these writers came to prominence after London was dead. And on the face of it, London's career would seem antithetical to these writers' shared experience with critical success and commercial failure. Their fiction was hard to read, with its dislocated syntax, its allusive and opaque language, and its absence of any comprehensible plot. London, on the other hand, was readable for almost anyone. He was the poster child for popular success. It would be strange if readers coming of age many years after the triumph of modernism had not absorbed a central axiom from at least two generations of teachers of literature: serious writing is difficult to understand and requires guidance from those to whom its meaning has been disclosed, much as the knowledge of Latin gave early scholars and priests a special status that set them apart from the untutored. But who needs a teacher for *Martin Eden*? The novel, unlike, say, *Women in Love*, can be read by any literate person without instruction.

Yet there is a first principle in talking about fiction with readers whose literary culture has a heavy dose of the "accessible"—that is, genre writing that includes pulp mysteries, legal thrillers, romance novels, and a range of other types. And that principle is that simplicity is a sophisticated manner achieved only with great discipline and enormous patience. Students can learn to distinguish between the art of simplicity and its sham pretender, accessibility, which in popular genres is formulaic structure and simplistic writing. A story by Hemingway or John Steinbeck, or one of London's short chestnuts, would be a perfect device for illustrating simplicity as a serious artistic objective. Martin Eden believes in this principle, and his success is London's nod not just to Stevenson and Kipling but to all writers who strive to convey the truth that they "see" in a manner that will enable others to see it as well. Eden says at one point that writers are the "giants" of the world, wittingly or not echoing Samuel Johnson's declaration in his great dictionary that the glory of a people derives from its authors. And London is not so far from the moderns that came after in his view of serious as opposed to popular writing, or perhaps in his recognition that a mass audience was not necessarily something to be proud of. Martin Eden finally conquers the world—the Grub Street world of pulp paper and the elevated world of hardcovers—and in the moment of his conquest is his defeat, for he realizes that his success was utterly capricious. It is such a turn of fate that London might have been channeling Hardy (except that Hardy was still living). In a way, the later modernists like Joyce and others who could not sell their wares were better off than London or Eden because they dissociated themselves as artists from the world, or rather they separated their art from all contingency, as if they were the purest of Kantians, form as purposiveness with no purpose. London, alas, was not made that way. Martin Eden was of the world, as was his art, and his art was of him.

The wonderful homage to Walt Whitman that London offers through Eden in chapter 14 is telling here, since the American bard, never named, stands for a writer whose world and art and being were so inextricably laced that only an image from nature could embody such a transcendent concept. As they picnic on a grassy hillside on a June afternoon, Eden says to Ruth, "I could write an epic on the grass," knowing full well that he is the grass and that what he celebrates the reader shall celebrate. The allusion sails right past the University of California–educated Ruth, who still feels compelled to mentor Martin in public speaking. This chapter provides a springboard for contrasting the openness of free reading with the limits of institutional education, much as Whitman unshackled poetry from its straitened verse forms.

Is *Martin Eden* a modern novel? London's career coincided with the emergence of a mass audience—that is, a readership far beyond the numbers that the midcentury Victorians were accustomed to, and one unwilling to give time to long books. Gissing ironically remarked in *New Grub Street* that paragraphs needed to be short in order not to strain the attention of these stressed and harassed new readers (ch. 33). With Stevenson and Kipling in the lead, these writers—London, Gissing, Arnold Bennett, H. G. Wells, John Galsworthy, and others—ushered in a professional literary class that expected to earn its living from writing. At the same time, they diverged from their contemporaries, such as Joyce, who, while insisting they did not write for art's sake alone, nonetheless elevated their art to a peak unreachable by any but the most intrepid of climbers. If these latter were "modern" artists, then all those "professional" workers in the fields were nothing but scribblers to the masses. Even more important, modern writers dealt with subject matter and form in a manner that was innovative and experimental while the scribblers were stuck in a tired and retrograde style.

From both vantage points, London was a modern writer manqué. Yet one of the characteristics of modern fiction was its open treatment of sexuality, and in *Martin Eden* London manipulates sex in a way that might have surprised Lawrence. Although the language is circumspect, his plot upends traditional expectations of male and female sexuality. Martin, strong, handsome, and irresistible to women, recalls in his periodic "visions" the women he has known in the past. The opening scene of the novel presents a powerfully written "portrait gallery" of women from San Francisco to Mexico to Japan to the South Seas. And in the present there is the beautiful and direct Lizzie Connolly, whose "bold black eyes" leave no doubt of her desire for Martin and, near the end of the novel, of her willingness to live with him on any terms. But Lizzie is immediately counterpointed with Ruth, whom this robust sexual male had invested with the kind of purity that can only be found in a Raphael portrait. The poor girl did not even have a chance. Martin's devotion to the immaculate object of his invention sustains itself for most of the novel. In a twist of literary history, London inverts the traditional sacrifice made for love (think Antony giving up all for one touch of Cleopatra) and instead extinguishes his hero's sexual life on the altar of his imagined romance.

Martin iterates his faith in love—"Love was the most exalted expression of life"—so many times that it becomes his defining passion, and his drive for success as a writer is a textbook example of Freud's principle. How London reconciles Martin's incalculable investment in a platonic idea with Herbert Spencer and evolutionary biology is a nice question, one certain to generate classroom controversy. But if London's bronzed god goes curiously tame before the fantasy of Ruth's perfection, it is Ruth herself that the novelist transforms into a sexual animal. From the start of the novel, when she is transfixed by Martin's neck, we see a woman who has no knowledge of sex repeatedly drawn by a desire she can neither resist nor comprehend. *Wanton*, *desire*, *fever*, *burning lips*, *blood*, *pulse*—these are the terms stitched into the sentences that dramatize the scenes that Ruth ravishes in against her conscious judgment. Her recurring compulsion to touch Martin's neck is simply a reaching out to his hard member. London even goes so far as to provide Ruth with an orgasm, in chapter 21, after an intensely evocative description of passion before a kiss: "So exquisite was the pang of love and desire fulfilled that she uttered a low moan, relaxed her hands, and lay half-swooning in his arms." But Ruth, ever the bourgeois, cannot die for love and rejects Martin because he is poor. When he hits pay dirt, however, and is the literary lion, she sneaks into his hotel room and offers herself to him. It is a damning scene, for her brother is waiting outside in the shadows, making it clear that the Morse family is offering her for sale. Lizzie Connolly's gesture, by contrast, comes out of unconditional love. Ruth, for one moment, turns into a working girl, while the real working girl exhibits a grace that Martin has finally come to value.

So what has London done? He has inverted the gender roles—the (sexual) male has become the lover of ideality while the (idealized) female has become the sexualized predator, a reversal perhaps worthy of Wilde, whose writing on gender and sexuality is the gold standard for the fin de siècle. Finally, it is impossible to read *Martin Eden* and not address the question of the hero's suicide, which cannot be reduced to London's oft-quoted remark about individualism versus socialism. Martin's overarching faith in a dream, like his younger cousin Jay Gatsby, has as its terrible consequence the inconsolable pain and despair that comes with the discovery of its falsity. Disappointment does not capture the emotion. Martin experiences the kind of despair that the later existentialists recognized—and of course he references Friedrich Nietzsche—and he does not have the resources to recover, having lost all desire, as Lizzie notices when she says he does not even see that women are looking at him with lust in their eyes. The novel is Martin Eden's story about becoming a writer and overcoming the odds in a world, as Damon Runyon said, that is always "six to five against," even if at the end he saw only the nada of Hemingway's "A Clean Well-Lighted Place."

NOTE

[1] Citations to *Martin Eden* are from the *Project Gutenberg* edition.

CLASS, POLITICS, AND IDEOLOGY

Jack London and Socialism

Jay Williams

To place Jack London and his socialist writings for students within the proper historical-political context, a class should cover certain crucial events and concepts: race relations, especially among whites, African Americans, and Asian Americans; the issue of the gold versus the silver standard; the concept of the cooperative commonwealth and the popularity of Edward Bellamy's *Looking Backward*; the increase of industrialization, unionism, and urbanism and the decrease in agrarianism and the diminishment of the American village; the Spanish-American War, the Mexican Revolution, and World War One; monopoly capitalism and the formation of trusts; immigration and nativism; the connection between women's rights and Prohibition; the hobo; and the rise and fall of socialism, especially its relations to craft unionism and the electoral process. One way to specify these large categories and so give students a way into them is to ask students to investigate certain key words of period. This exercise would give them not only the opportunity to recoup the historical definitions of terms crucial for understanding the period but also a sense of how far apart (or how close) this historical period is to their own time. A partial list of terms, which I am sure could be much longer, includes the following: *the hobo* versus *the homeless*; *realism* versus *romanticism*; *laissez-faire economics*; *direct action*; *use value* and *surplus value*; *waste*; *cooperation* versus *competition*; *degeneration* versus *eugenics*; *documentation*; *progress*; *class* and *class warfare*; *corporation*; *anarchism*; *craft unionism*; *altruism* and *nihilism*; *propaganda* versus *journalism*; *utopias* and *utopianism*; *alienation*; *wealth*; *nativism* and *nationalism*; and *evolution* versus *revolution*. When two students are each assigned a term in a pair that seems in opposition, the students should discover how much the terms actually complement each other; that is, the discussion should not degenerate into a competitive debate. Interestingly, some of these terms have biological as well as sociopolitical application, so for students with a scientific bent they may be doubly appealing. I would not necessarily recommend *Keywords for American Culture Studies* because its terms are too broad, but some students might find it useful. I would recommend Raymond Williams's *Keywords: A Vocabulary of Culture and Society*, from which a few of these terms have been taken.

London's involvement in the political sphere can be outlined by several key biographical events: in the summer or fall of 1895, he met Frederick Irons Bamford, Oakland's Christian Socialist reference librarian, an influential friend and founder of the Bay Area Ruskin Club; at a December convocation at his high school, London gave a speech similar to his first socialist essay, "Pessimism, Optimism, and Patriotism"; in December 1895, the *San Francisco Chronicle* subtitled London's first socialist essay "What Socialism Is" with the words "The Boy Socialist Defines the Meaning and Intent of the New Philosophy" (Wichlan 13; see also "Boy Socialist"). Soon after, in April 1896, the year when William Jennings Bryan and William McKinley campaigned for president, London joined the Socialist Labor Party (SLP); in February 1897, he was charged by police for speaking in public without a permit, a goal he and the SLP had hoped to achieve (Zamen 193); from 1896 to 1916, he formed and maintained professional relationships with the prominent socialist publishers Gaylord Wilshire and A. J. Wayland; he ran for mayor of Oakland on the Social Democratic Party ticket in 1901 and then later joined the Socialist Party; he lectured on socialism nationwide in 1905–06; he formed friendships and established correspondence with many prominent leftists of all stripes, including Emma Goldman (anarchist), Frank Strawn-Hamilton (walking delegate for the American Federation of Labor), Anna Strunsky Walling, and William English Walling (Socialist Party); his written work was praised by socialists both left and right, like Eugene Debs and John Spargo, and by communists like V. I. Lenin and Leon Trotsky; London published widely and read essays and books on class warfare, revolution, socialist economics, capital punishment, Prohibition and the suffragettes, and the definition of socialism. In fact, London, Upton Sinclair, and Debs were the only members of the Socialist Labor Party and Socialist Party who were known nationally (Moore 211), without being labeled criminals, as was Bill Haywood and others. Students could therefore do historical research on, say, the differences among socialists of London's time and compare socialist factions with current organized manifestations of leftist thought. It would be quite interesting, for example, for a student to gather material from the Democratic Socialists of America or the International Socialist Organization and find out how they view London and other historical forbearers.

So London's career as a writer—begun in 1893 and ended on the day of his death—and his socialist activities are coeval. However, before we explore and define his political activities and beliefs, we have to keep in mind that, above all else, Jack London was an author. He made his living almost exclusively by writing fiction, and he understood his professional identity as such. A fiction writer is what he trained himself to be, and a fiction writer is what he became. Unlike other major figures in American socialism, London excused himself from the cause from time to time whenever his writerly self demanded it.

Nonetheless, London was a consistent advocate for a particular ideology of American socialism. He was neither a propagandist (in the modern sense of the word) nor a theorist. He both advocated for and practiced socialism, and what he practiced coincided with what he wrote. As life and issues changed in his nation—sometimes with the rapidity many ascribe to modernity—and as his class status changed—from proletariat child and young man to upper-class adult author—he invariably focused and refocused on one element or another of his socialist program. But consistency within an evolving sociopolitical sphere was his trademark, and this essay tracks both his principles and the historical changes he faced. As Philip Foner has written, "three basic concepts which he drew from his initial reading of [*The Communist Manifesto*] were never to leave him, even after he resigned from the Socialist Party—the belief in the class struggle; the conviction that private ownership of the means of production and the interest of the majority of the people were opposed; and confidence in the inevitable emergence of Socialism" ("Jack London" 26).

In general, socialism to London meant a political aspiration for a more just and economically equitable American society based on noncapitalist principles, and it is worth noting how successful socialism was for however brief a moment in American history. In our age, when socialism is considered in some influential political circles as an evil on par with Cold War communism and even anti-American terrorism, it is somewhat amazing to think of an America that harbored a sustained and successful Socialist Party. In twelve years (1900–12) the Socialist Party increased its membership from ten thousand to one hundred and fifty thousand dues-paying members:

> It increased its electoral strength tenfold, from 95,000 to 900,000. It elected well over two thousand members to public office [from one member of Congress—Victor Berger—to many mayors, police chiefs, and other local officials]. It secured passage of hundreds of reforms, and contributed to the adoption of many times more. . . . It publicized inequities in American economic, social, and political life, and participated in the struggle to restore substance to the nation's democratic ideals.
>
> (Kipnis 422)

Never again would a third party in America achieve so much electoral success. During World War One, the nation found socialism incompatible with its ultimate capitalist goal—world military and economic superiority—and never looked back. Students should therefore be encouraged to think of how many issues advocated by radicals at the turn of the previous century are now commonplaces. What are the connections between the principles of socialism and the actions—whether inside or outside the electoral process—the socialists performed? How comfortable would these early socialists feel in today's political sphere? What would they applaud? What would they fight against?

We can now turn to a small sampling of London's overt political writings and enormous body of fiction to discover his individual "attempt to unite a certain ideology with art" (Rideout 3). His first explicit socialist essay—"Pessimism, Optimism, and Patriotism"—was followed by "What Socialism Is," a title that turned the clichéd interrogative "What Is Socialism?" into a simple declarative. Although the former was written for his high school magazine the *Aegis*, it shares many similarities with his newspaper writings and can be seen as a prelude, a warm-up, for his first submission to the *San Francisco Examiner* in December 1895—"What Socialism Is"—and to his submissions to two other Bay Area newspapers in 1896, in his last months of high school (*Letters* 1: 3, 7). "Pessimism, Optimism, and Patriotism" is a retort to two essays published that year in the *Aegis*, both of which advocated universal education, though one is written from the point of view of the privileged classes (the optimists) and the other from the lower classes (the pessimists). He was actively engaged in debate, just as he had been on the road in the spring of 1894, when he apparently first encountered serious discussion about socialism. Written in February 1895, "Pessimism, Optimism, and Patriotism" mentions Ralph Waldo Emerson's essay "Compensation," quotes John Ruskin, and, most significantly, draws on *The Communist Manifesto*; as Foner has pointed out, "Jack London may have read little else of Marx and Engels, but it was from the *Manifesto* . . . that he obtained the fundamental concepts of his socialism" (25). Echoing Marx and Engels, London writes, "[I]f we could wipe out, 'root and branch,' every optimist in the land, and become a race of pessimists, then could we prove the shadow lengthening across the American landscape to be a phantom." And he concludes with a direct call, a kind of mix between Thomas Paine and Marx and Engels, to his audience: "Arise, ye Americans, patriots and optimists! Awake! Seize the reins of a corrupted government and educate your masses!" ("Pessimism" 18). Though siding with the pessimists, London argues that education is beside the point if economic conditions are not bettered first. The essay proved prophetic, and the author became the experiment from which data was collected: poverty was a major reason he left the University of California, Berkeley, after one semester. Students should readily identify with the problem London faced paying for school and could examine the socioeconomic and political conditions surrounding their own enrollment in college.

London was fascinated with Marx and Engels's conjunction of communism and the figure of the specter. "What Socialism Is" begins with the Marx and Engels's theme: "Socialism and Christmas. How incongruous this specter, stalking forth when all is joy and merry-making" (13). Marx and Engels intended their manifesto to expose the notion of communism as a boogeyman: "It is high time that Communists should openly . . . publish their views . . . and meet this nursery tale of the Spectre of Communism with a Manifesto of the party itself" (473 [ed. Tucker]). At the same time, they represented the agent of the next period of revolutionary change, the proletariat, as a ghost. The manifesto closes famously with the lines, "Let the ruling classes tremble at a Communistic revolution. The proletarians have nothing to lose but their chains" (500). Of course, chains bind slaves, and this image is the standard way of reading these lines. But the fear of a ghost, often pictured in the nineteenth and twentieth centuries as a figure wrapped in chains—especially Charles Dickens's ghost of Christmas past—would naturally cause a person to tremble, and so in the *Manifesto* the proletariat/ghost comes to haunt the bourgeoisie, comes to overthrow their economic stranglehold on the poor much as a ghost overthrows one's reason. London, as we saw in "Pessimism, Optimism, and Patriotism," shared this revolutionary goal with Marx and Engels, though wiping out the optimists is not the rhetorical method they had in mind, at least at the time of the writing of the *Manifesto*. Violence might proceed from the publishing of views, but London in 1895 was already at the point of advocating violence. Socialism for him was a specter, but not because it was created by the bourgeoisie to scare the people away from revolutionary change; it was a specter because it was a very real power, a power invested in the working class that would violently change American society. If one was going to believe in ghosts, and London of course vacillated in any number of ways and in any number of contexts, he at least thought they should be invested with revolutionary power. Here is a subtle change in rhetoric from Marx to London, and it is important for understanding how London conceived of the power and manipulation of ghosts. Marx and Engels deny the reality of the ghost in favor of asserting the very real force of communism and its principles clearly, in the light of day, brought forth in the *Manifesto*. For London, however, it matters not if socialism is a ghost because ghosts can be just as real as the material world. Their power to effect change makes them so.

London's intuitive ontology at this age relied on a fundamental confluence between life and the afterlife. While his two early essays show how he responded positively to Marx and Engels's rhetoric of spectrality, as Jacques Derrida calls it, and learned from it how to mix spiritualism and politics, there was a fundamental difference between the figure of the ghost in London's work and the figure of the ghost in Marx. To reiterate through Derrida,

> Marx does not like ghosts any more than his adversaries do. He does not want to believe in them. But he thinks of nothing else. He believes rather in what is supposed to distinguish them from actual reality. . . . He believes enough in the dividing line of this opposition to want to denounce, chase away, or exorcise the specters but by means of critical analysis and not by some counter-magic. But how to distinguish between the analysis that denounces magic and the counter-magic that it still risks being? (*Specters* 46–47)

That is, once one practices what Derrida analyzes as conjuration, one already is invested in the power that one wants to deny. London's resistance through a lifelong process, however, to the reality and power of the specter grew weaker and weaker. London became, in this way, more of a Derridean than a Marxist, though his comfort level with spectrality is not as great as Derrida's, and he certainly never abandoned his leftist social consciousness. As Derrida points out, Marx did not want "to know what everyone alive knows without learning and without knowing, namely, that the dead can often be more powerful than the living," whereas London refused to relate "everything back to life only on the condition of including there death and the alterity of its other without which it would not be what it is" (48). Marx and Engels, however, in a line that Derrida does not cite, did not deny the power of the dead: violence, they say in the *Manifesto*, is a natural result of bourgeois capitalism, which creates forces of competition that go beyond its control, like the magician and "the powers of the nether world" (13). Although both Marx and London see materialism as infected and influenced by spiritualism, for London the character of spiritualism differed and the spirit world exerted its own brand of realism. Call it a theatrical realism. London would always connect spirits with the staging of his mother's séances. To make someone believe in specters or ghosts, whether of persons or of communities of persons—that is, political parties—one needs to present a performance. One engages in theater, and one senses the theatrical throughout London's life in socialism, whether it is as an actor dressed as a tramp in the East End of London in 1902 (to write *The People of the Abyss*) or as a capitalist in Vera Cruz in 1914 (to cover the American invasion of Mexico) or as a writer lecturing from a platform.

One more point needs to be made about his definition of socialism. London is careful to include mental labor and the exercise of talent in his discussion of the accumulation and distribution of wealth. He was proletariat with an eye on brain work. He of course favored an economic system that did not forbid the lower classes from entering the intellectual spheres of medicine or writing. No one has ever thought that London felt guilty for leaving behind his workingman's roots; he strenuously proclaimed that that kind of life would have killed or crippled him, as it did so many, and his will not to earn money with physical labor is admired by readers of all classes. (This has larger, theoretical implications when it comes to interpreting his fiction; that is, briefly, anytime London characterizes writing or the profession of authorship as machine-like or Tayloristic one knows he is portraying a false artist; for London, writing was always a deeply spiritual act.) But here in these early essays, when he is so close to the border between physical and mental labor, we see him describing his turn from the former in theoretical terms. It is a broad-minded conception of socialism, realistically taking into account the multifarious nature of American labor. He wanted from the very first to become a writer's socialist. Students, especially those who are first-generation college students, should be encouraged to think of how their own intellectual labor would fit into London's philosophy. How does the labor of their parents compare to their own in college? What is the difference between manual and intellectual labor? Why, typically, is the former unionized, but not the latter?

Throughout the rest of his career, London, for the most part, never contradicted the principles of socialism he enunciated in these first essays; much of what he later wrote, in *People of the Abyss*, *War of the Classes*, *Revolution*, and even *The Iron Heel* (as much a work of nonfiction as it is fiction), gathers and presents new data to support the socialist cause. But I want to take a quick look before we turn to the fiction at another early essay that placed socialism in what most Americans saw as an exotic locale. Even among Klondike millionaires and in the midst of national gold fever, London analyzed the northern gold hunt in socialist terms, lest we think that he took a year off from politics to simply hunt gold.

London wrote "The Economics of the Klondike" in August 1899. Its socialist application to the Klondike strike of 1896–98 was simple and straightforward: the strike was a disaster for the individual miner. He wrote that "$220,000,000 have been spent in extracting $22,000,000 from the ground." Leave it to London to show how one of the richest gold strikes in United States history seems paltry compared with the cost to the laborers. This simple economic fact underlies all his Klondike fiction; that is, any tale seemingly about the heroism of individual miners is undercut by the economic reality of Northern class differences. But one realizes that London, in 1899, was on the verge of losing twice. First, he was one of the exploited laborers in 1897–98. Second, his stories threaten to become Bret Harteish in their anachronistic nature (students should compare Frederick Jackson Turner's "The Significance of the Frontier in American History" with London's essay). If, as London predicts, "the frontiersman will yield to the laborer, the prospector to the mining engineer, the dog-driver to the engine-driver, the trader and speculator to the steady-going modern man of business," where goes the romance of the Yukon, the mysterious appeal to readers in the Southland? ("Economics" 72, 74). This essay easily could have been titled "The Future Economics of My Authorship," and students might be asked to read it with London's later novel *Burning Daylight*. Certainly London intended to play out the streak as long as possible, but at the same time he knew that he had to continue writing club and urban-life stories (like "The Proper 'Girlie,'" "The End of the Chapter," and "Semper Idem") and boys' adventure tales (like *The Cruise of the* Dazzler), all composed immediately after "The Economics of the Klondike." Not surprisingly, then, his next two novels that take place in the North—*The Call of the Wild* and *White Fang*—focus on dogs, not human beings. Thus, in this essay he is in effect announcing the departure of Sitka Charley, Stanley Prince, Mrs. Eppingwell, the Malemute Kid, and the others. Small wonder, too, that he was in the middle of the Children of the Frost series, whose central thematic is the rapaciousness of white miners. When the gold and, with it, the members of the white race disappear from the North, thought London, the Native Americans will still remain.

Socialism works overtly and covertly throughout his work, helping to blur the difference between fiction and nonfiction, between life and art. London once wrote to a casual correspondent, "All my . . . books ooze socialism" (*Letters* 3: 1021). Students should consider not what London's fiction tells us about London's beliefs but rather two main questions: How does a given story dramatize political beliefs? What were the effects of the dramatization on the reader? London's stories, that is, can portray characters who did not believe as he believed, and we cannot literalize his characters' beliefs and make them into London's; we have to apply critical tools to read his fiction that we don't use when we read his nonfiction. Nonetheless, I would argue that the stories are meant to inspire his readers to become socialists or to keep the cause alive. Crucial questions for students might include the following: using the words *propaganda*, *realism*, *romanticism*, and *documentation*, describe and define the differences and similarities between fiction and nonfiction. What rhetorical devices does London use to indicate that a work is a piece of fiction? a piece of nonfiction? What information about American society is the narrator communicating to the reader? Is it at odds or in agreement with what the characters do? Are we meant to argue with the narrator? with the characters? Are there rhetorical markers signaling us to enjoy London's fiction as an aesthetic object, as art for art's sake? If so, what sort of conflict arises stylistically between the dramatization of characters' lives and of American sociopolitical conditions? What is the nature of the conflict between entertainment and social activism?

Take, for example, three stories written in the first half of 1909, while London was also writing his novel *Adventure*: "The Strength of the Strong," "South of the Slot," and "A Piece of Steak" (on the dating, see Jay Williams, "Jack London's Works"). He is a year away from having completed *Martin Eden*, a novel of a writer who as a worker is alienated not from the act of composition but from the acts of selling and distributing his product, as Chris Gair has pointed out (*Complicity* 136); that is, Martin Eden applies his Taylorized work habits to the acts of typing, recording, and sending out his work, thus setting the stage for a fatal ennui that, London makes clear, could only happen in a capitalist society. If Eden had a proper socialist consciousness, he would have been saved. "The Strength of the Strong" repeats this moral, though the story begins with a seemingly different moral—"Parables don't lie, but liars will parable"—attributed to someone named Lip-King, actually London's humorous rendering of Rudyard Kipling's last name into a prehistoric name. (And students will see how some of the key words—*propaganda*, *journalism*, *realism*—immediately come into play and how they are intertwined with the ostensible themes of the story, notably, individualism and cooperation.) An individual must have a collective identity—as London said in his nonfiction, socialists are social—and this principle governs modern writers like Eden as well as the cave men in "The Strength of the Strong." The story ends with the vision of a futuristic, peaceful, socialist society in which various tribes have foresworn war. As London wrote to one of his editors, "some time ago, Kipling made an attack on Socialism in the form of a parable or short story, entitled 'Melissa,' in which he exploited his Jingoism and showed that a co-operation of individuals strong enough to overcome war meant the degeneration of said individuals" (*Letters* 2: 830). Given that both Kipling and London were journalists and fiction writers and familiar with each other's work, fruitful comparisons can be made by students between these two writers, as well as more traditional comparisons between London and others such as Stephen Crane, Frank Norris, and Ernest Hemingway. For other, less obvious comparisons, students could compare London with politically engaged fiction writers such as Sarah Orne Jewett (especially given Jewett's interest in photography [see Jay Williams, "Introduction"]), Frederick Douglass, Charlotte Perkins Gilman, and Emma Goldman.

London develops the continuity between cooperation among prehistoric humanoids and cooperation among modern human beings in a different way in the very next story he wrote, "South of the Slot" (completed 6 February 1909). Freddie Drummond is a sociology professor at University of California who writes mainstream analyses of class distinction in America that the capitalists hail but that London's narrator calls "pernicious" and "immoral" (1580). Drummond performs his research by dressing as a working-class stiff named Bill Totts, much as London did in the East End and Mexico, and the story is about his eventual disavowal of his professorial life in favor of the life of the proletariat. Totts is even likened to an earlier evolutionary form of Drummond, having more in common with Drummond's "dim forbears" than Drummond himself (1586). While London (and the narrator) lived in a third space—that of left socialism, like Debs and others who regarded craft unionism as complicit with capitalism—Drummond and Totts fight the traditional labor war between industrialist and workers. Socialism in fact does not even make an appearance in the story, and as a result the battle that ends the story and completes Drummond's transformation into Totts leaves the reader without a solution to the labor war even though this prominent apologist for capital produced "no more books on economics and the labor question" (1594). The absent solution is of course the socialist's cooperative commonwealth. The story makes clear that our sympathies should rest with the worker, and not with the writer of false consciousness—Drummond—who, like Bug in "The Strength of the Strong," sings the dominant hegemony's songs and writes its socioeconomic treatises. But peace will come only with the advent of socialism, not with their mere silencing.

London wrote the third story we will consider, "A Piece of Steak," four months later. Tom King, a proletariat boxer, is like Bill Totts and like several prehistoric characters in "The Strength of the Strong." He is "like a modern working-man" but gets his food "in the old, primitive, royal, animal way, by fighting for it" (1632). Like the other two stories, and countless others by London, "A Piece of Steak" dramatizes the worst effects of capitalism on the working class. It not only robs workers of rightful prosperity but also blinds them to the reality of their condition and renders them unable to see beyond class warfare; recall that in "South of the Slot" Totts, says the narrator, "lacked the perspective to raise him above class-consciousness." Like Tom King, Totts "really wasn't able to see beyond the next meal and the prize-fight the following night at the Gaiety Athletic Club" ("South" 1585). (To cement the connections between these two stories, London has King fight his last fight at the Gayety Club, even though Drummond (a noted boxer and, as Totts, a habitué of the Gaiety Athletic Club) lives in San Francisco and King in Sydney, Australia.) King believes to the very last that a proper meal was the difference between success and failure, and throughout the fight he sees that something larger—his age, the natural downward progression of the prizefighter—will end his career. But he cannot see the largest picture, the fact that his family is starving, not because of his age or the lack of meat, but because of capitalism. Thus, for London, the worker is often portrayed in fiction and nonfiction as a foolhardy or ignorant workbeast in an attempt to wake him or her up to the reality of capitalism. Long Beard in "The Strength of the Strong" sums it up at the end: "[W]e were all fools, except those who were fat and did no work. . . . Some day all the fools will be dead and then all live men will go forward. The strength of the strong will be theirs, and they will add their strength together, so that, of all the men in the world, not one will fight with another" (1578, 1579). This of course is not the strength of the boxer but of the cooperative commonwealth birthed by socialism.

This story may be the most challenging to students. They will want to especially examine how London works their emotions to identify with or not identify with the lower classes. The question of London's personal wealth will undoubtedly surface, and the instructor can use this moment of seeming contradiction to reintroduce key words such as *wealth*, *alienation*, *waste*, *surplus value*, and *use value* to guide students through the tangle of author-narrator and author-audience relations. One could also enumerate the number of socialists who were not proletariats—William English Walling, Anna Strunsky Walling, Gaylord Wilshire, and others—and think how in our own time dot.com millionaires, Hollywood actors, sports figures, and other wealthy Americans help advance liberal and reformist causes. Words such as *cooperation* and *cooperative commonwealth* and *altruism* come to mind as guides to solving the seeming paradox of the wealthy socialist. Helpful questions might include the following: Is wealth a marker of individualism? What are the sources of wealth? What are the connections between wealth and labor? What did London see as the source of his own wealth?

A class on London's socialism, therefore, could use his essays—and any of the socialist ones, like "How I Became a Socialist," "Revolution," and "The Class Struggle"—to lay the foundation for the study of his fiction. Students will quickly see how his centrality for understanding socialism cannot be overstated. Jack London's life traced his party's evolution as he himself went from proletariat author to upper-class author. Though his authorial life took off in unforeseen directions that made it incompatible with his life in the working class, he never lost his talent for articulating in manifold ways what he thought was best about socialism.

Teaching *The Iron Heel*

Paul Lauter

The Iron Heel (1908) is not an easy book to teach, and yet it is an important one. Like Sinclair Lewis's *It Can't Happen Here* (1935) and Philip Roth's *The Plot against America* (2004), it imagines the onset of fascism in the United States. London's novel is interesting because it presents an argument about socialism, features structural peculiarities, and provides images of London both as radical lecturer and idealized activist. Each of those points of interest, however, brings with it pedagogical problems that I wish here to address.

One of the first things critics, and often students, say about *The Iron Heel* is that it is a very "talky" as well as an oddly divided book. And it is. The first nine chapters consist mainly of a series of lectures, generally delivered by Ernest Everhard and often taking dialogue form. These dialogues lay out the central tenets of scientific socialism as London understood it, about which he regularly lectured during the first decade of the twentieth century. The remaining sixteen chapters mostly narrate a dystopian future: the repressive actions of the fascist-like oligarchy, the "Iron Heel," and the resistance developed by the revolutionaries; these chapters present less talk and more action. That structural divide is complicated by the frame within which the story is staged: the Everhard manuscript, as it is called, is supposed to have been discovered some seven centuries after the events narrated and is presented, complete with an introduction and notes by one Anthony Meredith, a somewhat comical academic figure. Critics in the past have valued this frame so little that they have omitted it from the text of London's novel, as was the case in the Hill and Wang edition introduced by Max Lerner that was for many years the only available text. This bowdlerization of London's book has at least the virtue of raising with students what the point of the frame—or, rather, frames—might be. For while the central figure of the novel is, or seems to be, Ernest Everhard, the narrator is his wife, Avis; in fact, we see rather little of Ernest in the second, activist half of the novel. Why present Ernest at two removes, as it were, through Meredith's "editing" and Avis's narrative? Discussion of the structural characteristics of the novel leads in a number of useful directions: Do the frames enable London to retain a "realist" narrative stance, something of a difficulty given the fact that the plot ends in catastrophe for all the central figures? Who could for London speak Job's words, as Ishmael does at the conclusion of *Moby-Dick*: "And I only am escaped alone to tell thee"? Does placing Avis at the center of the narrative represent London's effort to provide something of a female, perhaps even a feminist, lens through which to view a decidedly "masculine" set of actions? Is it London's expectation that his readers will identify with Avis, particularly as she models the learning process the first nine chapters are designed to encourage? Does constructing Ernest's audience as female require that London give Avis in the second half of the novel a decidedly activist, even heroic, profile? There are, I think, no definitive answers to such questions, which makes them all the more interesting for classroom discussion.

And, of course, why does London devote more than two-fifths of the book, the first nine chapters, to a series of lectures and dialogues configured more like a basic course in early-twentieth-century socialism than an action novel? Does that work? To answer those last questions, I want to focus on the first nine chapters, which seem to me to represent London's efforts to bring the ideas of scientific socialism to as wide an audience as he could reach. We see in these chapters a form of fiction, somewhat akin to platonic dialogues, harnessed to ideological and political goals.

The foreword, supposedly written seven centuries later by the putative editor of the Everhard manuscript, Anthony Meredith, describes Ernest's work primarily as "his elaboration and interpretation of working class philosophy. 'Proletarian science' and 'proletarian philosophy,'" Meredith writes, "were his phrases for it" (5).[1] The terms, Meredith continues, show "the provincialism of his mind," though it is not clear why that's the case, especially given Meredith's own comment—a basic premise of scientific socialism—that "historical events" could "have been predicted with the same certitude that astronomers to-day predict the outcome of the movement of the stars" (6–7). Meredith also insists that unlike other forms of social development—"primitive communism, chattel slavery, serf slavery, and wage slavery"—the Iron Heel was not a necessary stepping stone "in the evolution of society" but an unnecessary "step backward." It was neither necessary nor inevitable, he argues, thus suggesting that London's novel is directed toward forestalling the imposition of the Iron Heel on early-twentieth-century America. Implicitly, I think, the argument of the book is that preventing the horrors narrated in the final sixteen chapters depends on learning the lessons laid out in the first nine. While these lessons may seem somewhat dated—they are rooted in a form of industrial capitalism no longer dominant—I want to suggest that their larger implications remain of interest, both historically and, with some adjustment, in terms of contemporary political values.

The initial lesson, laid out in chapter 1, has to do with the power of a scientific as opposed to what Ernest calls a "metaphysical" "method of thinking." "Your method of reasoning," he says to the clergymen gathered for dinner in the Berkeley home of Avis's professor father, "is the opposite to that of science" (14–15):

> The metaphysician reasons deductively out of his own subjectivity. The scientist reasons inductively from the facts of experience. The metaphysician reasons from theory to facts, the scientist from facts to theory. The metaphysician explains the universe by himself, the scientist explains himself by the universe. (15)

Scientists formulate the circulation of the blood, discover America, build granaries and bridges, and drain swamps, all the while metaphysicians spin "airy fancies." To explain the voyages of discovery, Ernest claims that it was not the thinking and speculation of metaphysicians that prompted such activity. Rather, it was certain material conditions: "Bread and butter, silks and jewels, dollars and cents, and, incidentally, the closing up of the overland trade-routes to India [by the Turks] were the things that caused the voyages of discovery." Ernest's test of truth is "the facts." As Avis reports, "He bristled with facts. He tripped them up with facts, ambuscaded them with facts, bombarded them with broadsides of facts" (18). Ernest questions not the motives of his antagonists here but their starting points and ways of thinking. It is these that the scientific socialist London wishes to shape and so must change: start with "facts," that is, material conditions, and move from them to theorize about the shaping of society. This emphasis on the operative material conditions seems to me central to understanding social phenomena with which students daily engage, like the indebtedness they have incurred (see, e.g., Jeffrey Williams), the privatization of the costs of higher education, and the limitations of courses available to them. Likewise, many of those teaching the book must deal with the exploitation of "contingent" faculty members (see, e.g., *Education*), as well as the impact of the worldwide financial meltdown on their chances for obtaining a job, much less for ever retiring.

But a scientific approach to understanding society, while necessary, is not sufficient. The second chapter of the novel addresses what was then—and remains today—a critical issue for socialists: namely, class struggle. Avis tells us that she has read Everhard's books and is impressed with his arguments and his clarity. Yet there is something she does not like: "He laid too great stress on what he called the class struggle, the antagonism between labor and capital, the conflict of interest" (25). She confronts Everhard in terms that remain familiar to every political campaign then or since: "'You foment class hatred,' I said. 'I consider it wrong and criminal to appeal to all that is narrow and brutal in the working class. Class hatred is anti-social, and, it seems to me, anti-socialist'" (26–27). Everhard's response is, first, to distinguish class struggle from class hatred: "[W]e foment no hatred. We say that class struggle is a law of social development. . . . We do not make the class struggle. We merely explain it, as Newton explained gravitation" (27). His explanation proceeds along classical Marxist lines, in terms of both the history of class struggle and its supposed inevitability. He roots the conditions of the working class in the history of enclosures and the development of the factory system in the eighteenth century (31). And he lays out the inevitability of class struggle in simplistic terms determined by the fundamental selfishness of the parties:

> . . . [T]he workingman, being selfish, wants all he can get in the division. The capitalist, being selfish, wants all he can get in the division. When

> there is only so much of the same thing, there is a conflict of interest. This is the conflict of interest between labor and capital. And it is an irreconcilable conflict. As long as workingmen and capitalists exist, they will continue to quarrel over the division. (29)

But they should not, Bishop Morehouse and Avis protest. We should all be able "to get along," to use Rodney King's hopeful words. Yes, there are wrongs in the industrial system, but these are "due to the ignorance of the capitalist class" (34), as the bishop puts it. Once they know the truth, Avis and the bishop argue, they will "mend all that is wrong." The problem for them is thus not class struggle but a lack of "communication." Here again, I think, while the nature of the system has changed profoundly, the question of intent has not. The recent history of Western finance capitalism, which has produced today's immense disparities in income and wealth, may be suggestive—for example, subprime loans and their resulting profits and foreclosures.

It is precisely at this point in the novel, at the end of chapter 2, that London introduces the workingman Jackson and his missing arm. Over the two following chapters, Avis tests her theory that social problems are "due to ignorance" and that knowing the truth will produce change among capitalists or those who are tied to their machine. She interviews Jackson; his supervisors; a reporter friend; Jackson's lawyer; the corporate lawyer, Colonel Ingram, who defeats Jackson's suit for the loss of his arm; as well as major stockholders in the Sierra Mills and their wives. In short, she investigates the facts of one case, that of Jackson, and their implications. Jackson's arm becomes her equivalent of Mao Tse-tung's "Report on an Investigation of the Peasant Movement in Hunan." What she discovers is a "tacit conspiracy against Jackson. . . . But this tacit conspiracy grew large. Not alone was it aimed against Jackson. It was aimed against every workingman who was maimed in the mills" (52)—and, beyond that, at every workingman. Or, more precisely, she discovers that class conflict is the fundamental law of capitalist society, marked especially by self-righteousness on the part of those with whom she had, up to now, shared values—or so she had thought. And she finds, talking with the wives of the two major stockholders of Sierra Mills, that she cannot get anywhere appealing to what she had thought were their values: "And they were sincere, these two women. They were drunk with conviction of the superiority of their class and themselves" (55). What Avis also discovers, apart from class conflict, is the pervasiveness of industrial accidents as well as the efforts to minimize their costs, if not always their causes. It can be telling, once again, to propose that students examine today's industrial landscape (e.g., the case of Agriprocessors, the kosher meatpacking company in Postville, Iowa, that was raided by immigration authorities and widely accused of terrible safety procedures). They may, like Avis and readers, be stripped of illusions about "lack of communication" and become ready to face capital in all its naked power with London's characters. That confrontation takes place in chapter 5, "The Philomaths."

In this chapter, Ernest delivers a lecture at the meeting of the Philomath Club, a gathering of ruling-class gentlemen and ladies held at the home of a socially prominent member. He indicts their materialistic, commercial values, the commonness and selfishness of their lives. To this, they remain, as he had predicted to Avis, largely indifferent. They become enraged, however, when he threatens that the working class will "take your governments, your palaces, and all your purpled ease away from you" (64). His primary charge against them is that the "capitalist class . . . [has] mismanaged society." Because the modern worker is so much more productive than the caveman, he argues, "one would conclude . . . that under a capable management of society modern civilized man would be a great deal better off than the cave-man" (65). But he isn't, as poverty, child labor, and the general misery of workers demonstrates. "In face of the facts that modern man lives more wretchedly than the cave-man, and that his producing power is a thousand times greater than that of the cave-man, no other conclusion is possible than that the capitalist class has mismanaged." "You have failed in your management of society," he concludes, "and your management is to be taken away from you" (66). To this analysis and this threat, the Philomaths respond with incoherent rage, so incoherent, in fact, that Avis—London, really—does not reproduce their arguments. For the issue here is no longer a correct approach to social analysis; it is, rather, to bring to the surface the basic question of power.

That question is articulated by the one Philomath who is presented as calm and coherent, Mr. Wickson, an odd character who reappears periodically throughout the novel. He characterizes Ernest as a dangerous bear: "We will hunt the bear. We will not reply to the bear in words. Our reply shall be couched in terms of lead. We are in power. Nobody will deny it. By virtue of that power we shall remain in power. . . . There is the word. It is the king of words—Power. Not God, not Mammon, but Power. Pour it over your tongue till it tingles with it. Power" (72–73). And Ernest accepts the challenge: "Power. It is what we of the working class preach" (73). The power of the ballot, initially, but if victory in the polls is denied, then, repeating Wickson's very words, "[W]e shall answer you; and in roar of shell and shrapnel and in whine of machine-guns shall our answer be couched" (74). The argument about "mismanagement," a common enough argument in socialist circles of the early twentieth century, thus dissolves into a contest for power. And the question of power rapidly moves from the strategy of the immediate early-twentieth-century moment—winning through the ballot—toward the likelihood of armed struggle. London thus places violence on the agenda both as the ultimate, indeed only significant, strategy of capitalism, but as an eventuality that socialists must in response consider.

The debate with the Philomaths raises a number of riveting questions, both about social dynamics and about London's own politics. Most obviously, is violence a necessary component of fundamental social change? Is London attracted to violence and, if so, on what basis? Cleanth Brooks, R. W. B. Lewis, and Robert Penn Warren, in their anthology of American literature, render

London's politics as those of adolescent resentment: "[W]hat attracted London to Marxism was less the dream of a society perfected in justice than the drama of a class war fulfilling his own need for apocalyptic violence" (Brooks 1633). Brooks, Lewis, and Warren were, in some sense, right: violence and rage are the common coin of many London stories, some of which students may be reading. Where they misunderstand, I think, is that for London class struggle rather than adolescent fantasy is the source of "apocalyptic violence." What London saw quite clearly is that revolution is not a tea party but a necessarily brutal fight over power. The powerful do not cheerfully cede their power; it is seized from them, if possible, by whatever means come to hand, boxing and guns in "The Mexican," a blockade and chunks of coal in "South of the Slot," forms of a strike in "The Apostate" and "The Dream of Debs." Political violence is not, that is, a function of London's perverse desire but a consequence of what he saw as the grim process of serious social change. The question that may have to be addressed in the classroom is thus political more than psychological.

"Violence," the black power activist formerly called Rap Brown once said, "is as American as cherry pie." Yet do we really understand the violent hatreds that have motivated acts like those at Oklahoma City or on September 11? or the diet of suicide bombings to which we have become all but accustomed these recent years? Do we grasp the rage that fueled the Chinese Cultural Revolution? or, closer to home, that led strikers to run burning railroad cars into a Baltimore & Ohio roundhouse in 1877; white men to sell trophies consisting of fingers and bones taken from the burned corpse of Sam Hose, lynched near Atlanta; or New York's finest to invade for the umpteenth time the Stonewall bar or for the queens in it to fight back? or for Bill Totts of London's "South of the Slot" to rain down chunks of coal on the coppers of his time? Rage and violence are not only—and perhaps not at all—childish. They are terrifying, savage, and inhuman, but also, as Frantz Fanon has pointed out, liberating and occasionally, as in "South of the Slot" or "The Mexican," in some respects even joyful. Not to have felt the impulse to pour down large chunks of coal and rock on the denizens of the boardrooms of Enron, Global Crossing, AIG, Merrill Lynch, and the rest is not to have felt the rage of class violence in contemporary America. The Bushies did their best to divert that rage toward Saddam, with what success we all know. But the point here is not to analyze that macho administration's psychic policies, and less so still to celebrate rage. It is, rather, to ask how the rage and violence expressed both by Wickson and Everhard function in the novel and what students' genuine responses to that expression might be. Rage and class violence are ideas London knew well and caught intensely, sometimes with humor, sometimes in confusion, always with the primary knowledge gained on the job, on the road, and in the jail. Though it is worth pointing out that he, himself, did not join in the violence he seems to encourage.

It is within the context of this looming conflict, "the shadow of an oligarchy" (78), that the remaining dialogues of the book take place. The primary one emerges in chapters 8, "The Machine Breakers," and 9, "The Mathematics of a

Dream," a lengthy argument between Ernest and representatives of small business and the "middle class." These are the "Progressives" of the early twentieth century: "Their creed was, 'Bust the Trusts'" (89). Theirs is the liberal program of the day:

> They advocated government ownership of such trusts as the railroads and telegraphs, and excessive income taxes, graduated with ferocity, to destroy large accumulations. Likewise they advocated, as a cure for local ills, municipal ownership of such public utilities as water, gas, telephones, and street railways. (89)

Breaking up the trusts, with their efficient machinery and the methods that allow them to undercut smaller manufacturers, would, they believe, enable them to continue to bring in profits for themselves. Every part of that paragraph opens out into possible paper subjects for students engaged with the novel's politics or the history of social reform in America. However, calling these small businessmen "machine-breakers," Ernest poses another way:

> Let us not destroy those wonderful machines that produce efficiently and cheaply. Let us control them. Let us profit by their efficiency and cheapness. Let us run them for ourselves. Let us oust the present owners of the wonderful machines, and let us own the wonderful machines ourselves. That, gentlemen, is socialism, a greater combination than the trusts, a greater economic and social combination than any that has as yet appeared on the planet. It is in line with evolution. We meet combination with greater combination. (98)

The remainder of the argument is an elaboration of this statement: an explicit explanation of Marx's labor theory of value and a demonstration both of the inevitability of imperialism and, likewise, of how the middle class will be forced either into the camp of the oligarchy or into that of the proletariat. While the debate is itself at once interesting and dated, I think London's point is as much the style of Everhard's argument as its content. "I have demonstrated to you mathematically the inevitable breakdown of the capitalist system," he asserts, and he pursues his listeners and readers with the historic necessity that contradictions in capitalism must lead toward a final conflict over "the ownership of the machines" (111). "If labor wins," he continues, "your way will be easy."

> "But suppose the trusts win in this battle over the ownership of the machines and the world?" Mr. Kowalt asked.
>
> "Then," Ernest answered, "you, and labor, and all of us, will be crushed under the iron heel of a despotism as relentless and terrible as any despotism that has blackened the pages of the history of man. That will be a good name for that despotism, the Iron Heel." (112)

It is, I think, the "scientific" logic of Ernest's argument here, as much as his conclusion, that is London's point. In fact, the political fat is in the fire by now, in the novel if not yet in turn-of-the-twentieth-century America. However scientifically accurate and persuasive his arguments, Everhard cannot achieve an alliance with the small businessmen or, later, with labor aristocracy. Thus divided, the opposition to the Iron Heel must for centuries fail. The question for the novel *The Iron Heel* is whether its forms of analysis are sufficiently persuasive to head off the dangers that London seemed, at least some of the time, to see standing in the road of socialism, the dangers of persistently stupid self-interest in the face of the facts, the dangers of complacency and division in the face of the gathering power of the oligarchy.

There is another set of dangers that a discussion of this book, and other London texts, must engage: the idea of socialism as he develops and expresses it. *The Iron Heel* embodies the contradictions of London's socialism: socialism, as an expression of working-class values (R. Williams), emphasizes solidarity and collective, as distinct from individualistic, action as central to its achievement. Yet London and his representative in the novel, Ernest Everhard, are supremely individualistic in expression and demeanor. Ernest is conceived and described by Avis as a kind of superman: brilliant, martial, exciting, above all masculine. Furthermore, insofar as a proletariat emerges onto London's historical stage it takes the form of the "people of the abyss" rather than the instruments of historical transformation. From one point of view, this is a serious flaw in the novel as political tract: almost everything progressive that happens comes about through the efforts of heroic individuals. Or of faceless underground "fighting groups" whose adoption of terrorist tactics mirrors that of the Iron Heel itself. On the other hand, such contradictions open the novel to critique of the sexist (and racist) ideology that severely limited the socialism it advocated. Needless to say, examining the meaning and values of socialism has not been a high priority in American education. Oddly, however, the attacks made on President Obama's programs as "socialist" have had the effect of raising interest in the idea, which has, since the demise of real-world socialism at the end of the Cold War, resided in deep obscurity. One major virtue of *The Iron Heel* and its companion piece, *The People of the Abyss*, is that they force a reader of our time to consider the roles played by white and male privilege and the cultures they evoke in vitiating the kind of socialist program to which London subscribed. In other words, these books are as interesting, analytically, as much for how they are caught up and constrained in the cultural imperatives of their time as for how they open out into the politics of our own.

NOTE

[1] Citations to *The Iron Heel* are from Auerbach's 2006 edition.

Religion, Rationality, and the Course of History in Jack London's *The Iron Heel*

Aaron Shaheen

Admittedly, teaching Jack London's socialist-utopian novel *The Iron Heel* (1908) is not an easy charge. While I have actually heard one of my more radical-minded students proclaim, "This is the best novel ever!," more often I have gotten cooler responses. Some students—usually those who grew up reading *White Fang* and *The Call of the Wild*—were surprised, if not disappointed, to learn that London was a vocal Marxist. Others' dissatisfaction has stemmed not necessarily from London's Marxism but from the novel's inability to provide an engaging plot, one that should be able to sail successfully between the Scylla of abstract global events (the world wars, international labor revolts) and the Charybdis of minutia (Ernest's long discussions of dialectics over Dr. Cunningham's dining room table). Still others feel that the novel is just plain boring.

For nearly all the students who dislike the novel, the foreword and accompanying footnotes written by Anthony Meredith, the twenty-seventh-century scholar who recovers and reprints the Avis Everhard manuscript, are irrelevant. Though I tell the students to read Meredith's additions just as faithfully as they would the main narrative, they do so begrudgingly, complaining that such details only get in the way of a story that is already bogged down in Marxian dialectics and larger-than-life characters. Only after discussing the novel for a day or two do they come to realize Meredith's importance. Without him, this novel would more plausibly be the disappointment that students initially perceive it to be; but with him taken into full consideration, *The Iron Heel* not only proves highly intelligent and deeply innovative but also provides students with a way to chart the progress of religion and faith-based epistemologies in the modern Western world.

In fact, one can argue, as I do in the classroom, that the bulk of the novel—the Avis Everhard manuscript—is relatively meaningless unless we have this fundamental quandary of Meredith's with which to frame it. "The Rise of the [Iron Heel] Oligarchy," as Meredith explains in the introduction,

> will always remain a cause of secret wonder to the historian and the philosopher. Other great historical events have their place in social evolution. They were inevitable. Their coming could have been predicted with the same certitude that astronomers to-day predict the outcome of the movements of stars. Without these other great historical events, social evolution could not have proceeded. Primitive communism, chattel slavery, serf slavery, and wage slavery were necessary stepping-stones in the evolution of society. But it were ridiculous to assert that the Iron Heel was

> a necessary stepping-stone. Rather, to-day, is it adjudged a step aside, or a step backward, to the social tyrannies that made the early world a hell, but that were as necessary as the Iron Heel was unnecessary. (6–7)[1]

Though nowhere mentioned in this passage, religion ultimately helps readers understand what Meredith asks, which is why the Marxian trajectory of history from bourgeois oppression to proletarian supremacy took as long as it did. For students to unpack this important passage fully, instructors will need to provide them with at least a surface understanding of *The Communist Manifesto*. In it, Karl Marx and Friedrich Engels chart the history of Western society through a series of dialectic struggles, seeing the historical hostilities between the "[f]reeman and slave" in ancient times, the "lord and serf" in the Middle Ages, and the "gild-master and journeyman" in the early modern period as the culmination of the current-day (that is, mid–nineteenth century) antagonism between the bourgeoisie and proletarians (50–51 [ed. Malia]).

But in order for instructors to bring the discussion around to religion, it is also necessary to talk about what little we know of Meredith's twenty-seventh-century society and, further, to look at how that society is for London a fulfillment of certain Marxian principles. In the first footnote from chapter 1, for example, we learn that Meredith refers to the early twentieth century as "the Christian Era" (12). Presumably, then, we might suspect that Meredith's era, the Brotherhood of Man, is not Christian—nor is there any sign from the novel that religion even persists into the twenty-seventh century.

Why might Christianity no longer thrive in the Brotherhood of Man? Again, instructors may need to provide their students with information about the role religion plays in Marxist thought. Certainly, the most famous quote from Marx on the subject comes from his "Contribution to the Critique of Hegel's *Philosophy of Right*," which calls religion "the opium of the people" (115). This quotation, though, is deeply susceptible to misinterpretation, for without its full context it sounds like an attack on religion outright. For that reason, instructors should provide the full passage, which states: "Religious suffering is at once the *expression* of real suffering and the *protest* against real suffering. Religion is the sigh of the oppressed creature, the heart of a heartless world, just as it is the spirit of spiritless conditions. It is the *opium* of the people" (115). Given this broader understanding of what Marx means by his reference to opium, we find that religion is not so much a problem for the oppressed in society as it is the means by which the oppressed attempt to soothe themselves in a world that constantly strips them of their humanity. This passage suggests, moreover, that for all its lip service to religion, capitalism is really the force that has pulled the Western world out of the Middle Ages (steeped as it was in a faith-based epistemology) and into the industrialized world. This new capitalist world, as the *Manifesto* declares, "has drowned the most heavenly ecstasies of religious fervor, of chivalrous enthusiasm, of philistine sentimentalism, in the icy water of egotistical calculation" (53). More to the point, capitalism has created a world in which "all that is holy is profaned, and man is at last compelled to face with sober senses his real conditions of life and his relations with his kind" (54). Thus it is capitalism, not socialism, that catalyzes a secular view of the world, and the extent to which the oppressed masses rely on religion as if it were opium is in reality the degree to which the masses are forced into a world that sees them as little more than mechanical cogs. If Meredith refers to Avis's time as "the Christian Era," he does so not necessarily in derision but with the Marxian acknowledgment that with the oppression of capitalism lifted, the masses no longer need to seek recourse in religion to dull the sting of exploitation. That solace will be found instead in equality and shared economic prosperity. In other words, the Brotherhood of Man does not repudiate the rationalist influence initiated by capitalism; rather, it relies on rationality to show that religion is merely an emotional reflex among those battered by oppression.

Though we know relatively little about Meredith, we do learn that he is a figure of ascendant rationality. Students can find evidence of this rationality in the early pages of Meredith's introduction. In assessing the recovered manuscript's values, he states:

> Nowhere do we find more vividly portrayed the psychology of the persons that lived in that turbulent period embraced between the years 1912 and 1932—their mistakes and ignorance, their doubts and fears and misapprehensions, their ethical delusions, their violent passions, their inconceivable sordidness and selfishness. These are the things that are so hard for us of this enlightened age to understand. History tells us that these things were, and biology and psychology tell us why they were; but history and biology and psychology do not make these things alive. We accept them as facts, but we are left without sympathetic comprehension of them. (5–6)

More than anything, then, what seems to separate those living in the early twentieth century and those living during the Brotherhood of Man is the latter's heightened rationality. After a close reading of the passage, instructors may need to explain the difference to students between the irrationality embedded in "mistakes and ignorance," "ethical delusions," and "violent passions" and the arationality categorically embedded in religion. Religious-minded and nonreligious-minded students alike might take offense to the suggestion that religion is irrational. Yet what is instrumental to the progression of the class discussion is the consensus that even if religion is not irrational, it is arational insofar as it is a faith-based epistemology—a method of investigating the world that does not rely on empiricism for the development of its conclusions. (By making this distinction carefully and respectfully, I have managed to avoid a different kind of "class revolt.") With a careful reading of Meredith's foreword, it nonetheless becomes readily apparent that the novel sees the Brotherhood of Man as antithetical to both the irrationality of violence and the arationality of religion.

With this premise set, instructors can now return to Meredith's main question: why did the Brotherhood of Man take so long to come about if it only needed one more evolutionary step (the dictatorship of the proletariat) to reach fruition? Ironically, it may very well be rationality, the human being's chief instrument of discernment, that prevents humankind from fully understanding the world of Avis and Ernest Everhard. In other words, Meredith cannot see that religion and other nonempirical-based epistemologies played a much larger role in both the rise of the Iron Heel and the Marxist-informed insurgencies that opposed it. For the Brotherhood of Man to succeed, its forerunners needed to purge religion from their ideology, a process that evidently took three centuries to complete. But of what, instructors will ask their students, did this religion of the revolutionaries consist? The simple answer: revolution.

To explain how a revolution based on rationalist principles falls back on itself and becomes arationally religious, I use Max Horkheimer and Theodor Adorno's *Dialectic of Enlightenment*. Horkheimer and Adorno confront and attempt to explain the fascist world around them by looking at the curious development of Enlightenment thinking in the West. In their classic formulation, "Myth is already enlightenment, and enlightenment reverts to mythology" (xviii). They then go on to explain that no sooner do "enlightened" thinkers use rational and empirical processes to expose religious myth and superstition than those very processes become mythologized themselves:

> For enlightenment, anything which does not conform to the standard of calculability and utility must be viewed with suspicion. Once the movement is able to develop unhampered by external oppression, there is no holding it back. Its own ideas of human rights then fare no better than the older universals. Any intellectual resistance it encounters merely increases its strength. The reason is that enlightenment also recognizes itself in the old myths. No matter which myths are invoked against it, by being used as arguments they are made to acknowledge the very principle of corrosive rationality of which enlightenment stands accused. Enlightenment is totalitarian. (3–4)

Those instructors who consider using Horkheimer and Adorno in their discussions should expect students initially to struggle with the concepts. In fact, I recommend making individual copies of the above passage so that students can reread and annotate it for better comprehension. As further clarification, I often give examples from London's time that show how technology and empirical-based epistemologies took on a divinity of their own. I mention Henry Adams's "The Virgin and the Dynamo" and the godlike railroad in Frank Norris's naturalist epic *The Octopus* as two contemporaneous illustrations. If I have audiovisual technology at my disposal in the classroom, I show them Evelyn De Morgan's 1909 painting *The Worship of Mammon*, explaining that Mammon was a pagan god of wealth who in modern times has come to represent capitalism, itself a product of the Enlightenment. (Bishop Morehouse mentions Mammon in a similar context in the eleventh chapter.) Yet the best way to ensure that students understand this concept is to have them consider this dialectic in their own lives. How many of us have come to imbue our modern conveniences with a type of divinity? Doesn't flying on an airplane require a certain faith in technological devices too complex for most of us to understand? Hasn't video surveillance become so pervasive that it is now tantamount to the eye of God?

In a previously published essay on *The Iron Heel*, I have used Horkheimer and Adorno's premise in *Dialectic* to explain "complex humanism," a term I define as "the dialectical give-and-take between rational-based and faith-based epistemologies." Moreover, complex humanism holds that "religion has not receded [in the Western world] as much as it has adapted or accommodated itself to the demands of modern life" (Shaheen 36). Perhaps more than any other character in the novel, Avis Everhard exemplifies complex humanism. Starting out in the novel as daughter of a bourgeois professor, Avis becomes an adherent to Marxism in much the same way an infidel might convert to orthodoxy. In fact, the reader's first glimpse of Ernest is at the Cunningham home, where he has been invited by Avis's father to argue against the religious "metaphysicians," namely Bishop Morehouse and the theologian Dr. Hammerfield. As the argument unfolds, Ernest delineates the difference between his approach to apprehending the world and his opponents' approach: "The metaphysician reasons deductively out of his own subjectivity. The scientist reasons inductively from the facts of experience. The metaphysician reasons from theory to facts, the scientist reasons from facts to theory. The metaphysician explains the universe by himself, the scientist explains himself by the universe" (15).

But if the metaphysician argues from subjective experience, as Ernest claims, then his greatest socialist devotee, Avis, is guilty of exactly that problem. Upon seeing Ernest first enter her home, Avis is struck by his muscular build and rugged good looks. And whatever appeal Ernest's conversation with Hammerfield and Morehouse has for Avis's inductive-based intellect is clouded by her emotions, if not her sexual impulses: "My like for him was founded on things beyond intellect and argument. Regardless of his bulging muscles and prize-fighter's throat, he impressed me as an ingenuous boy. I felt that under the guise of an intellectual swashbuckler was a delicate and sensitive spirit. I sensed this, in ways I knew not, save that they were my woman's intuitions" (23). If Anthony Meredith is unable to understand why the oligarchical Iron Heel took so long to collapse, he might find early indication of the reason for this delay in Avis's explanation of her initial encounter with Ernest. In it, Avis seems to be far too ensconced in the same mythmaking processes that Ernest's inductive empiricism resists. This encounter is impressed upon her through emotion. If Ernest is at heart a materialist (a dialectical materialist in particular), it seems odd, if not contradictory, that she sees him not as a three-dimensional human being but as a metaphysical manifestation: a spirit. Moreover, Avis cannot rationally articulate her feelings for the proletarian leader; rather, she relies on intuition to explain herself. But what is intuition, exactly? It is at its core a way of understanding the world by transcending the five senses that serve as the bedrock for empirical investigation.

In fact, Avis's "conversion" to scientific socialism is so intense that it turns Ernest from her "eagle" (as the title of the first chapter indicates), to her savior: Christ. This development of her vision is antithetical to Marxist socialism on at least two counts. First, by invoking American iconography in her initial depiction of Ernest, Avis runs counter to Marx and Engels's claim in the *Manifesto* that the proletarian revolt is ultimately international in scope: "The working men have no country. . . . National differences and antagonisms between people are more and more vanishing," they assert (72, 73). But even more important, by likening Ernest to Christ, she reverses the flow of history, which sees capitalism as the spark that brings the modern Western world first to secular materialism (while tolerating religion as long as it makes one's economic exploitation bearable) and second to socialism. At the microcosmic level, Avis's developing allegiance to Marxism ironically provides a temporal extension for capitalism by bringing Western history back to an earlier phase of intellectual development; instead of attesting to "all that is sacred is profaned," Avis ensures that all that is profaned is again made sacred.

Once Avis's conversion to socialism is complete and she has married her Christly Ernest, she makes another retrogressive claim, showing the extent to which the "dialectic of enlightenment" can explain her religious fervor: "The Revolution took on largely the character of religion. We worshipped at the shrine of the Revolution, which was the shrine of liberty. It was the divine flashing through us. Men and women devoted their lives to the Cause, and newborn babes were sealed to it as of old they had been sealed to the service of God. We were lovers of humanity" (179). This particular passage so exemplifies Horkheimer and Adorno's premise that it offers itself up to a lengthy unpacking with students. There are particular tensions in the passage that instructors can point out, including the one embedded in the "shrine of liberty." Should we believe Anthony Meredith's Marxian view of history, that individual liberty is the very thing that renders shrines and other sites of worship obsolete? And by elevating "cause" to "Cause," Avis's manuscript evokes a kind of allegorical demarcation that mystifies the historic-economic processes that keep laborers oppressed. By turning revolution into a religion of sorts, revolution becomes mystified, and in such a state Ernest's methodical analysis of social evolution becomes less and less plausible.

Once students gain a certain comfort level with the contradictions embedded in Avis's development from bourgeois daughter to proletarian insurgent, instructors can then ask them to look for other areas of contradiction. One productive way to extend this discussion is to look at Bishop Morehouse, whom Avis calls "a favorite of mine" (12). Why, one might wonder, is Avis partial to this man? Certainly he is friendly and intelligent, but, perhaps more to the point, his own conversion to socialism is filled with the same ideological contradictions as Avis's (Shaheen 44). In fact, Morehouse's socialist religiosity is even more pronounced than Avis's, and students can benefit from a close reading of his speech to the members of the ambiguously named I. P. H. in the chapter "The Bishop's Vision." In the speech, for example, he not only suggests that Christ was a protosocialist but also likens his own socialist conversion to Saul's conversion to Christianity while on the road to Damascus (83).

If Avis Everhard and Bishop Morehouse show on the microlevel how an empirical-based epistemology cannot easily separate itself from irrationality or religious arationality, students should suspect that the revolution she helps lead is equally conflicted. Just before the United States Capitol is bombed and Ernest (now a member of Congress) is arrested in a setup, the revolutionaries dispatch secret agents into the Oligarchy's membership. They find, however, that their own camps are equally infiltrated. As Avis recalls in those days of mounting tension, "We permeated the entire organization of the Iron Heel with our agents, while our own organization was permeated with the agents of the Iron Heel" (177). In presenting a scenario in which the revolutionaries have become indistinguishable from the Iron Heel, the narrative further suggests an answer to Anthony Meredith's question concerning the delay of the advent of the Brotherhood of Man. Simply put, since Avis, Morehouse, and their revolutionary cohorts are unable to purge themselves and their doctrine of its metaphysics, they are bound to reinscribe within their own ranks the same ideological underpinnings of Dr. Hammerfield and other members of the Oligarchy.

Moreover, the People of the Abyss, the dregs of the Chicago slums who finally break out in chaotic fury under the oppression of the Iron Heel, show further evidence of the trend I have outlined. Though theoretically these people are the ones for whom the socialist revolution is meant, their embittered passion makes them uncontrollable. Avis sees them as a grouping of "misshapen monsters blasted with the ravages of disease and all the horrors of chronic innutrition—the refuge and the scum of life, a raging, screaming, screeching, demoniacal horde" (233). As Alessandro Portelli explains, the members of this mass "have no specific social role and identity, no class stake in the Revolution. . . . The ease with which they [or the revolutionists] can 'pass' into the oligarchy as agents shows that no objective reason prevents them from joining its ranks—or from imitating it once they seize power" (189). Such amorphousness, whether ideological or collectively corporeal, is the fitting adjunct to a revolution that itself can be indistinguishable from the capitalist forces it opposes. Garthwaite, the agent charged with rescuing Avis from the Chicago slums, suggests as much when he laments, "Friend and foe are all mixed up. It's chaos. You can't tell who is in those darned buildings. Try to find out, and you get a bomb on your head. Try to go peaceably on your way, and you run into a mob and are killed by machine-guns, or you run into the Mercenaries and are killed by your own comrades from a roof. And on the top of it all the mob comes along and kills you, too" (243). The revolutionaries and the masses they try to lead therefore show that passion and rationality are not so easily separated in the modern Western world. How such a separation could supposedly develop by the twenty-seventh century was apparently beyond Jack London's own scope of explanation; for even though the People of the Abyss provide readers with some concrete clues as to why the Oligarchy retained its power for three centuries, the novel says absolutely nothing about how the Oligarchy ultimately lost its force—about how, in other words, reason broke out of is dialectical symbiosis with emotion in order to reign supreme.

Admittedly, *The Iron Heel* presents significant challenges for students and instructors alike. London himself confessed that his plans for the novel fell well short of his expectations; it was for the author "a labor of love and a dead failure as a book" (qtd. in Whalen-Bridge, *Political Fiction* 92). Yet while students may experience frustration with the novel's ideological intensity, its frequently flat characterization, or its sweeping description of world events, they can use the text to learn about the complexities involved in charting modern history and thought. Too often I have seen students fall into the simplistic trap of thinking (within or outside a Marxist framework) that what is bad today will be better tomorrow—that temporal progression implies improvement. Such assumptions can be dangerous because they are predicated on the view that time moves in a straight line. Yet history has shown us that the forward lurch of time can just as easily resuscitate past failures. Perhaps history is most useful for showing us how and where we have not learned from the past. For all its artistic flaws, *The Iron Heel* encourages readers to look deeper into the conflicted impulses embedded not just in history but in themselves as well.

NOTE

[1] Citations to *The Iron Heel* are from Auerbach's 2006 edition.

"The Call of the Underworld": Teaching Class, History, and Literary Naturalism in Jack London's "South of the Slot"

Robert M. Dowling

During a sweltering Midwestern summer between my freshman and sophomore years, I happily landed a maintenance job at my university's athletic department. It was the first time I was truly on my own, living a hand-to-mouth existence, and mostly earning my own way. In what I considered a grand show of appreciation for being offered the position, I worked three times harder than any other man on the crew (they were all men). Less than a week on the job, I was tasked with scrubbing every toilet in the football stadium. It was a Big Ten arena equipped with bathrooms for tens of thousands of mostly drunken fans, and the toilets had been ripening for months since the last game of the season. I scrubbed each individually, a ghastly morning's work, but with no complaint. I snappily reported back and headed off to my next assignment.

My colleagues there, full-time maintenance men I too quickly assumed to be allies, soon after conducted a rather terrifying intervention. Apparently, I hadn't received their all-too-clear-in-hindsight message with the toilet duty. They lured me into the locker room, formed a circle around me, and the leader hotly demanded, with the barely implicit threat of bodily harm, for me to "knock it off." And so I did. I was making them look lazy, perhaps, but more important they believed that their full-time pay didn't warrant the kind of work ethic I brashly exhibited. The supervisor utterly ignored my dip in performance. No doubt he understood, as I had not, that in the fall I would return to my books and professors, poetry readings and parties, while the other men would scrub those brackish toilets for a pittance as long as their jobs would last.

Jack London's short story "South of the Slot" (1909) opens with Freddie Drummond, the author's bookish, genteel protagonist, in an analogous situation while performing "piece-work" (unskilled labor) at a cannery in San Francisco. Drummond's associates reward his overzealous work habits, as mine had, "with scowls and black looks, and made remarks, slangily witty and which he did not understand, about sucking up to the boss and pace-making and holding her down when the rains set in" (1288); also relevant to my experience, Drummond "was interviewed by his fellow workmen, who were very angry and incoherently slangy. He failed to comprehend the motive behind their action." But unlike me, Drummond does not capitulate. "He refused to ease down his pace and bleated about freedom of contract, independent Americanism, and the dignity of toil," provoking a "crowd" of workers who "jumped on his ribs, walked on his face, and stamped on his fingers" (1288). In this way the men render his body, the finely tuned engine that propelled his work ethic along, incapacitated for a week.

In London's text, Freddie Drummond, a professor of sociology at the University of California ("Freddie" is old-time Berkeley slang for "frat boy" [Dooley 159n]), has taken the position to collect material for a book-length study on labor, part of a larger Progressive Era project to inform the industrialists and managers who owned and operated San Francisco industries about the inner workings of their laborers' minds. Drummond titles the chapter following the attack "The Tyranny of Labor" (named for an actual antilabor piece published in the magazine *Manufacturer and Builder* [1892; Theisen 105]). Today's students may not know about backhanded Progressive Era tactics of easing out labor unrest, but most have experience in the routinized workforce, and many have lived through episodes similar to, if not always as violently aggressive as, Drummond's and mine. Some recount it with laughter, some with anger, and many, like Drummond, with utter incomprehension. That's as good a place as any to start a participatory discussion of "South of the Slot."

London wrote "South of the Slot" as a satiric treatment of middle-class progressives' naive and self-serving attempts to engage in the notorious class struggle that in many ways defines turn-of-the-twentieth-century America. But as a work of literary naturalism, the story also superbly lends itself to richly textured discussions in high school and college-level English classes on class conflict, the broader history of the period, and a host of integral literary matters as well. This essay is therefore organized around these three interwoven approaches to teaching London's story: class consciousness and conflict, historical sources and the Progressive Era, and literary naturalism and narrative.

Jack London, in a newly recovered 1905 interview, concisely remarked that "the history of society has been that of class struggle" (Ruh and Scharnhorst 70). It's therefore helpful for students to tackle class-consciousness and conflict in "South of the Slot," the story's most significant themes, by asking them to list on the board the attributes of the protagonist's vastly divergent personae, Freddie Drummond and "Big" Bill Totts: middle class / working class, "Cold Storage" / "Big" Bill, socially inhibited / gregarious, vegetarian / loves sausages and bacon, temperate/drinker, boxer/brawler, prude/womanizer, and so on. In this way, students might consider the divergent bourgeois Victorian and working-class cultures as London perceived the rift—an unnatural state versus being true to your ancestral-biological self. Instructors can then point out that for the middle class, as literary historian Eric Schocket has written, "Workers and the dispossessed appear to be alternately appealing in their seeming freedom and camaraderie and horrifying in their lack of self-regulation" (118). Students should try to reconcile the paradox inherent in this perspective, always referring back to the characteristics of Drummond/Totts they have published on the board.

A helpful follow-up discussion would address London's class-based divisions within the framework of the cultural Marxist Antonio Gramsci's concepts of hegemony and counterhegemony (dominant culture vs. subculture) and contradictory consciousness (how bourgeois morals and manners serve to undermine working-class consciousness and vice versa; see Gair, "Hegemony" 74–

76 and Dowling 49, 77), as well as theories on American hegemony by Alan Trachtenberg, T. J. Jackson Lears, and others. With the aid of these theoretical frameworks, students can tease out how this cultural conflict plays out in the contemporary world: Does a hegemonic culture dominate in the United States today? If so, does the Internet exacerbate or diffuse the conflict? Why is there no Labor Party in the United States when one exists in virtually every other modern democracy? Why do so many workers in the United States vote Republican, the party that would appear to be least representative of working-class interests? (This can partly be explained by the fact that American laborers often don't want to be associated with labor; getting away from labor is the American Dream, and their children deserve better.) And so on.

From the opening paragraphs, London makes clear that Drummond has set out to master working-class culture in order to break workers' will to protest in order to contain their potentially harmful influence on bourgeois life. Fredric Jameson's concept of "strategies of containment" is a particularly useful tool for helping students understand some of the ways "South of the Slot" is working. Amy Kaplan points out that the strategy Jameson describes—that of the deliberate isolation of a working-class neighborhood in order to destroy it—is both used and counteracted by texts such as those that Freddie Drummond publishes ostensibly for the benefit of the captains of industry: "by containing the threats of social change, realistic narratives also register those desires which undermine the closure of that containment" (10). In "South of the Slot," the titular "Slot" refers to an "iron crack"—a literal, physical boundary of containment—that steers trolleys down the center of Market Street in San Francisco. London's narrator specifies that the Slot acted as a "metaphor that expressed the class cleavage of Society" (1287). Instructors should ask students if their own cities or towns contain "slots" of this kind. My students at Central Connecticut State University usually choose Prospect Street, a class- and race-based line of demarcation that starkly divides downtrodden Hartford from affluent West Hartford. It's then useful to question why people choose to visit less affluent neighborhoods in the first place—philanthropy, thrill seeking, etcetera—always asking at what point each motive might be harmful or beneficial to either the districts' inhabitants or slumming outsiders.

Freddie Drummond is a professional sociologist, and although most students know the term *sociology*, it is important to ask them to define the field as best they can. Once arriving at a workable definition (the study of social groups, perhaps), we can establish a helpful distinction between realism and naturalism, which trend toward sociology, in contrast to modernism's emphasis on psychology, the study of the individual mind. What's Drummond's purpose as a sociologist? He wishes to study and write about working-class culture—fair enough. But we must press the class further so they might ascertain Drummond's ultimate goal.

Drummond's readership consists of railroad presidents and managerial staff members, who buy tens of thousands of copies of his work and distribute them to their laborers, most of whom undoubtedly toss them in the nearest trash can. According to the narrator, Drummond's first book, *The Unskilled Laborer*, "was hailed everywhere as an able contribution to the literature of progress, and as a splendid reply to the literature of discontent. Politically and economically it was nothing if not orthodox" (1287). London's narrator makes this even clearer to his audience when he compares Drummond's socioeconomic writing with the popular conformist works "Message to Garcia" (1899), by Elbert Hubbard, and *Mrs. Wiggs of the Cabbage Patch* (1902), by Alice Rice. The narrator reveals a political and moral abhorrence toward these texts, as he indicates of Drummond's work that "in a way, it was almost as *immoral* as the far-famed and *notorious* 'Message to Garcia,' while in its pernicious preachment of thrift and content it ran 'Mrs. Wiggs of the Cabbage Patch' a close second" (1287; emphases mine). (London's earlier story "The Apostate" [1906] is a direct assault on Rice's work.) The central irony of "South of the Slot" is that the middle-class professor's quest to "contain" the dissenting will of the working class eventually leads to his proletarianization. Discussing the concept gentrification in contrast to proletarianization can prove rewarding. I've found it surprising how few, if any, students have heard the more popular term. But once given an explanation, they find themselves well able to provide telling examples from their own towns, cities, and even rural districts.

Drummond immerses himself over a six-month period in the district South of the Slot in order to master its working-class inhabitants' slang, or "argot"; eating and drinking habits; sexual openness; and style of dress. Drummond, "being a natural linguist," not only dresses like his subjects but also, more important, incorporates their speech. Only by studying their language can Drummond fatefully adapt himself "more intimately to follow their mental processes" and subsequently create his working-class alter ego, "Big" Bill Totts (1288). The importance of language to understand divergent cultures was a recent development in the social sciences at the turn of the twentieth century, and it's critical to indicate to students how the trend is borne out in the emergent dialect writing of the larger realist movement in the works of such writers as Mark Twain, Charles Chesnutt, and Finley Peter Dunne.

London's story should also be explained as a tongue-in-cheek indictment of a genre of reform literature written by leftists and conservatives alike that Schocket has termed "class-transvestite narratives." He defines this term as "tales of temporary guise" that expose middle-class "attempts to close epistemological gaps through cross-class impersonation" (110). Schocket argues that class-transvestite narratives are part of a larger struggle for "middle-class revitalization" rather than their often self-styled rationale to aid the working class. Middle-class ennui—the "hopeless cramp of the bourgeois psychology" (916), as London puts it in his novel *Martin Eden* (916)—can be found in popular films like *Mary Poppins* and *Pleasantville*.[1] It's useful to ask students what, if any, impact traditionally disenfranchised groups—such as the working poor, new immigrants, and racial minorities—might have on the wider Anglo-American middle-class culture, always having them be careful not to resort to condescension or generalizations.

Recent scholars identify several direct connections to London's protagonist, any one of which could be researched for a complete essay on London's story in the context of American labor history and the Progressive Era—the management guru Frederick Taylor, the evolutionary theologist Henry Drummond, and the notorious labor leader "Big" Bill Haywood, to offer a few examples (see Theisen). Especially analogous to Freddie Drummond was Princeton University's Walter Wyckoff, the intrepid assistant professor of political economics who tramped across the United States throughout the 1890s working numerous unskilled labor jobs and collecting material for his celebrated two-volume study *Workers: An Experiment in Reality* (1897). Wyckoff's vagabond journey significantly ended in San Francisco, and he died at age forty-four in 1908, a year before "South of the Slot" was published. Similar to Drummond, Wyckoff openly expressed anxiety over his taste for the "primal needs" and their attendant "instinct" for "liquor and lust" (qtd. in Schocket 118). London's story can thus be read as a combination sympathetic obituary and cynical send-up of Wyckoff and his career.

Moreover, by assigning Freddie Drummond's would-be fiancée the name Catherine Van Vorst, London clearly evokes the genteel muckrakers Bessie ("Mrs. John") and Marie Van Vorst, the coauthors of *The Woman Who Toils, Being the Experience of Two Ladies as Factory Girls* (1903). An undercover exploration of two self-professed "ladies," *The Woman Who Toils* delves into the working and leisure-time behavior of women laborers across the country. The practice of crossing class boundaries that was in vogue for a middle-class "gentleman" like Wyckoff also attracted respectable "ladies" like the Van Vorsts. Other examples from the period include Helen Campbell, Rheta Childe Dorr, and Cornelia Stratton Parker. The trend has never truly died out: students will often make the connection to more contemporary sociological studies that are often taught in high school and college classes like Barbara Ehrenreich's *Nickel and Dimed*, and they should be asked whether such practices are justifiable sociological journalism or simple marketing gimmicks produced by intrepid authors and trendy publishers.

Once a reasonable distinction between realism and naturalism has been made in class—at its most basic, whether characters' have agency over their lives (realism) or are controlled by external and internal forces (naturalism)—identifying "South of the Slot" as one or the other always generates a productive debate. Both students and scholars alike tend to overlook the naturalistic qualities of the piece, inappropriately labeling it realism as opposed to naturalism because of its historical content, along with passing over some of the more deft literary sleights of hand contained in the work. For instance, it's useful to ask students why London switches the focal point from Drummond to Catherine Van Vorst in the riot scene (1297). The two most likely reasons, ones that students initially find difficult to grasp, are that Catherine's point of view emphasizes the "riotous savage" aspect of Drummond and that London illustrates the naturalistic loss of control that renders his character incapable of observing the situation dispassionately.

London's naturalism reveals larger implications about the author's assessment of class consciousness and American cultural politics as well, an observation that has as much relevance for students today as for those in his own time. Freddie Drummond recognizes that he must choose between Mary Condon and Catherine Van Vorst. In choosing the latter, London shows how Drummond attempts to distance himself from the human race. Students can nicely contrast the naturalism of London's piece to the realism of the mixed-race author Chesnutt's character Mr. Ryder in the story "The Wife of His Youth" (1898). Students should also be made aware of the terrific impact Darwin's theory of evolution had on perceptions of mankind's relation with the natural world at the turn of the twentieth century. The theory that human beings belong to the animal kingdom was and still remains abhorrent to many, and it is that upheaval that London confronts in *The Call of the Wild* (1903), *The Sea-Wolf* (1904), *White Fang* (1906), and "South of the Slot."

My students recalled that in the 2007 presidential primaries, the Republican candidate Mike Huckabee expressed contempt at the idea of being related to apes; it was then added that Woodrow Wilson voiced utter incomprehension as early as 1922 when a journalist asked if he believed in the theory of evolution. "Of course, like every other man of intelligence and education I do believe in organic evolution. It surprises me that at this late date such questions should be raised" (qtd. in Streissguth 188). As a man of "intelligence and education," Freddie Drummond believes in Darwin's theory; however, "he was a trifle ashamed of this genealogy, and preferred not to think of it. Wherefore, probably, he practiced his iron inhibition and preached it to others, and preferred women of his own type, who could shake free of this bestial and regrettable ancestral line and by discipline and control emphasize the wideness of the gulf that separated them from what their dim forebears had been." In other words, by marrying Catherine he would widen "the gulf" between himself and the "weltering muck and mess of lower and monstrous organic things," thus attempting to breed himself outside the animal kingdom (1292).

After their first encounter with the story, the most common question in students' minds is whether Drummond suffers from multiple personality disorder. They should be given sufficient time to debate this point on their own. But London makes clear that Drummond is mentally sane, since he's ever conscious of his dual identity and experiences a moment of crisis in which he must decide between Condon and Van Vorst. Drummond's betrayal of the natural order by choosing Van Vorst, and therefore embracing his "Cold Storage" persona, results in his transformation in the final scene into a "riotous savage," a natural force whose "onslaught was like a whirlwind" (1297). Students can observe that London was responding to the genre of slum-reform literature discussed above by undermining their evolutionary concerns with a naturalistic and satiric twist.

Drummond never *chooses* to become "Big" Bill Totts. On the contrary, he decides on Cold Storage. Rather than demonstrate the agency Ryder employs by successfully opting to side with his southern black heritage, Drummond's fate is determined by natural law—"the call of the underworld, the lure of the free and open, of the unhampered, irresponsible life South of the Slot" (1294).

Students must ultimately deal with how "the call of the underworld" relates to London's famous "call of the wild." Only by answering this question can they truly arrive at the central irony of the story: instead of transforming the working-class in his image (gentrification), Drummond himself is transformed (proletarianization). If we compare the final scene of "South of the Slot" with that of London's novel *The Call of the Wild*, Drummond, now Bill Totts, "towered a head above the crowd," just as the dog Buck, after joining a wild pack of wolves, "may be seen running at the head of the pack . . . leaping gigantic above his fellows" (86).[2]

Instructors might then ask students to research instances of the kind of self-conscious restraint that leads to extreme or destructive, often hilariously ironic actions like Drummond's. With some direction, they'll find plenty of examples from more recent highly publicized scandals such as Rush Limbaugh's OxyContin addiction, Britney Spears's revolt against her wholesome girl-next-door image, and the Catholic Church's pedophile-priest epidemic, to provide some examples from my own classes. Even the story's narrative structure demonstrates the contradictions of London's protagonist. The historian Christopher Gair finds that the narrative arc of "South of the Slot" brings to mind the archetypal "newspaper storiette" London lambastes in *Martin Eden*:

> The formula consists of three parts: (1) a pair of lovers are jarred apart; (2) by some deed or event they are reunited; (3) marriage bells. The third part was an unwavering quantity, but the first and second parts could be varied an infinite number of times. (778)

Students will again find that they can easily conjure examples of this kind of "closed narrative," as Umberto Eco has coined the term for such formulaic stories, from present-day romantic comedies. In fact, it's possible to read "South of the Slot" as a romantic comedy in which, after surmounting a series of challenges, the hero finds himself in the arms of the underdog heroine. But London's use of this archetype still manages to subvert the typical boy-meets-girl formula given his satirical tone, which is designed to protest against the hypocrisy of the middle-class cult of respectability.

Jack London's best work, and "South of the Slot" undoubtedly rates among it, stems from the author's "marginal" status. London's actual identities ranged from hobo to landowner, oyster pirate to shore patrolman, socialist leader to popular author. Indeed, his often romanticized view of the working poor overshadows deep ambiguities regarding the impact of their lives on the American public. On first meeting his genteel love interest, Ruth Morse, Martin Eden, the eponymous protagonist of London's most autobiographical novel, recalls the working-class and immigrant types he's encountered over his short lifetime and characterizes them in his mind's eye as "the scum and slime of the human pit" (561).

London's genius lies, as with Walt Whitman, in his ability to write from numerous perspectives; though unlike Whitman's celebratory verse, cultural openness in London often leads to the kind of existentialist alienation that compels Martin to take his own life. Jack London was essentially an autodidact who, like Mark Twain and many American authors before and after them, transcended his working-class background while at the same time remaining mindful of the cultural contributions his native class presented to the stultifying "genteel tradition" into which they were thrust willy-nilly as the United States' most famous authors of their times. Also like Twain, London defies strict generic categorization—his fiction contains romance and realism, fiction and autobiography, bourgeois assumptions of superiority and proletarian rage, genteel self-satisfaction and "the call of the underworld." As with all of his finest work, the most beneficial lesson plans are those that attempt to elucidate and explore these contradictions in "South of the Slot."

NOTES

I would like to thank my graduate research assistant Douglas Duhaime for his assistance on this project.

[1] Citations to *Martin Eden* are from *Jack London: Novels and Social Writings*.

[2] Citation to *Call of the Wild* is from *Jack London: Novels and Stories*.

Androgyny and Sexuality in *The Sea-Wolf*

Anita Duneer

In a letter to his publisher, Jack London wrote about his work in progress that would become *The Sea-Wolf*: "My idea is to take a cultured, refined, super-civilized man and woman . . . and throw them into a primitive sea-environment where all is stress & struggle . . . and make this man & woman rise to the situation and come out of it with flying colors" (*Letters* 1: 337–38). London's "idea" clearly positions Humphrey Van Weyden and Maud Brewster as characters thrown into the same struggle for survival. But most first-time readers of *The Sea-Wolf* are as surprised to see Maud pulled out of the sea midway through the novel as are the seamen, one of whom exclaims, "May I never shoot a seal again if that ain't a woman!" (619).[1] Student readers, who up to this point have been immersed in Humphrey's physical and philosophical struggle to find his "own legs" and to rise up from under the amoral Captain Wolf Larsen, respond in a variety of ways to Maud's appearance. In a brief online response, one student wrote: "It changed the dynamics of the male relationships on the *Ghost*. From that point on, for me, it read like a romance novel, and it definitely detracted from the thematic unity of the text." Another student expressed an interest in the romance: "I was happy to see a woman enter the story. There's nothing better than reading about two people falling in love in the middle of destruction and murder and filth." A third student's response is more open-ended: "I agree that the story seemed to change after Maud enters. I cannot decide if this was something London intended or if it was unconscious." I use students' initial responses to this change in the trajectory of the plot as a starting point for closer analysis of the function and purpose of the female character and for an examination of a broader range of gendered topics throughout the text: androgyny, romantic love, sentimentality, and (homo)eroticism.

Many students who have not read anything by Jack London are aware of his reputation as an adventure writer, and they are often surprised by his emphasis on gender in *The Sea-Wolf*. I have taught *The Sea-Wolf* in two types of courses: an upper-division literature course, Women and the Sea, and a sophomore course on twentieth-century American literature for English majors. *The Sea-Wolf* was a natural choice for the former, a seminar I designed to explore the ways in which female perspectives and the female presence in sea literature revise traditional (masculine) versions of the maritime romantic ideal. I also found *The Sea-Wolf* to be an appropriate introduction to a literature course that emphasizes broad social and literary movements. As a product of its pivotal historical moment just after the turn of the century, London's writing presents conflicted views about class, race, ethics, and gender. Reading *The Sea-Wolf* through the lens of gender is an approach that can encourage students to deconstruct London's dichotomization of a number of literary, philosophical, or social tensions, such as romance/realism, idealism/materialism, leisure class / working class, civilization / savagery—the list goes on. It's useful to have a class discussion about the intentional fallacy; the student quoted above is not unique in pondering the distinctions between what London intended and what might have been unconscious. I posit that London's interest in androgyny—and what it signifies as an incorporation of opposing sexual or gendered attributes—implies, in a broader sense, his search for a philosophical middle ground that resists the various polarizations that he dramatizes throughout the novel. Precisely where he stands on any of these issues is a problem students can investigate through close readings of contradictions in the text.

Contexts: Naturalism and Gendered Literary Aesthetics

In the letter quoted above, London implies that the "underlying motif" (*Letters* 1: 338) is his characters' social Darwinian struggle and their success in summoning atavistic traits that allow them to survive by overcoming the debilitating effects of overcivilization: in other words, the degeneration—or feminization—of modern life. Students are inclined to link degeneration with savagery rather than with overcivilization, but it can be applied to both ends of the spectrum. To Humphrey, "The continual brutality around [him] was degenerative" (575–76), but as he first appears, his weakness is symptomatic of the "degenerate" effeminacy of the leisure class. Early in our reading of the novel, I introduce some of the key ideas and language associated with naturalism. Donna M. Campbell's *Literary Movements* Web page is extremely useful for definitions and examples. I also draw on Eric Carl Link's *The Vast and Terrible Drama* in presenting literary naturalism as a thematic response to philosophical and scientific ideas of the day, rather than as a genre. A consideration of the relation of London's naturalistic themes to his use of elements associated with the genres of both romance and realism is part of these early discussions of the text. I also frame introductory discussions of *The Sea-Wolf* with three factors, as identified by William B. Dillingham, influencing the literary climate at the turn of the century: the closing of the frontier, the feminist movement, and what some naturalist writers saw as a movement toward effeminate literary aesthetics (84–88).

To help students appreciate the discourse of masculinity in the national mythology of the West and the relation of masculine strength to manifest destiny and Anglo-Saxon superiority, I have assigned excerpts from Frederick Jackson Turner's "The Significance of the Frontier in American History" and Theodore Roosevelt's *The Strenuous Life*. According to Roosevelt, on the frontier "[t]here was scant room for the coward and the weakling. . . . The winning of the West was the great epic feat in the history of our race" (1156, 1157). In 1893, Turner declared the frontier closed, but for London the sea remained a frontier space where epic battles could still be waged.

I invite students to share what they know of traditional roles for male adventurers in American literature. They are likely familiar with heroes like Ishmael and Huck Finn, who go to sea or the river to escape what Leslie Fiedler calls "the busy world of women" (357). Students are aware that in most adventure stories women stay at home. We discuss the notion of separate spheres of Victorian female domesticity and male commerce (with the caveat that recently critics such as Cathy N. Davidson and Jessamyn Hatcher have challenged the ideology of separate spheres as an imagined construction that has shaped the way historians and fiction writers have viewed and represented American society). Although the epithet "'Sissy' Van Weyden" might imply that Humphrey was comfortable staying home with his mother and sisters, like other heroes of watery frontiers, he was "always trying to escape them" (582)—which he does, albeit involuntarily when the ferryboat accident propels him into the "miniature floating world" of the *Ghost* (506).

To complicate our discussion of gender and the masculine space of the frontier, I share with students an essay by London's contemporary, Frank Norris, "Novelists of the Future." Norris imagines a "muse of American fiction" who "will not flourish indoors" (13), and whose androgynous frontier spirit transports the artist outside to the real world:

> [T]he muse of American fiction is no chaste, delicate, super-refined mademoiselle of delicate roses and "elegant" attitudinizings, but a robust, red-armed *bonne femme*, who rough-shoulders her way among men and among affairs, who finds a healthy pleasure in the jostlings of the mob and a hearty delight in the honest, rough-and-tumble, Anglo-Saxon give-and-take knockabout that for us means life. (13)

In taking the female muse out of the parlor, Norris has in mind a particularly masculine literary aesthetic. This passage can be used to open a discussion about the literary climate at the turn of the century, in which London and his contemporaries were writing masculine adventure stories, knowing that a large percentage of their readers were women. There are numerous provocative possibilities for considering Norris's androgynous muse as evoking the style and themes of London's *The Sea-Wolf*. The image brings together elements of romance and realism in the juxtaposition of myth and real "life"; at the same time, the androgynous *bonne femme* disrupts essentialist assumptions about gender (while calling attention to them) and suggests correlations among gender, class, and race. It's crucial, of course, to discuss the celebration of what is "rough-and-tumble" and "Anglo-Saxon" as characteristic of the general xenophobia in San Francisco at the turn of the century and to address the celebration of Nordicism that Norris shares with London. Implicit in the representation of Anglo-Saxon masculine superiority is its antithesis—the feminized racial other. Furthermore, the subject of Norris's muse is the working class—especially those who work and play outdoors. I ask students to consider Humphrey and Maud's displacement from, in London's words, the "artificial, civilized life" (*Letters* 1: 337) and their rude entrance into the world of the *Ghost*. Does London imply that they must learn to take their "knocks" before they can appreciate and take pleasure in the "jostlings of the mob"? Do both Humphrey and Maud need to shake off their femininity and become more masculine—not only to survive, but to experience life to the fullest? This image of an androgynous muse can elicit ways for students to consider problems with the dichotomies of feminine civilization and masculine brutality, and it also shows how *The Sea-Wolf* complicates attributes stereotypically associated with gender, class, and race.

Textual Complexities: Gender, Class, and Race

Students are quick to notice London's use of gender binaries in Humphrey's struggle to develop manhood and his unexercised muscles, which at the beginning of the voyage were "small and soft, like a woman's" (513). Most students are fascinated by Humphrey's larger-than-life, hypermasculine depictions of Wolf Larsen but somewhat less impressed by his sentimental musings about the feminine, ethereal otherworldliness of Maud. Humphrey "likened them to the extreme ends of the human ladder of evolution—the one the culmination of all savagery, the other the finished product of the finest civilization" (648). Beginning with this dichotomy, I ask students to consider the ways in which character descriptions and shipboard status are coded as masculine or feminine, and what assumptions about gender underlie these roles.

One student writes, "Since originally there are no women on the ship, the men feel the need to treat the weaker men like women, the lesser sex. Hump is one of those men. When Wolf Larsen looks at Hump's hands, he says, 'Good for little else than dish washing and scullion work'" (500). This is the kind of student observation that can initiate close analysis of the description of characters and their corresponding positions on the ship. Recent studies of gender and seafaring can be helpful for class discussions about the gendered implications of shipboard hierarchy. Laura Tabili, for example, has argued that race, class, and gender in the masculine space of the ship are "dynamics that flow from the same power structure" (174). Like women relegated to "unskilled" and domestic labor, working-class men have been feminized "[a]t sea as on land, [by] manmade divisions of race and gender masqueraded as natural ones" (188).

Tabili's notion of gender as masquerade provides a good segue into a discussion of definitions from gender theory. Eve Kosofsky Sedgwick, for example, defines sex as "chromosomal" and gender as "the far more elaborated, more fully and rigidly dichotomized social production and reproduction of male and female identities and behaviors" (*Epistemology* 27). Judith Butler's theory of performativity expands on this idea of gender as socially produced and reproduced. For Butler, "Gender reality is performative which means, quite simply, that it is real only to the extent that it is performed" ("Performative Acts" 527). One "does" gender by performing an act that is already scripted, and to deviate from the script of how one acts as a "man" or "woman" can result in dire social consequences. The repetitive performance of gender (for example, through one's dress, gestures, or occupation) reifies the assumption of its naturalness. Performing one's gender "right," according to Butler, supports essentialist "configurations of bodies into sexes which exist in a binary relation to one another" (524). Instead of revealing the "true" identity of the performer, the performance reveals social expectations that deter deviation from gender norms: "the performance renders social laws explicit" (Butler 526). As my perceptive student has noted, the performance of gendered roles on the *Ghost* emphasizes the social hierarchy firmly in place before Humphrey appears on the ship—a structure that scripts masculine- and feminine-identified roles for the all-male crew.

This question of what one *does* versus what one *is* (or how one defines oneself) can be further explored in class discussion. Whereas certain roles on the ship are coded masculine—those of the sailors and seal hunters—the work associated with domesticity, or woman's work, is assigned to the cook (Mugridge) or the cabin boy (Hump, as Larsen names him), who cleans the captain's quarters and makes his bed. One problem of interpretation is that the associations of the savage-masculine as opposed to the civilized-feminine do not neatly break down in terms of class or race. Ironically, the most subservient of the working class—Thomas Mugridge, the Cockney cook—and the most civilized gentleman—Humphrey Van Weyden, "a scholar and a dilettante" (512), are feminized. What they have in common is that they are both products of generations of social-class immobility. Humphrey's initial impression of Mugridge is one of "hereditary servility," the embodiment of the working class, with "effeminate features running into a greasy smile" (492). Mugridge suffers because he accepts his station as a slave to other men and to his lot in life: "I'm already myde, an' myde out of leavin's an' scraps" (578). Humphrey is a weakling because, as a gentleman, he has not had to do anything for himself: as Larsen tells him, "You stand on dead men's legs" (500). In contrast, Larsen has escaped the poverty of his youth by working himself up from cabin boy to become a self-made "[m]aster and owner of a ship" (560). Students are interested in Larsen's rise and fall; some even consider him a tragic hero. Questions for class discussion may include the following: How is Larsen able to rise above his humble beginnings, whereas Mugridge is mired in his legacy of servitude? What do their personal stories suggest about the degree to which biological or social factors determine their success or failure? In what ways is masculinity implied in agency, self-reliance, and physical or social mobility?

Although the racial designations of the crew may not seem particularly obvious, in the context of London's emphasis on the superiority of Nordic, Viking, and Anglo-Saxon peoples the correspondence between race and status can be seen in the divisions between sailors and hunters: "The sailors, in the main, were English and Scandinavian, and their faces seemed of the heavy stolid order. The hunters, on the other hand, had stronger and more diversified faces, with hard lines and the marks of the free play of passions" (506). In racist, social Darwinian terms, "passions" and their relationship to sexuality are associated more with the lower, animal rungs of the evolutionary ladder, as opposed to the suppressed and controlled emotions of Maud, "the finished product of the finest civilization."

The relation between gender and race raises another set of problems. Humphrey's descriptions of the feminine beauty of Oofty-Oofty and the masculine beauty of Larsen, juxtaposed in chapter 15 and later in chapter 26, serve as dramatic contrasts. And even the individual descriptions are conflicted. Humphrey has difficulty categorizing Oofty-Oofty. As a "Kanaka" (a South Seas or Hawaiian islander), he would likely belong to the hunter category, but he is a "splendid seaman, so named by his mates" (586). Oofty-Oofty "was a beautiful creature, almost feminine" (590), yet Humphrey "knew the barbaric devil that lurked in his breast and belied all the softness and tenderness, almost womanly, of his face and form" (672). In contrast, Humphrey perceives Larsen as "the man-type, the masculine, and almost a god in his perfectness" (593). Still, even the godlike physique of Larsen exhibits feminine attributes: "His body, thanks to his Scandinavian stock, was fair as the fairest woman's" (593). Is racial difference the main determinant for Humphrey in describing these characters' embodiment of masculinity or femininity? Beneath Larsen's godlike physique also "lurks" a "barbaric devil." What essential, learned, or socially conditioned qualities make a man—or a beast, for that matter?

Humphrey's portrayal of Larsen as a sexual being most obviously reflects anxieties about his own body and masculinity. He is mesmerized by "the great muscles [that] leapt and moved under the satiny skin" (593). In a broader sense, the combined seduction and danger of Larsen's character evokes the often-feminized romance of the sea itself, or any number of mythical enchantresses who lure sailors to their destruction. Humphrey later imagines Larsen as a masculine embodiment of the archetypal femme fatale, Circe, who seduces, bewitches, and enslaves Odysseus's crew: "Wolf Larsen it was, always Wolf Larsen, enslaver and tormentor of men, a male Circe and these his swine" (673). Larsen's "terrible beauty" as a mythical seductress might be read as an unnatural marriage of masculinity and femininity (593). A question Sedgwick in *Epistemology of the Closet* asks in her analysis of homosexuality in Herman Melville's *Billy Budd* can be equally provocative for our reading of Humphrey's erotic gaze on Wolf Larsen's muscles (the effect of which Larsen is keenly aware of as he "command[s]" Humphrey to "Feel them" [*Sea-Wolf* 594]). "Is men's desire for other men the great preservative of the masculinist hierarchies of Western culture, or is it among the most potent of the threats against them?" (Sedgwick, *Epistemology* 93). What do we make, then, of London's depiction of the all-male social world at sea? By definition, it is a radical departure from the normative heterosexual society on shore. Is it a threat to social convention or a hypermasculine expression of the American frontier spirit? The danger expressed through Humphrey's imagination of an androgynous Larsen is an idea to which students can return after fleshing out the more "positive" possibilities of androgyny in Humphrey's relationship with Maud.

Entering the Critical Conversation

I have assigned two group activities to encourage students to develop skills in close reading and to draw them into the critical conversation. The first is a preliminary exercise in close reading. Groups are assigned one of the following topics for analysis:

> The scenes in which Humphrey and Maud are "rescued" by Wolf Larsen;
> The effect Maud's appearance seems to have on Humphrey and Wolf Larsen;
> The discrepancies between Humphrey's descriptions of Maud and what Maud actually *does* in the narrative;
> The progressive development or degeneration of the characters.

Each group chooses two specific passages to explicate. As students compare and contrast characters and situations, they consider the ways in which London's treatment of gender and use of gendered language seem conventional (e.g., what they might expect from a romantic or sentimental Victorian novel) and in what ways they suggest possibilities beyond convention. Then students offer conclusions about the ways gender shapes the narrative and social tensions in *The Sea-Wolf*.

The second assignment engages students in a larger scholarly debate about Maud's function and purpose in the novel. Two critical articles that present opposing interpretations of Maud's role in the text are Sam S. Baskett's "Sea Change in *The Sea-Wolf*" and Lee Clark Mitchell's "'And Rescue Us from Ourselves': Becoming Someone in Jack London's *The Sea-Wolf*." Baskett argues that London "is interested in showing a man and a woman who complement each other in an ideal androgynous union because each has a sense of individual identity that transcends conventional concepts of gender roles" (108). Mitchell arrives at a completely opposite conclusion: "The novel can only end by confirming what it wants to deplore: civilized behavior, class divisions, gender inequality" (332–33).

Mitchell reads the novel as "a rough Darwinian allegory of *homo erectus*" (321). In terms of gender, "The evolutionary process of standing up and walking on two feet represents for London . . . independence, moral heroism, and virile manhood. By contrast, lying down denotes dependency, death, cowardice, and ultimately (or so the novel asserts) femininity" (321). Mitchell notes that the novel exemplifies Butler's notion of gender as performative. Nevertheless, although he admits that there is more complexity in the narrative voice than in the characters (325), Mitchell emphasizes Humphrey's perspective over Maud's *performance*. In the earlier close reading exercise, students may have noticed the tension between Humphrey's impression of Maud's "fragility" and her actions (648): for example, she "mans" the tiller (my word choice) in an open boat for seven hours straight while Humphrey sleeps and helps him bail water during rough seas.

Baskett draws on external evidence to set up his reading of the Maud-Humphrey romance as a complementary resolution to the Larsen-Humphrey power struggle, replacing the social Darwinian survival of the fittest with a cooperative union. Citing examples from letters London wrote in previous years to publishers and love interests, Baskett illustrates that before writing *The Sea-Wolf*, London had already put a considerable amount of thought into the ideal of an androgynous relationship between a man and a woman.

Mitchell and Baskett both present exemplary models of close reading, in lucid, jargon-free prose accessible to most students. I divide the class into two groups. For homework, each student reads one of the articles and brings to class a paraphrase of the thesis and notes with "talking points" in response to the following questions:

> Does the critic make a convincing case for the thesis? Whether or not you agree with the critic's interpretation, has the article brought to your attention details that you had not previously noticed or considered? What one specific example do you find most illuminating? Is there a specific point with which you do not agree?
>
> How has your understanding of *The Sea-Wolf* changed after reading this article? If you were going to write a paper about gender in *The Sea-Wolf*, how would you position your argument with respect to these critics?

I make clear that even though the group assignment is structured as a debate to encourage lively interactions between points of interpretation, students do not need to completely agree with one argument or the other—that each of these critics makes valid points that can challenge and enrich students' individual readings of the novel. An analysis of the ways in which London both challenges and reinforces gender essentialism at the beginning of the twentieth century can challenge students to reevaluate their own assumptions about gender at the beginning of the twenty-first century.

After students have mulled over the relevancy of the various contexts for the novel that have informed our work in the classroom and many of their paper topics, we return to the initial response of the student who couldn't decide whether the change in the novel after Maud appears was "something London intended or if it was unconscious." Another student contends that the novel should stand alone, that knowledge of London's romantic state of mind and interest in androgyny should not be necessary for appreciating the work: "The androgyny isn't completely absent; it is just only recognizable after reading Baskett's essay." Ultimately, these problems can initiate productive conversations about the relation between text and contexts, the value and purpose of literary criticism, and the validity of any number of theoretical approaches to reading and writing about a literary text.

NOTE

[1] Citations to *The Sea-Wolf* are from *Jack London: Novels and Stories*.

Experimental Narratives: "Samuel"

Donna M. Campbell

If asked about the stories of Jack London, most students who know anything of his work would reply that he wrote about dogs, the frozen North, and adventure on the high seas. And they wouldn't be entirely wrong: with *The Call of the Wild* and *The Sea-Wolf* as his best-known work and stories such as "The Law of Life" or "To Build a Fire" appearing frequently in literature anthologies, London built his reputation writing vividly descriptive stories that emphasized the inherent drama of characters, often men, struggling in a pitiless environment or fighting one another for survival. He also pioneered a style that complemented these subjects, using strong verbs, vivid descriptions, and clear, vernacular phrasing to give strength and urgency to the action-filled narratives that were his specialty. This style became his trademark even as he branched out into other subjects, from the poverty in the East End of London in *The People of the Abyss* to the stories of Hawai'i and the South Seas that he wrote late in his career.

But London also wrote fiction in which he deviated from his usual narrative practices to experiment with form, theme, and subject matter. Chief among these experimental narratives is "Samuel," which differs from London's usual writings in its focus on a maternal female character, its unusually thick dialect from a region not typically associated with London, and its complex treatment of providence and fate. In providing an alternative perspective on his naturalistic philosophy, "Samuel" provides a contrast to the typical means of studying London.

"Samuel"

Students acquainted with "To Build a Fire" and *The Call of the Wild* are surprised to learn that London considered "Samuel" one of his best short stories, and, given London's popularity as an author at the time, they are also surprised to hear that he had trouble selling it. The magazine editors to whom London submitted the story apparently thought it too much of a deviation from his usual subject matter: the story made the rounds of twenty magazines before being sold "for a song" (*Letters* 3: 1308) to the *Bookman*, where it appeared in May 1913 (*Letters* 3: 1161). As its editors explained in an introductory note, the *Bookman* did not usually publish fiction but considered "Samuel" an "exceptional story" despite its lack of a "happy ending," largely because of its portrait of the "lonely, stubborn old mother" (Note to "Samuel"). Nearly a year later, London was still defending the story and complaining of the obtuse judgments of his work by most magazine editors, calling it a "real story" and still proclaiming it as one of his best (*Letters* 3: 1308). Written in 1909, "Samuel" was based on a tale that London had heard from a sea captain, and he may have meant that it was a "real story" because he heard it from a reliable source. But the story is also "real" in that it provides an accurate portrait of human nature grounded in psychological truth.

Set on Island McGill, half a mile off the coast of Ireland but a world away in its ancient Scottish customs and Hebridean dialect, the story begins with the arresting sight of an elderly woman carrying hundred-pound bags of grain up a set of narrow steps to a loft. Struck by her wide-set blue eyes, domed forehead, and air of "stable equilibrium," the unnamed narrator begins to question her and learns that she is Margaret Henan, seventy-two years old and "beholden tull no one" (1613), not even to her children, who refuse to help her. All her sons have gone to sea and come home again except "Samuel oz was drownded" (1613). But as he questions several villagers, the narrator learns that beneath this innocuous tale, Margaret's life is a story of family tragedy. From Mrs. Ross, his landlady, he learns the story of the first three Samuels: one died of the croup in infancy; the second was "cooked tull death" (1617) when he fell into a tub of scalding wash water at the age of three; and the third, the one whom Margaret mentions, was drowned at sea. Clara, Mrs. Ross's daughter, provides the additional information that Margaret named her sons after her brother, Samuel Dundee, who had earlier met a tragic end. Along with two other couples, Samuel Dundee and Agnes Hewitt had been married in a new church built from the stones of the old one, but after the men shipped out to sea the marriages were nullified because the new church had not been approved by the authorities in Dublin. The other couples were speedily remarried, but believing her husband lost at sea, Agnes drowned herself and their child rather than face the shame of its illegitimacy. When Samuel Dundee returns, he tries to kill himself while lying across her grave, living only long enough to spit in the minister's face and blaspheme as he died.

In honoring her brother by naming her sons after him, Margaret affronts the village's sense of propriety because she thus also honors his blasphemous legacy. After the deaths of the first two Samuels, the villagers predict disaster, but the third Samuel confounds their expectations and grows into a strong, intelligent man who becomes first a teacher and then a sailor. Faced with the mistakes of a drunken captain, he stays at the wheel during a storm and is drowned, thus fulfilling the supposed fate of the uncle for whom he was named. Hearing of his death, Margaret, at forty-seven, becomes pregnant once again and is convinced that, because "there be balance un all thungs" (1624), her last child of the twelve she has borne will be a boy. Margaret does have a son and names him Samuel, but the compensation for his tremendous physical strength and vitality is the utter absence of reason; he is mentally challenged, an "eediot" in the clinical and vernacular terms of the time (1625). Goaded by his three-year-old son's braying and animal-like behavior, Tom Henan kills this fourth Samuel and then hangs himself in the stable. Shunned by family members and surrounded by death, Margaret still insists that her one regret is not having yet another son, so that she could call him Samuel. When the narrator asks why, she replies, "Do a wee but of a name change the plans o'God? Do the world run by hut or muss, an' be God a weak, shully-shallyun' creature thot ud alter the fate an' destiny o' thungs because the worm Margaret Henan seen fut tull name her bairn Samuel?" (1627). Besides, she says, "Whu can tell the *why* o' like? . . . I *like* Samuel, an' I like ut wull" (1628).

Teaching "Samuel": Initial Approaches

When I teach this story, two issues crop up immediately: its thick dialect and the meaning of Margaret's obsession with the name Samuel. The issue of dialect is important, since it is both integral to the story and the biggest barrier to the discussion. Students accustomed to London's clear, vivid prose object that they did not understand some of what Margaret was saying or were initially confused. I usually approach the question of dialect in a few different ways, depending on the level of the class. The first is simply to read some of the passages aloud and then invite students to do the same; if "Samuel" is included in an American literature survey course in which students have read Mark Twain or Charles W. Chesnutt, they are already used to the technique of reading a few paragraphs aloud to get used to the dialect. After reading portions aloud, I ask if they have noticed any system or patterns that helped them "translate" the dialect. In "Samuel," for example, "tull" is "to"; "o" followed by a consonant sounds like a short "a" ("thot" for "that") or "u" ("onderstandun" for "understanding"); and most of the usages of "u" followed by consonants would in Standard English be rendered as a short "i" or "e" sound: "wull" is "will" or "well," depending on the context; "fut" is "fit," and so on. Writing a short list of these on the board usually encourages students to ask about other words that gave them trouble.

The immediate thematic issues that "Samuel" raises for students are those of moral responsibility and the workings of fate, especially with regard to naming. The first question to ask students is why Margaret behaves as she does in naming her sons Samuel. London provides at least three possibilities for interpreting Margaret's actions, and students can be asked to identify these and to discuss which they think is best supported in the story:

Margaret's actions cause her sons' deaths. This is the position of the villagers, but does it make any rational sense? Should superstitions govern one's actions? (It's often useful to ask students about superstitions of their own, such as athletes not changing their socks if they're on a winning streak.)

The deaths of Margaret's sons are predestined as part of a divine plan. This is Margaret's position; she refuses to see any cause-and-effect link between her actions and her sons' deaths and asserts that their destiny is shaped by the greater forces of Providence, by which she means God. Does the story support her idea? What does her belief in Providence say about Margaret as a character?

> Margaret's actions are irrelevant because random fate causes her sons' deaths. If students suggest that there is no cause-and-effect relation between the name and their fate, I ask if they think that London uses the name "Samuel" ironically, since it means "beloved of God." If students have already been introduced to the concept of naturalism, I ask an additional question: is the tragic outcome of Margaret's defiant action in naming her sons the typically ironic thwarting of human will that occurs in many naturalist texts?

The second question to ask students is about the power of naming: Why is it important? What meanings do we attach to names? I ask students to talk briefly about their own names, if they wish: Do you know how your name was chosen? Were you named after a relative? Do you use your first or middle name, and why? Where did you get your nickname? Is your name spelled in a unique way? What associations or connotations do you or others have with your name? If there is time, we talk more generally about the popularity of certain names in different generations and about recent scholarship on naming: some research suggests that children given names currently considered unpopular are often less well treated in school by teachers and peers, and other research demonstrates that certain types of names are highly correlated with status and success. Within the context of thinking about their own names and what they know of names, students can better understand the power of naming in London's story.

Providing cultural context on nineteenth-century naming conventions also helps students understand the differences between Margaret's culture of naming and their own. For example, sons were often given their mother's surname as a middle name or were named after a grandfather, whereas the first girl would be named after her maternal grandmother. Although students tend to find naming a child after its dead sibling to be a little morbid, it was not at all uncommon in the nineteenth century and earlier, when high child mortality rates ensured that most families would have one or more deceased children whom they might wish to memorialize by giving a new baby the name of a beloved child who had died. Traditional biblical names such as Samuel were more common, too, although Margaret's choice seems to derive more from liking the name than from its biblical connotations.

Teaching "Samuel" through Archetypes, Myths, and Fairy Tales

"Samuel" is more a character study than the usual action-filled London tales that students have read, and students need to recognize that there are two principal characters: the mysterious figure of Margaret and the questing narrator who tries to analyze the secrets of her psychology. The key question to ask is this: Why does the narrator find Margaret and her story so compelling? As we discuss the narrator's fascination with Margaret, I outline some of the ways in which London makes her a universal figure through his use of classical, biblical, archetypal, and folk or fairy-tale elements.

Classical Mythology

Since most students have had exposure to classical mythology, I ask them if they see any parallels between Margaret and the figures of Greek myths: for example, Jeanne Campbell Reesman compares Margaret to the goddess Athena because of the extensive eye and hand imagery used to describe her and the sacks of grain that she carries (*Jack London* 122), and, as the mother of many children, Margaret may also be linked to Niobe. The sacks of grain that Margaret carries would also link her to the greatest mother of all in Greek myth, the goddess Demeter (Ceres), who plunges the earth into winter while mourning the abduction of her daughter Persephone (Proserpina) into the underworld.

Christian or Biblical Parallels

Margaret's status as a mother also has religious overtones. As both Reesman and Earle Labor point out, Saint Margaret is the patron saint of women in childbirth (Labor, "Archetypal" 29), so Margaret's name is suitable to her position as a mother. Her endurance in the face of sorrow also recalls the *mater dolorosa*, or "sorrowful mother" of the Roman Catholic Stabat Mater Dolorosa, a hymn to the sorrows of the Virgin Mary, and the biblical Rachel of Matthew 2.18, who "would not be comforted" while weeping for her lost children. Unlike her classical and religious counterparts, however, Margaret does not weep without ceasing, which raises this question: Why does London present this mother figure as being beyond mourning or grief? Does her failure to mourn in conventional ways make her seem an unnatural mother?

Archetypes, Folktales, and Fairy-Tale Elements

In the summer of 1916, five years after writing "Samuel," London read Carl Jung's *Psychology of the Unconscious* and its theories of the collective unconscious and archetypes. Jung believed that human beings possessed a collective unconscious that stored memories from the earliest history of the human race and transmitted them to individuals. Among these were memories expressed as archetypes, universal human emotions and experiences that manifested themselves in the characters, symbols, and plot patterns of myth and legend. Common character archetypes include the anima, the persona, and the shadow, as well as characters that recur in folktales, myths, and literature, such as the old man, the trickster, and the great mother, or *magna mater*. Labor considers Margaret Henan to be an archetype of the great mother, "the avatar of that mysterious force through which all living creatures are brought forth inexorably to bloom and die in the great cycle of nature" (29). If London portrays Margaret as a figure beyond mourning, it may be because as a great mother she has the power of both life and death.

Because students have often studied the archetypal hero's journey as described by Joseph Campbell in *The Hero with a Thousand Faces*, I ask them if they see any elements of this quest, or of other fairy-tale elements or universal symbols, in the narrator's pursuit of Margaret's story. Other archetypal or fairy-tale elements that appear in the story include the following:

Universal symbols, such as earth, fire, and water. For example, the imagery of the sea and water usually signifies the feminine element, as when it becomes the "fierce old mother" in Walt Whitman's "Out of the Cradle, Endlessly Rocking." In "Samuel," water takes the lives of two of Margaret's sons, the second and third Samuels.

The common fairy-tale theme of the curse of a granted wish. Margaret's wish is to have a son named Samuel, and she gets her wish four times, only to see each son die in turn.

Trebling. Students are well aware that most fairy tales have three wishes, three villains, three tasks to perform, and so forth. Described as "trebling" in V. Propp's *Morphology of the Folk Tale*, this repetition "may appear as a uniform distribution (three tasks, three years' service), as an accumulation (the third task is the most difficult, the third battle the worst), or may twice produce negative results before the third, successful outcome" (74). In Margaret's case, London uses unconscious associations with trebling to confound the reader's expectations: the third son named Samuel should be the one most subject to a terrible fate, but "nothing happened. The whole island was confuted" as he grows up to be a strong, intelligent man far above the average of men on the island (1620).

The power of naming. Folktales and fairy tales also invest the process of naming with deep significance, so that the ability to name someone, or to discover a secret name, as in "Rumplestiltskin," grants power to the person who is able to perform that act.

Teaching "Samuel" as a Gothic Story

Students who read "Samuel" after reading stories by Edgar Allan Poe should have little trouble in drawing parallels between its gothic elements and those in works such as "The Fall of the House of Usher," "The Black Cat," "The Tell-Tale Heart," and "The Imp of the Perverse." London points to the Poe connection in the story by describing how the "Imp of the Perverse must have chuckled at the situation" of the technicality in church records that rendered three marriages invalid, including that of Samuel Dundee, and "the Imp must have held both his sides" at subsequent irony of Samuel's return after his wife's death (1619, 1620).

In reading "Samuel" after studying Poe stories, students are already familiar with several characteristics of the gothic:

- An atmosphere of gloom, terror, or mystery
- Elements of the uncanny (*unheimlich*) that challenge reality, including mysterious events that cause the protagonist to question the evidence of his or her senses and the presence of seemingly supernatural beings
- An exotic setting isolated in time or space from contemporary life, often a ruined mansion or castle. The building may contain hidden doors, subterranean secret passages, concealed staircases, or other such features associated with the place's past violence.
- Events, often violent or macabre, that cannot be hidden or rationalized despite the efforts of the narrator
- A disturbed or unnatural relation between the orders of things that are usually separate, such as life and death, good and evil, dream life and reality, or rationality and madness
- A hidden or double reality and narrative beneath the surface of what at first appears to be a single reality and its narrative. As Eve Kosofsky Sedgwick explains, a primary feature of the gothic is that the self is "massively blocked off from something to which it ought normally to have access" (12). The narrative arc of the gothic story thus leads to an exposure of what was once hidden, breaking down the barrier between the surface reality and the reality beneath the surface.
- An interrupted narrative form that relies on multiple methods—inserted documents, letters, dreams, fragments of the story told by several narrators—to tell the tale.

In outlining these characteristics for students, I ask them to think about the ways in which "Samuel" meets these criteria. First, London's narrator seems almost hypnotized by Margaret's remarkable eyes and the mystery she embodies, and the uncanny events that lead to the deaths of her sons only add to that mystery. Second, Island McGill is not only an exotic setting to the narrator but, with its isolation and the contrast it sets up between Scottish Presbyterian rationality and conventionality and Irish mysticism, a fit space for unusual events. Third, although the narrator does not learn the fate of the fourth Samuel until nearly the end of the story, the numbers of suicides and murders of children by parents fit the criteria for macabre and violent happenings. Fourth, as Charles Crow explains, in its narrative arc "Samuel" reveals "the secret of the home place"—the murder of the fourth Samuel—and portrays Margaret Henan as a gothic heroine who "radically mixes traditional standards of good and evil" ("Jack London's 'Samuel'" 86). Finally, the unusual device (for London) of having a tale interrupted by having it told by different narrators reinforces the classification of "Samuel" as a gothic story.

Although students who have read *The Call of the Wild* or other London stories are accustomed to violence in his works, the deaths and fights in those stories are immediate and logically motivated either by revenge or by the law of survival of the fittest. In "Samuel," by contrast, the causes of the deaths are mysterious and inexplicable, motivated apparently simply by Margaret's preference for a name. Linking London to the gothic and its elements of mystery is important, for it helps to illustrate the ways in which London was attempting to tap into a more supernatural or mystical vein in explaining human behavior, one that would lead to the unexplained mysteries in late symbolic stories like "The Red One."

Teaching "Samuel" as a Regional Story

Although I have also used "All-Gold Canyon" when teaching local color fiction, "Samuel" provides a good example of this form as well. Like Sarah Orne Jewett's *The Country of the Pointed Firs* or the short stories of Mary E. Wilkins Freeman, "Samuel" contains several local-color characteristics: a remote, insular community; rural folkways; thick dialect; characters with little education who have lived in the place for generations; the preservation of the past in the present; and an individual who questions or challenges the community's standards. Teaching "Samuel" as a part of local-color fiction allows discussion not only of the themes of individual and community but also of the ways in which it lends itself to feminist interpretations.

Students reading "Samuel" after discussing local-color stories such as Freeman's "A Church Mouse" or Jewett's "The Foreigner" are quick to pick up on the ways in which Margaret, like Hetty Fifield or Mrs. Captain Tolland, risks ostracism by violating community standards. Steeped in Presbyterianism and the "old ways," the islanders speak with one voice, with the lone holdout the dissenter Margaret. Indeed, the islanders' voices appear in the story as a kind of Greek chorus to the tragedy of Margaret and her sons, commenting on, explaining, and at times condemning the actions that she takes. In writing about the depiction of community in the story, Laura Bedwell identifies the chief conflict as that between Margaret's heroic individualism and the islanders' narrow-mindedness, a conflict that the story resolves in Margaret's favor when the narrator converts to her point of view. The theme of individual versus community is universal, not specifically a local-color theme, so students can link "Samuel" to other works that use it as well.

In looking at the story from a feminist perspective, I ask students to find examples of the way in which London gives Margaret masculine attributes. Her physical strength, her habit of smoking a pipe, her "callous thumb" (1626), and, less obviously, her stubbornness in the face of opposition are stereotypical masculine traits. Another and less obvious masculine trait or privilege is that Margaret insists on naming her sons instead of allowing her husband to do it, as was customary, and, in the islanders' estimation, this usurpation of male power offends God and leads to her sons' deaths. Moreover, if Margaret's naming practices are indeed responsible for the deaths of her sons, as the villagers assert, the implication is that she has put her own desire—the desire to have a son named Samuel—above what is best for her children, in effect sacrificing their lives so that she can exercise her individual will instead of subsuming it for the good of family and community. That the narrator, and the story, presents this in a neutral rather than a disapproving fashion hints that Margaret's wishes are to be considered as much as those of any man in the story, a feminist position.

Moreover, two of the story's subplots lend themselves to feminist analysis. The first is the story of Agnes Hewitt and Samuel Dundee, whose lives are ruined because a petty bureaucratic error in the establishment of the new church means that they are not legally married. Although the three couples affected by the error clearly believed their marriages valid, the legalistic insistence on the written word—the patriarchal *logos*—instead of the maternal law of feelings results in the death of Agnes, Samuel, and their child. In other words, patriarchal culture, rather than Margaret's stubbornness, sets the violent events of the story in motion. The second is Margaret's determination to conceive another son after the third Samuel is drowned. Although the islanders are disturbed by Margaret's naming of her sons, they are even more scandalized by her desire to have another son at the age of forty-seven, finding it "unnatural and ungodly" that a woman should still be capable of bearing children, and thus of being sexual, at an age when culture demands that women resign their sexuality and already be mothers. With the declaration "I LIKE," Margret exemplifies the ideas of Ralph Waldo Emerson's "Self-Reliance," such as "Trust Thyself—every heart vibrates to that iron string" (Emerson 34). Part of the fascination that the narrator feels for Margaret is this duality, the recognition that she embodies both the life-giving and the life-denying force, and hence the terrible power of the maternal body.

Two works of regional fiction work especially well when paired with "Samuel." The first is Rose Terry Cooke's "Freedom Wheeler's Controversy with Providence" (1877), which has the same plot: Freedom Wheeler is determined to have a son named after himself. He is thwarted by various means, including the deaths of several wives, the spirited insistence of one wife that she be allowed to name the child, and a horrific accident in which Freedom trips while holding the newly baptized Freedom, falls on the child, and crushes him. Freedom finally gets his way when he gives up his quest, deferring to his new wife Melinda in the matter of naming, after which she decides to call the baby Freedom. In contrasting this treatment of the subject with "Samuel," issues of gender, fate, and naming all help show how London's story differs from this early version of the same theme, with Freedom submitting to the laws of providence as Margaret continues to deny their power. The second work is Edith Wharton's *Ethan*

Frome (1911), which echoes the form of "Samuel." Like "Samuel," *Ethan Frome* opens as an unnamed narrator, a visitor to the remote New England village of Starkfield, watches as Ethan Frome walks across the village square to get his mail. Intrigued by the ruined figure that Ethan has become, the narrator, like the narrator in "Samuel," seeks out a variety of village informants, including his landlady, to learn Ethan's story. An engineer by profession, the narrator pieces the story together from fragments gleaned from the townspeople, a method that London's narrator also employs, and, like London's narrator, he conjectures about Ethan's life with a mixture of philosophical detachment and empathy for Ethan's plight.

London's "Samuel" is one of the more unusual works in his canon, an experiment in form and subject matter that looks toward his later work. That London strove to make "Samuel" a genuine experiment in method is suggested by one of the story fragments, which is told by Gavin McNab, the bosun of the third Samuel's boat. By subordinating his usual subject matter, the exciting story of a man's heroic actions during a storm at sea, to a minor segment rather than making it the major focus of the story, London indicates that this is a serious experiment in form. And by refusing to tie the story up neatly in either fable or parable format with a clear lesson, he moves away from the method of his earlier fiction and branches out in a new direction with a new tolerance for ambiguity. The departures in form, theme, style, subject matter, and character make this story a worthy companion piece to the earlier fiction with which students are familiar.

Teaching Contradictory Representations of Gender, Race, and Ethnicity in *Martin Eden*

Debbie López and María DeGuzmán

Jack London's complicated and, from a perspective of gender and ethnoracial equity studies, conflicting views on sexual, racial, and class identity make for strange balancing acts in his work. London's semiautobiographical novel *Martin Eden* offers students an excellent entry into the tensions in his work, moving as it does between seemingly opposed aesthetic, philosophical, psychological, and sociopolitical positions. Some of the binaries that the text explores include aestheticism/utilitarianism, high art / low art, art / work performed, idealism/materialism, culture/nature, human/animal, equality/inequality, freedom/enslavement, and—the focus of this article—masculine/feminine and whiteness/blackness (DeGuzmán and López 100). When teaching the novel to upper-division students, we recommend first inviting them to examine specific passages that initially appear to present ideological dualisms concerning gender or race and ethnicity. Second, we suggest students look for thematic comparisons and connections in other works of American literature, particularly those focusing on the relation between authority or authorship and success. Last, in relation to the gender issues that London explores, we examine his allusions to British literature. Nineteenth-century American writers promoting a distinctively American literature frequently characterized British authors in general, and the Romantics in particular, as dreamy (and, suggestively, effeminate) aesthetes. Martin Eden presents himself as an impassioned realist in chapter 36, but the novel as a whole represents him as a Romantic artist. Intimately related to gender are the ways in which London's references to race, ethnicity, and nationality define the protagonist of *Martin Eden* in relation to his destiny, or, more to the point, his doom.

The title of this article was inspired by the passage in which the working-class Martin begins to discover that his feelings for the wealthier, educated Ruth Morse are different from those he has had for any other member of the female sex:

> His gaze wandered often toward her lips, and he yearned for them hungrily. But there was nothing gross or earthly about this yearning . . . They were lips of pure spirit, and his desire for them seemed absolutely different from the desire that had led him to other women's lips . . . He was not conscious of this transvaluation of values that had taken place in him . . . Her penetrative virginity exalted and disguised his own emotions, elevating his thoughts to a star-cool chastity. (609)[1]

This passage often prompts a bolder student to question who is doing the penetrating here. Patriarchal assumptions about the relative values of male and female are transposed, as are the conditions of passive virginity and active penetration. The oxymoronic phrase "penetrative virginity" captures in microcosm the gender play of the passage and of the book as a whole.

Such questioning from students can open the way for discussing the rise of the new woman and general concerns regarding gender and sexual politics with —to use Elaine Showalter's phrase (adopted from the novelist George Gissing)— "sexual anarchy." Such a discussion can in turn lead to an exploration of Martin's ambiguous gender position as author in an age when female writers so dominated the periodical press that one male author complained, "[T]he monthly magazines are getting so lady-like that naturally they will soon menstruate." Also, as Showalter notes, at the turn of the century, three-quarters of published books were by female authors (77).

Martin's depiction is further complicated in passages that reflect what Judith Butler has called "the interwoven vectors of sexuality and race" (*Bodies* 173), including passages such as the following:

> He had not dreamed he was so *black*. . . . He *twisted* his arm, rolled the biceps over with his other hand, and gazed underneath where he was least touched by the sun. It was very *white*. . . . Nor did he dream that in the world there were few pale spirits of *women* who could boast fairer or smoother skins than he—fairer than when he had escaped the ravages of the sun. (586–87; our emphasis)

Later in the novel, Ruth is described as listening to Martin like Desdemona to Othello (DeGuzmán and López 100–02).

Moreover, Martin's otherness has been compounded by his encounters with characters who are assumed, by the Anglo characters, to be nonwhite foreigners, notably Mexicans. Martin's neck, so often a source of fascination for the pale Ruth, is not only bronzed but also marked by a scar from his encounter with "a Mexican with a knife" (562). For historic reasons, namely the Mexican American War of 1846–48, in which United States forces took a third of Mexican territory and the Mexican inhabitants of the northernmost reaches of Mexico found themselves to be aliens in their own lands, Mexicans, of the different so-called "foreigners" Martin does meet, hold the distinction of being the foreigners at home or the Natives alienated from home. Significantly, Martin is shown to be marked by the alienated Native, a mark that, semiotically speaking, brands him with difference from his "white," Anglo companions and relates him to a narrative about cultural conflict, conquest, and domination in which it is not at all clear that Martin is in a dominant position. He may be strong, but what does it mean that the Anglo, bourgeois Ruth, who ultimately seems to sap his strength, is drawn to a particular mark on his body that emblematizes his meeting with a Native who is "Mexican," at once a foreigner and an alienated Native of the United States?

These passages invite class discussion and take-home essay questions such as, How can Martin Eden be at once black and white—and not only black "brown" or associated with whoever falls outside the dominant black/white binary structuring of ethnoracial relations in the nineteenth- and early-twentieth-century United States? What does it mean that Martin is both black and white and also browned by nature (the sun) and by culture (his encounter with the Mexican)? How can he be a lower-class laborer when he is by "nature" so white that his whiteness contests that of upper-class women, whose very whiteness marks their status? How much of Ruth's fascination with Martin derives not just from the size of his neck (described as "heavy corded, almost bull-like" [566]) but also from the brand that it wears? And what do students make of Ruth's fascination? How does her fascination resonate with the contents of the novel as a whole? What are the greater cultural implications of that fascination in terms of gender or sexuality and race or ethnicity? How are issues of gender or sexuality and race or ethnicity related? How do they "shade," so to speak, into one another, and where do they seem to be in tension with one another? What can be made of these continuities and discontinuities?

Questions of class and status are central to the rise and fall of Eden, a not-quite-white-enough white man (if by "white" it is understood that certain ethnic and class markers constitute the right type of whiteness). A fair fellow yet also a rough, muscled sailor, he is thrust into Ruth's bourgeois world of ladies and gentlemen thanks to his chivalric saving of her ironically named brother Arthur—a heroic deed that Martin modestly discounts. This encounter recalls the standard first step in the Horatio Alger protagonist's rise, when he has the fateful opportunity to be of service to someone who will prove to be a patron. Yet instructors may need to point out this formula, since remarkably few students are now familiar with it, despite the fact that the phrase "a Horatio Alger" story continues to be used today. After first being introduced to that formula, they can go on to explore London's use of it through reading excerpts from Alger's paradigmatic *Ragged Dick*.

In over one hundred novels written between 1864 and 1899, Alger preached the doctrine earlier made popular by Benjamin Franklin: the path from rags to respectability is potentially open to any honest, industrious American. However, Alger's protagonists on the rise tend to be Anglo with a foil who is frequently Irish and who does not succeed on account of his lack of industry. With variations, Alger's formula for success is simple. His protagonist is either a country boy come to the city seeking employment to support his widowed mother back home or, more often, a plucky, streetwise city boy. That is, anyone might start selling newspapers on the street and wind up a William Randolph Hearst. (An interesting variation is in Emma Dorothy Eliza Nevitte Southworth's *The Hidden Hand*, in which a poor, displaced heiress cross-dresses as a boy to prosper as a "newsboy" in New York.) Of course, some chance event always introduces the protagonist to the benevolent businessman who will become his benefactor (as would seem to be the case in *Martin Eden*). In Alger's *Ragged Dick*, a wealthy man's child falls overboard from a ferry, and Dick, providentially, is there to help. Dick's success is sealed by his courageous saving of the boy, just as, in an ambiguous manner, Martin's saving of Arthur on a ferry seals Martin's ultimately unfulfilling success.

Attentive students will pick up on the discrepancy between Martin's perception of his romantically named, would-be patron Arthur and what readers are told of the latter, whose attitude toward Martin is exoticizing, commodifying, and ultimately objectifying. Martin "did not know that his [own] quietness [at dinner] was giving the lie to Arthur's words of the day before, when . . . [he] had announced that he was going to bring a wild man home to dinner and for them not to be alarmed, because they would find him an interesting wild man" (570). In contrast to Arthur, the touchingly earnest Martin and his campaign of self-improvement, involving better dental hygiene and pronunciation in a world characterized by decay, corruption, and affective incomprehension and ideological chasms between people, may remind one of Jay Gatsby, who follows a similar Alger-like program.

While it is worth pointing out to students that *Martin Eden*, like *The Great Gatsby*, is an Alger parody, the ethnoracial issues in London's novel invite its comparison with Alger parodies by African American authors. Ann Petry's novelistic Alger parody *The Street* (1946), for example, makes for fruitful class discussion. Written a few years before Ralph Ellison's *Invisible Man* (1953), Petry's work looks at Harlem in the aftermath of the promising decade, heralded by Alain Locke's anthology *The New Negro* (1925). Her protagonist, Lutie, is a perfect candidate for success in the world Locke envisioned. In addition to being African American and female, she has all the qualities of the Alger hero: she is intelligent, industrious, and scrupulously honest. Like Martin, she is a great believer in education: she attends night school after working all day and taking care of her child. Yet despite all this, by the end of Petry's novel Lutie, far from succeeding, has lost everything. A lustful, wicked neighbor frames her child, and the boy is put into court custody as Lutie, having been tormented into committing murder, flees Harlem on a train:

> As the train started to move, Lutie began to trace a design on the window. It was a series of circles that flowed into each other. She remembered that when she was in grammar school the children were taught to get the proper slant to their writing, to get the feel of a pen in their hands, by making these same circles. Once again she could hear the flat, exasperated voice of the teacher as she looked at the circles Lutie had produced. "Really," she said, "I don't know why they have us bother to teach you people to write." Her finger moved over the glass, around and around. The circles showed up plainly on the dusty surface. The woman's statement was correct, she thought. What possible good has it done to teach people like me to write? (435)

Petry's novel could be described as an example of gothic naturalism. Class discussion invites students to see that *Martin Eden* is also naturalistic. London presents Martin as a working-class man accustomed to hard labor who is inspired by his worshipful love of a bourgeois woman (Ruth) to teach himself how to read, write, handle algebra and trigonometry, and become a prolific writer only to discover that the bourgeoisie welcome him so long as none of his ideas challenge their paradoxically slavish master-class ideology or upset the narrow conventions of their existence. The novel represents the bourgeoisie as adherents to an ideology that helps them maintain their status quo, but that ideology is slavish because it keeps them from thinking in more universal terms and serves the interests of a class above them, which is represented by the late-nineteenth- and early-twentieth-century robber barons. Success brings Martin bitter disappointment because it comes at the price of the rejection of everything about himself and his existence that he values and considers genuine. Thus, he gains access to the dining rooms and salons of the bourgeoisie at the expense of who he is—a working-class man who obtains an education that he uses to try to address the social injustices he himself has experienced. Instructors can find countless passages in *Martin Eden* that show how Eden, despite his seeming advancement, is deprived of any fulfilling success by the pervasive ideology and stranglehold of the master class.

The novel's naturalism is especially evident when it depicts the forces, both material and psychic, ranged against the happy success of those who are neither white nor socioeconomically advantaged. Can they ever really make up for their disadvantages? At what cost? The intersections among race or ethnicity, class, and cultural access make London's work interesting to students studying the experiences and cultural productions of people of color in the United States. As Jeanne Campbell Reesman observes in the introduction to *Jack London's Racial Lives*,

> If he [London] spoke of his admiration for "Anglo-Saxons" and used racial stereotypes, especially in his nonfiction and novels, London's greatest appeal to readers around the world [and perhaps specifically in the United States] was and is his exposure of injustices committed in the name of class or racial superiority and heroic resistance against them. (2)

Reesman adds that many of London's stories represent nonwhite protagonists struggling valiantly against ethnoracial obstacles (6). One striking example of this kind of struggle is "The Mexican," a story that participates in racial stereotyping and yet aligns itself empathetically with the position of a young Mexican boy, a fierce believer in the Mexican Revolution who scrubs floors and later gets dragged into the bloody "Gringo" sport of prizefighting, at first just to earn enough to eat—but then for more. "The Mexican" was published in 1911, one year after the beginning of the Mexican Revolution. It portrays the revenge of one Mexican youth for atrocities committed against his parents during an attempted suppression of the revolution.

Martin, though white, is physically marked by characters represented as nonwhite, as in the case with "a Mexican with a knife" who cuts Martin's neck in a fight and leaves a scar (562). Teachers of this and other London texts should be aware that students of color and students from low-income families, regardless of ethnoracial identification, may draw strong parallels between the struggles of these characters, including Martin, and those with socioeconomic disadvantages in contemporary United States society. It may be useful to point out that references to London's work appear in the literary work of a number of Chicanos—for instance, the writer and scholar Américo Paredes and the attorney, political activist, and writer Oscar "Zeta" Acosta (who refers to "To Build a Fire" in a 1970 teleplay).

References to London's works from recent writers of color may not be familiar to most students. The 2006 Home Box Office film *Walkout* (directed by Edward James Olmos), based on a true story of the 1968 East Los Angeles walkouts on the schools discriminating against Mexican Americans, features a key scene in which Chicana/o students are reading aloud from London's 1904 novel *The Sea-Wolf*. Two of these students are corporeally punished for a brief exchange in Spanish about the meaning of the word "gong," which they find in London's text. Their school is bound by an "English only" rule. Arguably, the film deploys London's novel to suggest, by extension from descriptions of hierarchy, hazing, and torture aboard a ship composed largely of Nordic immigrants vying for power, the senseless, destructive social Darwinist brutality of an Anglo-run school that discriminates against students on the basis of their Mexican American ethnicity. Although in the film many students are being taught to read, they are being silenced at the same time. Olmos's film questions the purpose of learning to read in a society that will not allow certain groups of people to communicate in their own language; thus, like Petry's *The Street*, it highlights the challenges these groups face to write their own history, their own truths—to express the value of their own existence.

This is also the question asked by Martin, who abandons writing, deciding instead to travel to Tahiti aboard the suggestively named *Mariposa*, a ship whose name means not only "butterfly" or "moth" but also "whore" and "effeminate homosexual" in Mexican Spanish. Regardless of his escapist gesture, while on board he feels compelled to revisit a collection by Algernon Swinburne (DeGuzmán and López 117). Reading Swinburne's "The Garden of Proserpine" inspires Eden to commit suicide. This last instance illustrates the necessity for students to understand London's myriad allusions in the text and the extent to which these allusions connect to issues of gender or sexuality, ethnicity or race, and notions of personal and historical teleology—in the form of destiny, fate, doom. To this end, students might keep a running glossary of names new to them—both for their sakes and for those of their instructors, who may or may not have anticipated their students' unfamiliarity with London's interest in the social Darwinism of Herbert Spencer, much less the unexpected influence of British poets on London, so often considered a quintessentially American writer.

For example, with regard to the influence of British poets, Martin's friend Brissenden, modeled on London's friend George Sterling, advises, "[L]ove beauty for its own sake alone . . . and leave the periodicals alone. . . . You can read the magazines for a thousand years and you won't find the value of one line of Keats" (814). Students may readily pick up on the Keats reference, if only knowing his reputation as a very talented poet who died young. Both Keats and Brissenden were gifted writers who, thanks to tuberculosis, lived, to adopt Keats's phrase, "posthumous existence[s]" (qtd. in Bate 680). On the other hand, students may not readily see the connections between popular portrayals of "poor Keats" and Martin as a prototypical Romantic artist. Both were ostracized because of their class and celebrated by their admirers for their "negative capability" sensitivity that involves the capacity to see beneath the surface of things and dwell in the uncertainties and mysteries of the depths. This "negative capability" sensitivity involves courageous contemplation and understanding rather than pusillanimous measuring judgment. Martin's "gift [is that] of sympathy, understanding" (558). Martin Eden is, as one contemporary reviewer wrote, "a child of the slums . . . [but] with the delicate soul of a sensitive plant" (qtd. in DeGuzmán and López 109). More important, Keats's poem "Lamia" and its eponymous succubus snake woman offer one way to read Ruth, who imagines placing her hands on Martin's neck so that "all strength and vigor would flow out to her" (566). And one of the biggest fans of Keats's "Lamia" was Swinburne, whose poems figure in *Martin Eden*. What might seem like a confusing proliferation of references actually forms a matrix of cross-referencing associations between sensibility, effeminization, Romanticism, genius, hypersensitivity, degeneracy, outsider status, and doom.

The first work Martin seizes when entering Ruth's house is Swinburne's *Tristram of Lyonesse*, and he subsequently imagines championing Ruth as his Iseult. The repressed Ruth doesn't entirely approve of Swinburne—a hint of the difficulties to come, given that this particular poem is generally thought to champion natural love over Victorian inhibitions. Later in the novel, when the subject of Swinburne's "Dolores" arises, Martin recalls that it is a poem that he thoroughly understands. This is telling, in that "Dolores" celebrates "the raptures and roses of vice." As Swinburne writes: "And good shall die first, said thy prophet, / Our Lady of Pain" (134). So infamous was Swinburne for his morbid fascination with sadomasochistic love that he was parodied by *Punch* as "Swineborn" (Black 614). Hence, Martin's mispronunciation of the poet's name may be a well-informed insider's joke as well as a marker of class division.

The poem that sings Martin to his sea death is Swinburne's "Garden of Proserpine," which speaks of the underworld gardens guarded over by Pluto's wife, who rules with "cold immortal hands" (137). This is a poem about an era, specifically that of Victorian England, embracing its own dissolution. Everything in this Swinburne poem is about world weariness. Nothing is new. Everything is decaying or dead. The end of the poem denies new prospects altogether, including any promise of an afterlife or resurrection. But what, students might ask, of the new world Martin and the part it plays in "Eden's" demise? Why is *Martin Eden*, a novel whose title obviously calls attention to Eden and the idea of the New World, so heavily laden with doom, concluding as it does with Martin's suicide by drowning in the South Pacific? If nothing else, the novel would seem to attest to the impossibility of finding an uncorrupted world and happiness in the promised land of the United States while caught in a morass of sociocultural and philosophical contradictions. Instead of a new Eden, the reader finds a heaving and plunging that kill its protagonist, who *lifts* "his shoulders and half his chest out of water" to "gain impetus for the *descent*" (emphasis added), thus effecting a reverse birth into the exterminating ocean (930).

NOTE

[1] Citations to *Martin Eden* are from *Jack London: Novels and Social Writings*.

It's a Family Affair: Nativism and Ethnic Panic in Jack London's *The Valley of the Moon*

Gina M. Rossetti

In his novel *The Valley of the Moon* (1913), Jack London offers a seemingly nostalgic account of Billy and Saxon Roberts's return to a pastoral ideal located in California's Sonoma Valley. A closer examination of the novel reveals, however, a coupling of nostalgia and early-twentieth-century nativist principles. By invoking the term "pioneer family" as a euphemism for race and nation, the text offers a re-creation of the pioneer's pilgrimage to the West. That is, from the references to the pioneer-family stock to the settling of the West, the text offers a complex argument whereby nostalgia functions as an ideological tool that rationalizes the nativists' call for the return of the Anglo-Saxon. The era's philosophies of race and nation, as espoused by Gino Speranza and Charles Gould, offer insights into the ethnic panic that motivates Billy and Saxon. The couple's final emergence as landowners and overseers of ethnic prison laborers creates an American feudal order, suggesting that the Anglo-American identity manifest in the novel is steeped in a racialized, binary logic. It is important to note that teaching nativism in *The Valley of the Moon* does not rely on an anachronistic argument but situates the novel in a larger, ongoing, and complex web of ideas that framed the opening decades of twentieth-century American culture. Encouraging students to conceptualize London's novel in terms of its engagement with ideas, issues, and values of its time gives teacher-scholars the opportunity to show students how a literary text becomes the vehicle for representing its era's contested issues.

Contextualizing Nativism in The Valley of the Moon

In his 1923 text *Race or Nation: A Conflict of Divided Loyalties*, for instance, Speranza argues that American culture draws its origins from Anglo-Saxon stock, and, as a result, "through their kinship in spiritual and cultural traditions and antecedents, and the ennobling conditions of life and struggle in the new continent, they became a homogeneous people—the historic American stock—distinctly like-minded and peculiarly alike also in character, in outlook, and in ideals" (15). A philosophical opponent to assimilation, Speranza argues that immigrants not only become "more difficult [to] absorb because of their increasing bulk, but by solidifying their differences, they actually obstruct and resist such processes" (27). He rests the foundation for this claim on the conclusion that immigrants' numbers; their estrangement from American cultural traditions, which grow out of an Anglo-Saxon ancestry; and adherence to their race identities as immigrants create the conditions where "they become increasingly aggressive in their more or less consciously organized resistance to absorption until they gradually reach a point where they will actually attempt to impose their views and their principles, their interpretations, and their standards upon the historic American majority" (28).

For Speranza, immigrants are a threat to the unified culture and unfit to become agents in the institutions that govern their new nation. Once again, he establishes his claim along racial lines and asserts that "Anglo-Saxons are, and necessarily must be, better fitted in every way to manage institutions and systems which were developed by their own people, through the training and experience of centuries" (44). Speranza goes on to link the presence of the immigrant with the era's ongoing economic challenges, which he asserts were triggered by "both the 'suddenness' and the massiveness of our immigrant alienage which seriously threaten our whole social structure" (138).

One year earlier, Gould identifies the family as the central locus for his concerns about the role of the immigrant in American culture. In his *America: A Family Matter* (1922), Gould argues that just as "with animals physical capacity can be improved by care in breeding[;] man is no exception to this general animal law" (3). Consequently, Gould traces the development of ancient and modern civilization as one where societies were threatened by the influx and racial intermingling of alien peoples. As evidence for his claims, Gould relies on Darwin and asserts that "the importance of keeping the strain pure is paramount. It is the fundamental rule. Many instances are given by Darwin of the strong tendency in hybrids to revert, and thus their offspring lose the benefit of the good traits which careful selection in breeding had given their respective parents" (27). For Gould, racial purity is essential to a culture's survival: "[I]f the members of a tribe or people are of a common stock, speaking a common tongue, holding in common ideals and animated by the same sentiments, the result of their united action will create manifestations much more important than those of a state composed of a jumbled mass of unrelated elements. . . . [A] republic is possible only to men of a homogenous race, determined and united in intelligent control of their own affairs" (33, 163). If such an intermingling were to occur, Gould reasons, the result is that "we dissipate our fortune of American freedom and condemn the children to rub shoulders politically, not with their mates, but with strangers and foreigners whose sympathies are with each other and not with the American-born" (163).

For Speranza and Gould, American cultural identity is intrinsic. Consequently, the immigrant cannot possibly become an American because she or he was not literally "born" into this breed or tribe. These complicated race-nationality-origin ideologies in the opening decades of American culture provide a useful frame for teaching *The Valley of the Moon*.

What I seek to do in my classroom is place the novel in the frames of historical context and of the genre of romance to show students that the romance becomes a kind of nostalgia—a backward glance to an era that never was. This looking back espouses a vision for a new social order in which members of the tribe reclaim their lost Anglo-Saxon birthright in the soil of an unspoiled

Sonoma Valley. More explicitly, the American pastoral becomes a healing place for Saxon's and Billy's "threatened" identities: Billy's and Saxon's success comes to fit squarely in the era's nativist concerns, values, and principles. Among the questions I ask my students to consider: How does the novel express complicated and contradictory nativist principles? How does the novel's use of the pastoral connect the text to a broader literary tradition? What does the novel help us understand about its era and its original audience?

I am sensitive to my colleagues who express concern about framing a text in its nativist context: discomfort surrounding race issues can make some students shut down during class, short-circuiting the discussion. I recommend that the teacher incorporate trust-building exercises early in the course, so that students recognize the classroom as a space where they can explore difficult and challenging ideas without personal attack. While such an approach seemingly validates felt, personal responses over the analytic, I have discovered that students want to articulate the values that inform their frame of reference; in the end, such a practice provides students with an understanding of how competing frames can be better understood if noted and acknowledged rather than ignored. Once students learn that multiple frames of reference exist, and that such frames often drive interpretations of texts and ideas, the transition to the study of London's novel, which addresses troubling and problematic notions about race and American cultural identity, is smoother. One potential strategy that addresses the novel's context, while also meeting students "where they are," was suggested to me by Jeanne Campbell Reesman's scholarly approach to London's fiction, which makes use of Todorov's distinction between racism and racialism: "in the work of authors we must 'distinguish' between racism, which is a ubiquitous form of behavior, and racialism, or theories of race, whose heyday extended from the middle of the eighteenth through the middle of the twentieth centuries" (Todorov, qtd. in Reesman, *Jack London's Racial Lives* 34).[1] I ask students for examples of racism and racialism in the novel, and we discuss the Social Darwinian ethic that was pervasive at the time and persists today.[2] In putting such an approach into practice, the teacher can identify the major issues that dominate the text, as well as the critical tradition that informs London's scholarship and the literary traditions that inform his work. The teacher may want to divide the class into teams focused on one of these particular issues. In researching and applying them to the primary text, students can trace where ideas take root and where the limits to an idea or concept begin to emerge.

The Story of Settlement

The novel's foregrounding of nativist claims reveals itself in the story of Saxon's origins, which informs and sustains Saxon even in the midst of challenging financial circumstances. For instance, as she lives in the squalor of her brother's Oakland apartment, in which she must also endure her sister-in-law's verbally abusive comments, she focuses on "a very ancient chest of drawers." Further, she muses,

> she knew [the ancient chest of drawers] had crossed the plains with her people in a prairie schooner. It was of solid mahogany. One end was cracked and dented from the capsize of the wagon in Rock Canyon. A bullet-hole, plugged in the face of the top drawer, told of the fight with the Indians at Little Meadow. Of these happenings her mother had told her; also had she told that the chest had come with the family originally from England in a day earlier than the day on which George Washington was born. (7)[3]

This chest of drawers not only places Saxon in the context of Western pioneers but also posits her as a "pre-American" insofar as she is an antecedent to George Washington. This description has many implications for the novel's connection to the era's larger cultural context about race, nation, and family: First, the westward journey is reminiscent of the Puritans' treacherous journey and existence amid a "howling universe" populated by "hostile" Native Americans. Second, the furniture bears the scars of the family's dangerous and ultimately righteous settlement of the West. Finally, the journey as story and its accompanying props become the talisman that Saxon clutches as she attempts to survive her urban landscape, where her identity as a pure-blooded American is lost amid the poverty, deprivation, and immigrant inhabitants.

And it is this lineage that informs and shapes Saxon's frame of reference, which not only sets her apart from her fellow workers but also becomes the means by which she will find her mate and other true American: Billy Roberts. When she meets Billy, she explains her name's origin. She opines, "[T]he Saxons were a race of people—[my mother] told me all about them when I was a little girl. They were wild, like Indians, only they were white. And they had blue eyes, and yellow hair, and they were awful fighters" (21). Further, she explains this lineage to Billy in more practical, political terms: "[The Anglo-Saxons] were the first English, and you know the Americans came from the English. We're Saxons, you an' me, an' Mary, an' Bert, and all the Americans that are real Americans, you know, and not Dagoes and Japs and such" (21–22). Much like Speranza and Gould, Saxon employs nativist rhetoric to draw the boundaries around her and Billy, and she does so by invoking lineage, race, and nation. It is at this point that Billy offers his origins narrative. Billy states that "my folks lived in America a long time. . . . Anyway, my mother's folks did. They crossed Maine hundreds of years ago" (22). With this simple statement, Billy lays claim to a foundational birthright in American society that predates the nation's formation. As Saxon probes this story to ensure that they share a common, pioneer heritage, she learns from Billy that perhaps his father's ancestry is less known: "[H]e didn't know himself. Nobody ever knew, though he was American, all right, all right" (22). Continuing, Billy offers the following information:

> Roberts was the name of a gold-miner who adopted him. You see, it was this way. When they was Indian-fightin' up there with the Modoc Indians, a lot of the miners an' settlers took a hand. Roberts was captain of one outfit, and once, after a fight, they took a lot of prisoners—squaws, an' kids an' babies. An' one of the kids was my father. They figured he was about five years old. He didn't know nothin' but Indian. . . . Roberts adopted him, and that's why he don't know his real name. But you can bank on it, he crossed the plains just the same. (22)

This exchange is compelling because it fits the notion of a pioneering, Anglo-Saxon stock and works against the race primacy it posits. That is, Billy's ancestry is far less certain than Saxon's. What makes Billy an American is the story of his origins: the extent to which his tale reifies a nostalgia that envelops him in the lore of an American identity. He becomes an American because his father's conditions fit so rightly into a kind of early American captivity narrative in which his birthright as an American is restored to him through the rescue by the gold miner. In other words, Billy's father's whiteness and his Americanness are not erased by his immersion in Native American culture. Rather, Billy's father is discovered by another American pioneer who restores him to his rightful place. As a result, the idea of a common familial bond becomes a euphemism to draw a very narrow conception of that American—even while that definition appears to be rather dubious at best.

Billy's father's story of capture and redemption offers an excellent opportunity for teachers to introduce students to captivity narratives, some of which depict the captive's restoration into white society, and the consequent legitimization of the need to maintain strict racial boundaries. Students might compare Mary Rowlandson's captivity narrative with the story Billy tells and consider how immersion into Native American culture is something that both imperils the captive and holds out the possibility that, through the eventual rescue of the captive person, the entire community will reach salvation. In putting the texts together, students might identify how the threats to white culture manifest themselves and the extent to which the captive's restoration allows for the community to redraw its racial boundary lines.

Another useful context for Saxon and Billy's story of Americanness is the genre of the American pastoral.[4] Students might investigate how questions about liberation, selfhood, and individual freedom come to be posited onto the landscape, investing nature with the task of enabling human potential. The teacher may want to point students to Annette Kolodny's groundbreaking text, *The Lay of the Land*, which argues that the return to the land in the West becomes, in point of fact, a "regression from the cares of adult life and a return to the primal warmth of womb or breast in a feminine landscape" (5–6). One possible assignment entails having students analyze Saxon and Billy's journey into Sonoma by juxtaposing it with a novel from the American West tradition. Crucial to this assignment are the conventions and features shared by the texts and the status of the mythos of the West—the frontier had long since "closed" at the time of *The Valley of the Moon*'s publication. Students will gain a deeper understanding of London's original audience if they research the popular ideas and magazines that framed the era, especially as congested urban spaces often triggered a nostalgic return to the American West.

Nostalgic Narrative to Reality: Mrs. Mortimer

In the novel's last section, Mrs. Mortimer emerges as an integral figure who legitimizes Billy and Saxon's dreams, connects them to the Anglo-Saxons who "crossed the Plains," and reifies the family as the locus for American cultural identity in her retelling of their common story. It is on a kinship level that Mrs. Mortimer first sanctions their Anglo-Saxon mythmaking. When first meeting Billy and Saxon, Mrs. Mortimer notes her Anglo-Saxon roots:

> I'm of the old stock myself. . . . [M]y grandmother was one of the survivors of the Donner Party. My grandfather, Jason Whitney, came around the Horn and took part in the raising of the Bear Flag at Sonoma. He was at Monterey when John Marshall discovered gold in Sutter's mill-race. One of the streets in San Francisco is named after him. . . . [W]hy, you two dear children, we're almost like relatives. It's a breath of old times, alas! (344)

Mrs. Mortimer's proclamation that she, Billy, and Saxon are "family" only reinforces the novel's use of the term as a euphemism for race and nation. As a result, Mrs. Mortimer emerges as another branch in Billy and Saxon's metaphoric family tree, and she becomes the one who bears the textual evidence for the stories the couple tell about their family's contributions to this pioneer past. For instance, she provides evidence of Billy and Saxon's connections to actual history—the published poetry of Saxon's mother and the legend of Billy's father's capture—when she muses, "[Y]ou are historical, or at least your father is. I remember about him. The whole thing is in Bancroft's History" (344). The articulation of this statement, along with her presentation of Saxon's mother's published and bound poetry, connects these characters to the so-called Great Plains past and tightly draws the boundary lines of race and nation under the auspices of family. Moreover, Mrs. Mortimer's confirmation that Billy's father's story appears in a reputable historical text seemingly confers on it a legitimacy that it would not ordinarily have since his father's legacy and connection to this mythic past could well be questioned. Mrs. Mortimer's logic works as follows: if the story is published, then it is true. The subjectivity of history and the narrative quality of the historical tale are absent from Mrs. Mortimer's proclamations.

After Mrs. Mortimer provides Billy and Saxon with a confirmation of their common legacy, she imparts to them the essentials they will eventually need to become farmers in Sonoma. To lend further credence to the information she is about to impart, she informs them that, just as Billy and Saxon were urbanites, "[I]n the beginning I was a greenhorn, city born and bred. All I knew of the country was that it was a place to go to for vacations, and I always went to the springs and mountain and seaside resorts" (337). Here, Mrs. Mortimer evokes the image of the immigrant greenhorn but uses it in a manner that is estranged from its actual definition. While the immigrant is labeled a greenhorn because of his or her degrees of separation from American ways, this notion takes on new meaning with Mrs. Mortimer as she uses the term to comment on the extent to which she had become estranged from her own inborn American identity. In this comment, then, the urban landscape becomes a place not suited for the "real American," thus legitimizing the desire for Billy, Saxon, and others of Anglo-Saxon stock to take to the country and reinscribe it with American cultural identity. What makes Mrs. Mortimer's tale even more intriguing is that she tells Billy and Saxon that it was not physical strength that tilled her land and made her a profitable farmer. Rather, her profits came because of her intellect. As she notes, "I had been a librarian. I knew my way around books. First of all I'd read everything written on the subject, and subscribed to some of the best farm magazines and papers. . . . So, it is the head that counts" (338). From this initial tutelage, Billy and Saxon learn that recapturing an American landscape for Americans comes through intellect rather than through brawn.

What makes the discovery of Sonoma Valley all the more important for Billy and Saxon, then, is that it comes to represent the same virginal, unspoiled, and, more important, seemingly "empty" land that their ancestors had once encountered. As they come into the valley, they discover that "here were neither Asiatics nor Europeans. The scant population consisted of the original settlers and their descendants. More than one old man or woman Saxon talked with who could remember the trip across the Plains with the plodding oxen. . . . Old customs had changed little. There were no railways. No automobile as yet had ventured their perilous roads" (473). By arriving at this conclusion, Billy and Saxon's journey becomes much like their ancestors' trek from earlier times, which creates a clear and unbroken line between that pioneer past and their current circumstances. Indeed, as they reach this spot, Saxon declares, "I know I've never been here before but it's all so familiar! Why, I feel as if I was coming home" (479). This homecoming not only legitimizes their seemingly impossible on-foot journey from Oakland to Sonoma, but it also suggests that their survival comes because they are a chosen people who did not succumb to the desperate ends that their counterparts Mary and Bert suffered. It is at this point that they purchase the Madrono Ranch and send for Mrs. Mortimer, who provides them with further counsel and offers advice that once again links her to this pioneer couple. She implores Billy, "[D]o as I did. Cut out the middle man. Sell directly to the consumer." Further, she indicates that "this valley is just waking up. Here's your market. There isn't a competitor in the valley" (496–97). One would think that the prospect of settling the valley would contradict Billy's earlier claim in the novel that success need not stem from hard labor. On the contrary, Mrs. Mortimer advises that the couple should invest in convict labor, which she had done in her early farming days. In fact, she dispatches to them the use of her overseer, Mr. Hale, who, according to Mrs. Mortimer, "knows all about it himself. . . . There are plenty of Chinese and Italians there, and they are the best truck-farmers. You will kill two birds with one stone. You serve the poor convicts, and you serve yourselves" (500). This formula for economic success is predicated on the use of a zero-sum-gain principle against the immigrant, formerly imprisoned laborers.

This exploitative practice is not limited to prisoner labor. Rather, Billy devises a scheme whereby he will rent his horses to teamsters, who are desperate for the means to make a living; will offer them his business as their exclusive horse provider; and will, as a result, undermine the union to which he had once belonged. With economic security at hand, the novel closes with Saxon's confession to Billy that she has written to her brother and "asked him to ship up the old chest of drawers—my mother's, you remember—that we stored with him" (529). While initially confused by his wife's desire, Billy soon learns that this chest of drawers is important because of the baby clothes in it. Elated, Billy reveals, "[I]t's what I wanted, Saxon, more'n anything else in the world. I've been thinkin' a whole lot about it lately, ever since we hit the valley" (530). Unlike the labor-strife streets of Oakland that triggered Saxon's earlier miscarriage, the valley's fecundity leads to the most important conclusion that the novel might offer: the continued family line of this pioneer stock. Enraptured by the promise of new life, "they gazed far up the side of the knoll where a doe and a spotted fawn looked down upon them from a tiny open space between the trees" (530). In this concluding moment, Billy and Saxon extend the dream once imagined by their pioneer ancestors and find in an unspoiled landscape the means by which to continue this American family. As a result, the novel invokes the era's nativist principles and values to render Billy and Saxon's dreams a reality, and, in doing so, reifies the family as the controlling metaphor for race, culture, and nation.

NOTES

[1] Although in *Jack London's Racial Lives*, Reesman uses a psychoanalytic lens through which to interpret London's inconsistent and fraught treatment of race and I do not, her use of Todorov is nonetheless useful because his distinction opens up *The Valley of the Moon* for its treatment of race in ways that may put at ease students' and teachers' concerns about discussing race in class.

[2] Kaufman cites the problematic race ideology in *The Valley of the Moon* by painting London's fiction with a rather broad brush, asserting that London wrote "books that focused on race, books in which intense ideological fervor converted intended novels into xenophobic tracts" (97). See Rothberg for an acknowledgment that London's race ideologies are a part of a larger network of inconsistencies and contradictions. Crow situates

the text in terms of the California romance. He asserts a two-sidedness to this romance: California as a dispeller of dreams and California as the romantic fulfillment of financial fantasies ("Homecoming" 5–6).

[3] Citations to *The Valley of the Moon* are from the 1913 edition.

[4] See Buell's *The Environmental Imagination*, which traces the scholarly history that interpreted the use of the American pastoral. Buell indicates that what distinguishes newer scholarship from older is that the former "stresses even more than the older scholarship nature's function as an ideological theater for acting out desires that have very little to do with bonding with nature as such and that subtly or not so subtly valorize its unrepresented opposite" (35). While Buell's study raises questions about the absolute certainty that recent critics bring to the American pastoral, who figure the landscape as a passive theater onto which a burgeoning American identity transferred its real or imagined preoccupations and desires, his main argument in parsing the various approaches is to acknowledge that "the current revisionism has not gone far enough in stressing the 'imperial' cast of American pastoral ideology, and that it has gone farther than it should, by making insufficient allowance for American naturism's ideological multivalence" (36).

Teaching London's Margins: *A Daughter of the Snows* and Others

Andrew J. Furer

While Jack London scholarship—thanks to members of the Jack London Society and others—has made a significant return from the margins, as has the teaching of such central works as *The Sea-Wolf*, *The Call of the Wild*, and *Martin Eden*, the pedagogical potential of his vast oeuvre has been only minimally explored. Over the past two decades, however, I have found that many of his unjustly overlooked works can be very profitably taught. That is to say, one shouldn't be afraid to teach London's margins. Such texts, whether previously dismissed for obscurity, aesthetic shortcomings, or exoticism, can engage students powerfully in many ways, historically and transhistorically. London's marginalized texts, such as his first novel, *A Daughter of the Snows*; his late fantasy *The Star Rover*; or his socialist and antiracist stories—as much or more than his canonical works—reveal many key issues of his era related to gender, race, and class, as well as to the literary imagination, issues to which current students are strongly drawn.

A Daughter of the Snows, for example—which an informal survey of London scholars and others suggests that I have been alone, until very recently, in teaching—reveals that the "portrait of a [new] lady" often unveiled in realism and naturalism courses through such canonical writers as Henry James, Kate Chopin, and Edith Wharton is incomplete. London's idea of a new womanhood shows students that the author was a major contributor in reshaping the understanding of women's physical capabilities in this period, a role that he shared, to some extent, with Bernarr Macfadden, who promoted women's physical capabilities at a time when such advocacy seemed an endorsement of what many commentators of the era referred to as the "manly woman" or "mannish lesbian." I have found that through *A Daughter of the Snows* students dramatically come to see—in ways that echo our own time—how changes in perceptions of women's physical capabilities are inextricably intertwined with the sexual, political, intellectual, economic, and legal transformations represented in the fiction of the other writers just noted.

In this essay I first highlight strategies for overcoming some of *Daughter*'s significantly negative qualities, such as its extreme racism and aesthetic flaws, and show how it can be usefully taught in freshman and sophomore writing classes. Second, I discuss the value of teaching some of London's often overlooked multiracial short fiction, such as "Koolau the Leper" and "The Mexican," texts that provide a valuable external commentary on works by contemporaneous nonwhite writers, such as Sui Sin Far and Zitkala-Ša, unveiling, among other things, the complex interconnections of radical politics, race, and art in the Progressive Era. Third, I demarcate how teaching London's radical socialist works, such as "The Apostate," "South of the Slot," "The Dream of Debs," and *The Iron Heel*, reveals not only the prominence of radical socialist thought at the turn of the century and London's significant contributions to it but also the fact that even in an age in which socialism appears discredited, London's radical ideas resonate powerfully with many students. Last, I show the manner in which *The Star Rover* can engage students not only through the power and exoticism of London's imagination—a faculty that exceeds that of any author of the period in range and originality—but also through its cry for justice.

The pedagogical value of all these works lies in showing how engaging with London is crucial to understanding his era, in drawing students into an era they may think greatly distant from their own, and in provoking students to read more widely in London's works outside class, so that they might discover, among other things, the unique power of his imagination.

Teaching A Daughter of the Snows *in a Composition Seminar*

I first taught *A Daughter of the Snows* as a graduate student instructor of freshman composition at the University of California, Berkeley, in the early 1990s. Although I felt strongly that the novel had significant value in terms of its cultural work, the first time I taught it I was hesitant, given its many literary flaws. My doubts, however, were quickly erased as I continued to teach it.

One of the great virtues of the common practice of open-topic freshman and sophomore writing classes is that one can construct syllabi that ask non-English-major undergraduates to rise to meet the challenge of difficult special topics. I developed the Berkeley first-year writing seminar as a gender course, The American New Woman and the Construction of Gender, 1880–1915. In it, I taught *A Daughter of the Snows* alongside Henry James's *The Portrait of a Lady*, Kate Chopin's *The Awakening*, Sarah Orne Jewett's *A Country Doctor*, Edith Wharton's *The House of Mirth*, and other works. To my pleasant surprise, I found that the juxtaposition of London's model of the new woman alongside those of James and prominent female writers of the era turned out to be one of the most powerful strategies with which to engage writing students in the study of the new woman. Students uninspired by James's novel's elegance and psychological complexity, for example, or Chopin's intricate explorations of the strictures of the cult of true womanhood were captivated by the physical adventure of London's text and vice versa, leading to the wide range of essay topics that I have always found most effective in eliciting writing students' best work. Moreover, the James fans' enthusiasm not infrequently infected the London fans, and the reverse was also true, which became apparent when we conducted a workshop on a pair of essays on these texts.

Daughter's aesthetic weaknesses (London himself described it as a "failure" and said he had squandered enough ideas for a dozen novels on it) can be set in the historical context of the debate over the new woman, leading to a class discussion of the ways in which literary works can have significance aside from questions of artistic force and beauty (J. London, *Letters* 1: 240; C. London, *Book* 1: 384). A key example is the novel's challenging of the double standard when the protagonist, Frona Welse—during an argument with one of her suitors, Vance Corliss, over her treating the prostitute Lucile as a friend—directly subverts such bias, declaring, "Because you are a man, you may court contamination. Because I am a woman, I may not. Contamination contaminates, does it not?" (109). That is to say, in contrasting *Daughter* with works such as *Portrait*, students learn that a literary text is made important through the cultural work it does, not merely through its aesthetic qualities, a crucial idea to inculcate in underclassmen, especially since many high school English classes still use a "great books" approach that is based primarily on aesthetic criteria. In such a course, in this way, one of *Daughter*'s major weaknesses becomes a significant strength.

Furthermore, as awkward as the novel's romantic elements are, they have the virtue of exploring nontraditional relationships between men and women, as when Frona transforms the effete, overcivilized Corliss into a balanced figure who is able to survive in an elemental environment and to adapt to its subversive effects on conventional social values. We are told that "he was a product of the sheltered life" (75) and can thus benefit greatly from the example set by Frona, since she has been bred in the severe conditions of the Yukon. Moreover, while Frona remains chaste, she has a frank sexual appreciation for male beauty, unlike most female characters of the era, with the possible exception of *The Awakening*'s Edna Pontellier at one or two moments or the protagonist in another of Chopin's works, "The Storm": "it was a delight to her and a joy to look upon the strong males of her kind," with "comely" bodies and "muscles swelling. . . . If she felt impelled to joy in a well-built frame . . . why should she restrain? Why should she not love the body, and without shame?" (*Daughter* 87). This novel, in fact, describes forthright sexual feeling but depicts no sexual action— Frona and Corliss don't even kiss. In any event, the novel clearly represents Frona as a radically independent woman who deals with men as equals. At a time when more women than men are attending college and when Charlotte Perkins Gilman's "sexuo-economic" relation is, in complex ways, less significant than ever before, this novel's often inverted gender relations add significantly to its pedagogical value.[1]

Finally, despite its status as one of the most virulently racist of London's novels ("All that the other races are not, the Anglo-Saxon, or Teuton if you please, is. All that the other races have not, the Teuton has. What race is to rise up and overwhelm us?" [83]), I have been able to bring it profitably into class discussions of certain works of the Sioux writer Zitkala-Ša, especially "A Warrior's Daughter." Published in the same year as *Daughter*, both works represent the ideology of what I call "natural feminism," the restructuring of women's roles through a connection not so much to nature's fecundity as to its power, as represented, for example, by Zitkala-Ša's comparison of her protagonist, Tusee, to a panther—it is no accident, in this view, that each work's heroine is metaphorically the daughter of a powerful, naturally grounded force. One reviewer of *A Daughter of the Snows*—in language that could easily describe Zitkala-Ša's heroine—stated that London had "created a new woman, something elemental, physically almost savage, but with touches of the eternal feminine that prevent her being a man in petticoats" ("Elemental Maid" 40). London represents Frona, who "understood the physical world and the workings thereof," as a prime example of a new kind of "natural women" (*Daughter* 14, 111).

In my course Sex in White Gloves / Sex Red in Tooth and Claw: Courtship and Coupling in Realism and Naturalism—where we had time to delve more deeply into the historical context of the new woman—in addition to eliciting many of the same student responses described above, close reading of the novel and its contemporary responses led students to understand the often constrictive and disciplinary functions of the social construction of gender. The result was that four of twelve chose to focus on *A Daughter of the Snows* as one of the primary texts for their final research essays, usually comparing the work with those of Gilman and Chopin.

A Daughter of the Snows demonstrates the incompleteness of the portrait of the new woman unveiled through discussions of such canonical writers as James, Chopin, Gilman, Wharton, and Willa Cather. London's idea of a new womanhood shows scholars and students that London was a major contributor in reshaping the understanding of women's physical capabilities in this period and that he promoted female fitness at a time when such advocacy was unpopular and subversive, a role that he shared, to some extent, with Gilman and Zitkala-Ša. In ways that are provocatively echoed in twenty-first-century popular culture, students dramatically come to see how changes in perceptions of women's physical capabilities are inseparable from the sexual, political, intellectual, economic, and legal transformations represented in other new-woman fiction of the era. *A Daughter of the Snows* is an unjustly overlooked text that is crucial for understanding the discourse of gender at the beginning of the last century and that sheds new light on gender roles in the new millennium.

London's Multiethnic and Anticapitalist Short Fiction

Just as *Daughter*'s redefinition of gender roles makes it a timely text to teach, so too does the antiracism of London's multiethnic short stories. At a time when many classrooms are more ethnically diverse than ever before, London's overturning of his era's racial hierarchies allows students to see themselves in the past.

In my Basic Writing class, in which many were working-class, nonwhite, and the first in their families to go to college, students identified powerfully with the struggles of Felipe Rivera, of "The Mexican," and Koolau, of "Koolau the Leper," each victims of racial oppression and unfair treatment who triumph over their Euro-American oppressors. One immigrant Latina student found a special, personal resonance in Rivera's rage over his family's treatment in Mexico and his isolation in the new Anglo culture in which he found himself. Several students were surprised to find echoes of their own struggles in century-old texts by a white author. "The Apostate" had similar resonance with many of these students, who had experienced—or were still enduring—mind-numbing, menial jobs.

Although predominantly from middle-class backgrounds, the students in Literature of Social Change also reacted strongly to these works. This elective course allows me to teach a wide range of London's works, including four short stories, two novels, and four socialist essays. The course as a whole presents materials from multiple genres and media and focuses primarily on two adjacent eras, the progressive and the interwar eras.

All works discussed in the course are placed in substantial historical context. For the class's first half, including the London section, this means covering major Progressive Era developments, such as industrialization, the growth of labor unions and activism, urbanization, American imperialism, the new woman debate, the burgeoning socialist vote, the neurasthenia "epidemic," and so on. The London section of the course, moreover, is preceded by course segments titled "War and Remembrance" (highlighting Bierce's antiwar fiction); "Social Change and the City" (covering the Ashcan school, Riis, Crane, and Lombroso); "Remaking Womanhood: The New Woman and the (Re)construction of Gender" (featuring Gilman, Chopin, and Veblen); and "Progressivism and Race" (featuring Chesnutt, Dunbar, Du Bois, Zitkala-Ša, Far, and Norris). For a number of these authors, as for London, fictional works were juxtaposed with their nonfictional works—for example, Far's "Mrs. Spring Fragrance" with "A Plea for the Chinaman" (1896) and Zitkala-Ša's "The Soft-Hearted Sioux" with "Why I Am a Pagan"—to highlight why writers would choose fiction to convey messages of social change, as well as what the effects of the diverse strategies employed by these writers (and other artists) are. Thus, by the time we get to London, the students are well prepared to examine his unique engagement with issues of social change.

After presenting an introductory lecture on the author, I divide this segment of the course into a socialist section and a race section, followed by one that considers *The Star Rover* as perhaps the most unusual example of the era's literature of social change, since it is a novel of astral projection as much as it is a manifesto for prison reform. Students discovered powerful resonances in London's anticapitalist stories, such as "The Apostate," the protagonist of which, Johnny, they came to understand as doubly victimized—as a worker under industrial capitalism and as an exploited child who is forced into the world too soon yet who is prematurely old. One Literature of Social Change student, like several in the Basic Writing class, found Johnny's alienation from his labor echoed in her own. She wrote in her journal (weekly written commentaries were a required part of the course) about her part-time job at a law firm, where, in her "social pit" of a cubicle, she felt like a cog in a machine filing papers and stuffing envelopes. She went on to note that in "How I Became a Socialist," London's description of having socialism hammered into him is highly evocative because it shows the irony of capitalism forcibly creating the seeds of its own destruction; she found this irony heightened when the essay was juxtaposed with "The Apostate," which represents the mechanization and alienation that factory workers experience as mere cogs. In reference to London's other socialist works, another student remarked that in the context of *The Iron Heel*, "The Dream of Debs" seems to suggest not only the power of organized labor but also its limits, since the workers return to their old jobs, with the implication that even more radical measures may be necessary. Several students found "South of the Slot" compelling in its depiction of a class-based "double-consciousness," and in its expression of the complex psychology of an author who had moved up from the working class to the upper middle class and beyond. The story depicts a character, Freddie Drummond, who is strongly drawn to move in the opposite direction, going from the constraint and monotony of one to the fire and freedom of action of the other, as Bill Totts. On the whole, students preferred Totts to Drummond, finding London's own raffish charisma in the former. Clearly, the particular combination of London's socialist texts represented in this course fired students' imaginations, often leading them to sophisticated insights into the author and his era.

Another Literature of Social Change student highlighted the doubly victimized status of the eponymous hero of "Koolau the Leper," who is oppressed because he is not white and because he is a leper. This student wondered why it was that London seems repeatedly drawn to doubly victimized characters and suggested that portraying such characters was a powerful strategy with which to effect social change through literary means. She also commented on the way in which Koolau is still a leader at the end of the story even though his fellow lepers have abandoned him since we, as readers, have been recruited as his followers. The pairing of "Koolau" and "The Mexican" has worked very well for me in several courses. The juxtaposition of these texts leads students to ponder the manner in which London forces his readers inside his texts, compelling them to engage his major characters as part of an audience within the text. The same student who commented on how Koolau eventually becomes our leader found significance in the way in which Rivera in "The Mexican" becomes more admirable the less admirable the boxing crowd finds him. She thought this transformation heavily ironic, since London's white readers (then, if not now) could easily have found themselves to be part of such a crowd. For "Koolau," we become part of the audience for his speeches; in "The Mexican," we become both members of the junta, observing and puzzling over the source of Rivera's donations to the cause, and of the boxing audience of his final match, screaming at him to go down.

The Star Rover as Manifesto and Fantasy

Students in Literature of Social Change, after reading London's socialist and multiethnic, antiracist texts, both contextualized by reviews, letters, and other documents, move on to *The Star Rover*, which London thought of as "a punch against prison conditions in California." He continues:

> I'm trying to get some of these ideas over to fiction readers. Do you know that today it is possible to sentence a man to solitary confinement in California? That it is possible for us to hang a man for assault and battery? That, in fact, last year in 1913 we did hang a man for assault and battery? Jake Oppenheimer was hanged for assault and battery here in [our] own State, in California. The straitjacket still obtains in our prisons. Didn't you know that? (London, Interview)

As his daughter, Joan London, noted a quarter of a century later, "into this extraordinary and little-known book he flung with a prodigal hand riches which he had hoarded for years, and compressed into brilliant episodes notes originally intended for full-length books" (362). Thus the novel can appear to be a strange two-headed creature, a novel of social change grafted onto an episodic science fiction or fantasy novel. It yokes together widely disparate vignettes, each of which might indeed have been expanded into its own book-length work. My students actually found the novel more engaging and provocative because of its dualism. Some linked its astral-projection theme to a tendency in London to have his characters overcome physical and social obstacles by finding an image or idea that gives them a source of infinite power—for Rivera, for example, the importance of the revolution and the need to prevent the kind of slaughter that destroyed his family. For Darrell Standing, *The Star Rover*'s protagonist and narrator, the central idea is that of using mental discipline to transcend physical discipline, of overcoming injustice by taking command of one's imagination and spirit, an idea that I contextualize in class by linking it to the underground railroad codes incorporated into Negro spirituals, and then back to *The Iron Heel*, with its secret signals and subterranean networks of revolt. Some students found London's attempt to combine the highly imaginative genre of fantasy fiction with a message of social change highly successful; others were—at the very least—compelled by the imaginative riches represented by a novel that told so many stories spread over such a wide swath of space and time, from Jesus's Jerusalem to medieval Korea, prehistoric Europe and the nineteenth-century Mountain Meadows massacre, to mention only a few.

Defining the London canon is a complex project, since even his major works, while more widely taught than a decade or so ago, still do not show up as frequently as they should in English department syllabi. A casual survey of online college course catalogs shows that semesters or even years go by in some departments without any of London's works being taught. This might seem a reason to choose to teach only his major works; however, I feel strongly that this would be a mistake. As illustrated by the student responses noted above, some of London's oddest works, such as *The Star Rover*, exert a powerful effect on today's students, not only opening up a new world for them but also allowing them to find themselves within it.

NOTES

I wish to thank the students in the following courses for their hard work and class comments: at the University of California, Berkeley, English 1B, 27, fall 1993; at Fordham University, ENLU 1010, fall 2005; ENEU 3675, spring 2006; ENLU 3656, fall 2006; and ENLU 3675, spring 2007. Special thanks to those students in ENEU 3675 and ENLU 3656 who completed questionnaires, including Steven Borba, Christina Shanahan, Erik Herron, Nicola Kissane, Lauren Cartelli, Rachel Walker, Monique Diman, and to others who chose to remain anonymous.

[1] Gilman defines the "sexuo-economic relation" in *Women and Economics* as one in which the breadwinning male becomes the total environment for the passive, dependent female, replacing the rest of the natural and social world in which she would otherwise get her own living: "By combining the human sex-relation with the human economic relation, we have combined a permanently individual process with a progressively collective one. This involves a strain on both, which increases in direct proportion to our socialization, and, so far, has resulted in the ultimate destruction of the social organism acted upon by such irreconcilable forces" (106).

Representations of Gender in Two Versions of *The Sea-Wolf*

Jeff Jaeckle

This essay considers how gender in Jack London's 1904 novel *The Sea-Wolf* and Michael Curtiz's 1941 film version can be discussed in lower-division courses on literary naturalism and film adaptation. I draw on scholarship by Sam S. Baskett ("Sea Change"), Vinnie Oliveri, and Tony Williams ("From Novel to Film") during the course of discussion. However, students are not required to read these essays in their entirety to engage in the conversation; instead, they review the most fruitful quotations from this scholarship in a handout. These discussions work best over the course of two seventy-five-minute class periods, with the first devoted entirely to the novel and the last devoted to a comparison of the novel and the film, which students screen outside class. I also recommend placing the published screenplay, edited by Rocco Fumento and Tony Williams, on library reserve. These class discussions have four principal aims: to encourage close reading practices by requiring that students identify references to gender in *The Sea-Wolf*; to facilitate thoughtful debate about Jack London's often complicated representations of gender, sex, homoeroticism, and androgyny; to develop critical viewing habits by having students engage with a film adaptation of the novel; and to broaden the students' knowledge of film terminology. I recommend that instructors conclude these discussions with a take-home essay assignment (5–7 pages) that asks students to compare the novel to the film and to consider how these texts represent gender and what these representations ultimately convey to audiences.

As a preface to the opening discussion of gender in *The Sea-Wolf*, which the students have already read in its entirety, I devise a homework assignment for optional credit that requires them to highlight occurrences of the following variant terms: *man*, *woman*, *male*, *female*, *masculine*, *feminine*, *manhood*, *womanhood*, *gentleman*, and *lady*. I then instruct them to create a document listing these occurrences, grouped by character, to keep track of their findings and to facilitate discussion. Finally, I ask them to review the handout and to locate evidence from their findings that supports or detracts from the arguments made by Baskett, Oliveri, and Williams.

The discussion tends to open with comments about the novel's blurring of gender, with students observing that the male characters are often feminized. Students point out that the narrator, Humphrey Van Weyden, admits that he "shrieked aloud as the women had shrieked" aboard the sinking *Martinez* (487) and has muscles "small and soft, like a woman's" (513); Cooky, too, observes that Hump's skin is "more like a lydy's than any I know of" (492).[1] Students also note Hump's references to femininity in his descriptions of the seal hunter Oofty-Oofty, who is said to sleep "as placidly as a woman" (586) and whose body,

Hump notes, "I should call feminine" (593). Even Wolf Larsen, whom Hump claims is the "man-type," has a body "fair as the fairest woman's" (593). After writing on the board these and other quotations the students provide, I pose the question, How do these depictions of male characters as feminine influence the novel's plot and themes? This question elicits a variety of responses centering on the notion that the depictions challenge the hypermasculine sailor archetype by showing the characters to embody feminine traits and roles.

To aid in this discussion of gender blurring, we turn to Baskett's argument that Hump's feminine descriptions of himself and the other male characters are part of the novel's broader valorization of "an ideal androgynous relation between men and women" ("Sea Change" 93). Through his experiences with the masculine yet feminine characters of Larsen and Oofty-Oofty, Hump "slowly claims an androgynous sexuality" (99). It makes sense, then, that Hump also admires the stereotypically masculine characteristics of his lover, Maud Brewster, including her financial independence, ignorance of dressmaking, and wearing of a "boy's cap," which Hump eventually exchanges for a "man's cap" (656, 687). Some students raise objections to this argument by citing Hump's frequent references to Maud's feminine weakness and fragility in comparison to his masculine strength. They cite, for instance, Hump's repeated comment that Maud is "only woman after all" (687). They also stress that Hump and Maud actually assert their culturally constructed genders instead of using gender-neutral language. In the novel's concluding dialogue, for instance, Hump proclaims, "My woman, my one small woman," and Maud responds in agreement, "My man" (771).

To facilitate this new direction in the conversation, we review Oliveri's argument that the novel, instead of advocating for an ideal androgynous relationship, actually dramatizes Hump's "efforts to become masculine and to repress Maud's masculinity" (99). According to Oliveri, Hump desires to prove his masculinity to himself, Larsen, and Larsen's crew; this masculinity, however, "must be constantly defended; it never becomes a stable, internalized identity" (108). With this critical perspective in mind, students begin to read Hump's emphases on Maud's weakness and fragility not only as his denial of an androgynous ideal but also as a means of defending his masculinity at her expense. Yet students also read Hump's descriptions of Larsen and Oofty-Oofty as a means of demonstrating that all men possess feminine qualities. If so, students ask, then doesn't this tactic support Baskett's argument that Hump advocates for an androgynous ideal?

This question usually brings us to the end of the first discussion period. I ask students to consider before the next class how Curtiz's 1941 film adaptation of *The Sea-Wolf* treats these topics of androgyny and gender suppression. The students complete another homework assignment for optional credit in which they note every reference to gender in the film's dialogue and vocal performance, gestures, and costuming.[2] We begin by discussing the similar representations of gender in the novel and film, such as the comment made by Cooky (played by

Barry Fitzgerald) about Hump (Alexander Knox): "You're soft, like a woman."[3] Students are quick to observe, however, that despite this overt commentary on Hump's feminized body, the film often omits many of the novel's references to gender and sexuality. Students note, for instance, that the film removes any reference to Wolf's (Edward G. Robinson) womanliness and Hump's homoerotic fascination with Wolf's physique. Whereas the novel's Wolf Larsen displays the "perfect lines" of his masculine yet feminine body for Hump to gaze upon, Robinson's Wolf remains fully dressed throughout the film (593). Hump even omits commentary on Wolf's physique when giving his impressions of Wolf's character. Hump notes, "Skip the physical description. That's obvious." I provide some context for these omissions in the film by explaining that they stemmed in part from the "Hays Code" (or, Motion Picture Production Code of 1930), which banned any references to homosexuality or "sexual perversion." Because the topic of censorship can easily consume the entire class period, I gradually shift the discussion from the significance of these omissions to the instances of gendered language that the film *does* incorporate.

Students observe that when the film's characters make explicit reference to gender, these observations often have less to do with sexuality than with social class and broader questions of humanity. They point, for instance, to the character of Ruth Brewster (Ida Lupino), a thief and prostitute quite unlike the wealthy poet of the novel, Maud Brewster. When first aboard *The Ghost*, Ruth passes as a sophisticate by adopting an upper-class Eastern accent. After the crew learns of her criminal background, Cooky proclaims, "She's not a lady. She's one of us." Students suggest that Cooky's criticism here is not about gender (Ruth's perceived masculinity) but rather about class (Ruth's "common" social status). A useful follow-up question is, Does Cooky's overt joke about social class belie a tacit commentary on wealth and education as effeminate? This commentary appears in the novel, for instance, when the crew attributes Hump's weakness and fragility to his privileged lifestyle. We keep this line of discussion open by turning to George Leach's (John Garfield) use of gendered language. After Wolf Larsen threatens to beat him for insubordination, Leach exclaims, "He isn't talking to a dog; he's talking to a man." Students note that, just as *lady* in the earlier example had more to do with class than gender, the word *man* here is not opposed to *woman* but to *dog*, thereby drawing a distinction not between genders but species.

To guide the discussion at this point, we turn to Williams's argument that the film adaptation focuses primarily on issues of social class and national politics. Williams claims that the film's screenwriter, Robert Rossen, who was involved in 1930s Hollywood radicalism, rewrote London's novel as an "allegory of the brutal world of the post-Depression era" plagued by industrial capitalism and fascism ("From" xxii). These concerns arguably subsume questions of gender into those of class and power. Even though Ruth and George are of different genders, they are both working-class characters that suffer at the hands of the dictatorial Wolf Larsen. Williams's critical approach encourages students to return to the topic of omissions and to note how the film's relative lack of gendered language works in tandem with the inclusion of plural pronouns. Students point, for instance, to Leach's insistence that Ruth and he possess an unquenchable drive for freedom:

> What I got inside of me Larsen can't get at. . . . I can't explain it. It's just something that tells me to go on fighting. That tells me that there's something for people like us. . . . Men like Larsen can't keep on grinding us down because we're nobodies. That ain't true. We're somebodies.

Even though Leach explicitly aligns Larsen with "men," he does not fixate on gender binaries but rather on the powerful versus the oppressed, describing the latter as "people," "us," "we're," and "somebodies." A useful follow-up question here is, Does Leach's use of plural pronouns suggest that the film ultimately valorizes androgyny? Students are often divided on this point. Some argue that George and Ruth are helpmates that together (with Hump's assistance) defeat Larsen, while others assert that George remains the film's clear male hero who saves the comparatively passive female Ruth. Because this debate often brings us to the end of the second discussion period, I recommend that the students use these ideas as the basis for their essays.

At the conclusion of these discussions, my hope is that students have become better equipped to identify and analyze scenes in literature and film that engage with issues of representation, censorship, and the blending of gender and social class. If these discussions are successful, then students will approach future texts with improved abilities to read closely, to think critically, and to engage productively with scholarship.

NOTES

[1] Citations to *The Sea-Wolf* are from the 1992 Oxford World's Classics edition.

[2] See Williams's "Hollywood and *The Sea-Wolf*" for thorough histories of London's involvement with Hollywood and the numerous film versions of *The Sea-Wolf* produced since 1907.

[3] All dialogue is quoted from my transcription of the film.

Legend to Lesson: Five Decades of Teaching Jack London

Earle Labor

Although it has been nearly eight decades since I first heard the call of Jack London as a grade-schooler, I've been teaching Jack London courses for only five decades. In late September 1965, I received a letter that would change the course of my life as well as my career. King Hendricks, head of the English department at Utah State University, had been favorably impressed by my work on Jack London. As a result, he wrote asking if I would be interested in teaching a five-week Jack London undergraduate course, along with a graduate seminar in literary criticism, the following summer. "It would give you an opportunity to work in the materials that we have here at Utah State," he added. "I don't think I've told you before, but Shepard has given to our library many of London's manuscripts and other rare documents. You would find much original material here to work on."

Hendricks and his wife, Barbara, had been Charmian London's friends and, following her death in 1955, remained close friends with the Shepard family. Jack's nephew Irving was the owner of the Jack London Ranch as well as executor of the London estate. He and King had recently collaborated on the edition of London's letters published by Odyssey Press, a major contribution to London scholarship.

I didn't hesitate to accept Professor Hendricks's offer, and the next summer my family and I drove our new sky-dome Buick station wagon across country to one of the most beautiful university campuses in America. (Utah State University is situated on a mile-high plateau at the mouth of Logan Canyon, overlooking the verdant Cache Valley and the city of Logan.) When King took me over to the library, I saw there was indeed "much original material" in the large collection Irving Shepard had donated: not only manuscripts of London's works but also letters, many letters—especially from Charmian's correspondence. And much more besides. "I don't think Irving realizes how much he's sent us," King remarked, for here was truly a treasure trove of Londoniana, second only to the monumental archives at the Huntington Library in San Marino, California.

Among all the other rare items was the 1902 *Youth's Companion* containing the first version of "To Build a Fire." A cursory examination immediately substantiated London's own explanation that he wrote this story "for boys merely" and that he was "absolutely confident that beyond the motif itself, there [was] no similarity of treatment whatever" between this and the later version he wrote "for men" ("To Richard" 544).[1] The very beginning of the first version is notably different from the later one: "For land travel or seafaring, the world over, a companion is usually considered desirable. In the Klondike, as Tom Vincent found out, such a companion is absolutely essential. But he found it out, not by precept, but through bitter experience" ("To Build a Fire [1902]" 56).

The narrator has announced at the outset that this is an exemplum: a short piece of fiction used to dramatize a moral lesson in the weekly sermons being preached to America's young citizens by the *Youth's Companion*. The moral is clearly stated, the protagonist is given a symbolic name (many of the readers would have learned in their Latin classes that *vincere* means "to conquer"), and it is implicit that he will survive his ordeal.

Note, in contrast, the opening sentences of the 1908 story:

> Day had broken cold and gray, exceedingly cold and gray, when the man turned aside from the main Yukon trail and climbed the high earth-bank, where a dim and little-travelled trail led eastward through the fat spruce timberland. . . . It was a clear day, and yet there seemed an intangible gloom over the face of things, a subtle gloom that made the day dark, and that was due to the absence of the sun. ("To Build a Fire [1908]" 136)

No didactic hint here—only a foreboding of doom for the protagonist, who is given no name. Whatever lesson is to be learned rests on the reader's philosophical shoulders.

It is easy to understand why the 1902 story was not reprinted for over sixty years. It appeared in the summer 1967 issue of *Studies in Short Fiction*, appended to an essay King and I wrote about our discovery—while the 1908 version has been reprinted countless times since its initial publication.

Next in that summer of 1966 was my Jack London course. The class consisted of fifteen students: large enough to justify my lectures but small enough to allow for group discussions. Because our term was limited to five weeks, we used only one textbook. Harper's Perennial Classics *Great Short Works of Jack London*.

The edition, while limited in geographic scope, contained ample selections for this short term: the full texts of *The Call of the Wild* and *White Fang*, plus a half-dozen Northland stories and my editorial commentaries.

The course gave my students a substantial introduction to the first major version of London's symbolic wilderness: the Northland saga. Our examination of the two novels showed why they had become popular classics. Furthermore, I was able to provide typed copies of the 1902 "To Build a Fire" to compare with the version in our text, which helped my students understand the difference between a good moral fable for the young and a truly great story for all ages. I also related the following advice, which London had given his friend Cloudesley Johns about writing effective fiction:

> Don't you tell the reader [what he or she is supposed to think]. BUT HAVE YOUR CHARACTERS TELL IT BY THEIR DEEDS, ACTIONS, TALK, ETC. Then, and not until then, are you writing fiction and not a sociological paper upon a certain sub-stratum of society.
>
> And get the atmosphere. . . . The reader, since it is fiction, doesn't want your dissertations on the subject. . . . BUT PUT ALL THOSE THINGS WHICH ARE YOURS INTO THE STORIES, INTO THE TALES, ELIMINATING YOURSELF. . . . AND THIS WILL BE THE ATMOSPHERE. . . . And for this, and this only, will the critics praise you, and the public appreciate you, and your work be art. ("To Cloudesley" 531)

Reading aloud the entire opening paragraphs of the two versions of "To Build a Fire" clearly validated London's advice and demonstrated why his fiction had been praised by the critics and appreciated by the public.

I made another discovery while reading aloud some passages in *The Call of the Wild*. For example, I read the opening paragraphs of chapter 7, "The Sounding of the Call," instructing the class to note the change of mood created by certain words like "fabled lost mine," "quest," "tragedy," and "shrouded in mystery," which revealed the subtle transformation from the naturalistic to the mythic world in which Buck would undergo his transformation from devoted sled dog to awe-inspiring "Ghost Dog." After reading this first paragraph, I skipped down to the fifth—one of my personal favorites in the novel:

> The months came and went, and back and forth they twisted through the uncharted vastness, where no men were and yet where men had been if the Lost Cabin were true. They went across divides in summer blizzards, shivered under the midnight sun on naked mountains between the timber line and the eternal snows, dropped into summer valleys amid swarming gnats and flies, and in the shadows of glaciers picked strawberries and flowers as ripe and fair as any the Southland could boast. In the fall of the year they penetrated a weird lake country, sad and silent, where

> wild-fowl had been, but where there was no life nor sign of life—only the blowing of chill winds, the forming of ice in sheltered places, and the melancholy rippling of waves on lonely beaches. (405–06)

The vivid poetic description shows the influence of one of his favorite authors, Edgar Allan Poe. But when I read it to my class that morning, it showed me something else I hadn't noticed before—how skillfully the author had woven his spell, so subtly that only at that moment, after having read the passage many times, did I suddenly sense the anachronism. I asked my students, "Did you catch that? Did you hear something totally odd and unrealistic?"

They didn't.

"Stop and consider for a minute: try to envision the characters realistically. They've got to be strong and hardy, extraordinarily tough to survive what they've gone through—very macho, in fact. Also think about their appearances—couldn't be very neat or very clean. Now look again at what they're described doing. Picking strawberries. Fine. Wild strawberries are good to eat, and these men have probably been living on a lean-meat diet for months. But wait a minute: Stopping to pick flowers? Come on! Can you really see it, now that you look again? I mean, these guys are anything but 'flower lovers.' They're driven by gold fever, not aesthetic fervor. Here's my point—it just hit me: London, practicing exactly what he had preached to Cloudesley, created his 'atmosphere' so effectively that we were completely charmed, unaware of the weird anomaly."

I've been teaching Jack London's fiction now for a half century, and I have discovered new referents and resonances time and time again. In the summer of 1972, as the recipient of a grant from the Huntington, I was reading through the vast collection of materials the library had received from Charmian London and the Shepards. In one box of memorabilia I uncovered a clipping from the 15 July 1900 *Sunday [San Francisco] Examiner Magazine*, a full-page illustrated article headlined "California Girl's Wild Ghost Dance" (Ferguson). Inset at the bottom of the page was Henry David Thoreau's description of the Society Islanders' "night-born gods," who were held in greater awe than their "day-born gods."

Lillian Ferguson, author of the article, related the story of Annie Mitchell, "a woman who dared." Dared what? I wondered. I read that, at the age of sixteen, Annie had been sent from home in California to live with relatives in Indian Territory (Oklahoma), where she had been made a virtual work slave on the farm. After enduring this joyless servitude for several years, she ran away, joined a tribe of Ponca Indians, and married Little Bow, the tribal medicine man. She enjoyed a greater happiness living with the Indians close to nature. She even went so far as to invent a "ghost dance" that celebrated Little Bow as the Messiah to whom the Great Spirit had announced the end of the world "when all the whites would be killed, dead Indians restored to life, and all the game returned to this earth." But her happiness took a tragic turn when curious white settlers intruded to see what the Indians were up to and the tribe fought to drive them away. The militia was called out to stop the melee, and Annie was arrested, charged with inciting a riot, and put in jail. Noting that Annie is "back at the point where she started," Ferguson concludes that "[s]he is a prisoner, longing for freedom."

It is an interesting newspaper piece—but more interesting were the marginalia. In London's own inimitable scrawl were these fragments: "And then I knew I was night-born. . . . That Thoreau was a wise man. I wish I knew more about him. I could have made him a good wife."

Recalling a story titled "The Night-Born" I had read several years earlier, I went down into the library basement, pulled from the London shelf a copy of *"The Night-Born" and Other Stories*, and carried it back up to my desk in the reading room. As I began rereading the story, I was amazed by what I now saw but had failed to appreciate on my previous reading: not only was the narrative remarkably complex (three different points of view), it was also a powerful indictment of the sordid "man-mean city" versus the clean, virginal wilderness of "no man's land." But most astonishing: it was a virtual grab bag of archetypal images.

During the years since my initial reading, I had discovered the work of C. G. Jung and his study of those symbols that reverberate universally in our "collective unconscious." Here Jack London exhibits what Jung would eventually call the "visionary mode," in which the artist articulates universal images accessed through the unconscious. To summarize quickly: the story begins as an anonymous member of an elite men's club in San Francisco mourns the fate of a clean-living young boxer killed in the prize ring the night before—victim of the "grotesque sordidness and rottenness of man-hate" that now plagues the city. "Here was Youth, clean and wholesome, unsullied—the thing of glory and wonder for men to conjure with," says the narrator of the fallen young gladiator (263). At this point a second character named Bardwell quotes Thoreau's passage about the night-born, which prompts "old Trefethan, bald-headed and dewlapped," to tell about the odyssey he had made during the prime of his life into an "uncharted and unnamed" flower-swept subarctic Eden, where he encountered a magnificent Eve figure named "Lucy," who was chief of an Indian tribe. Bardwell and Lucy: obviously symbolic but hardly archetypal names. What about Trefethan? Odd name—but we'll come to that later.

Trefethan recalls that Lucy was sitting on top of a robe of white swan skins: "I have never seen anything like that robe," he tells his fellow club members. He describes Lucy herself as "a full-bodied woman, and royal ripe . . . a regular She-Who-Must-Be-Obeyed" (265–66).

At this point in the story, I began to sense a deeper symbolic import. J. E. Cirlot's *Dictionary of Symbols* had become one of my basic interpretive keys, particularly useful in unlocking the inner doors of Jack London's stories, even though written well after London's death: Cirlot's dictionary is based largely on the Jungian insights that London's work anticipated and that London himself was reading toward the end of his life. (I always remind my students that we don't want to read anything *into* a story, but we do want to read *out* all that its context will sensibly justify.) Cirlot explains that "[t]he white swan [was] sacred to Venus [and] in poetry and literature is an image of naked woman, of chaste nudity and immaculate whiteness. . . . In sum, the swan always points to the complete satisfaction of a desire [and symbolizes] the mystic centre and union of opposites" (322).

Lucy now tells her own story to Trefethan, recounting how she had been "frontier-born, of poor settlers, and you know what that means—work, always work, work in plenty and without end." She says she became "plumb sick at times" just to get out and enjoy the natural world. "I wanted to run nights like a wild thing, just to run through the moonshine and under the stars, to run white and naked in the darkness." When the farm failed and her family was forced to migrate to Seattle, Lucy found work in a factory, then as a "hash-slinger" in a cheap café (267).

Desperately longing to escape the drudgery, she married an older man who was going to start a restaurant in Juneau. She admits she didn't love him and that she found out too late he had married her because he needed a wife "to save paying wages" to a waitress. After "toiling for four mortal years," she had a "vision." It came to her in a scrap of newspaper that quoted Thoreau's "Cry of the Human" and celebrated the Polynesian night-born gods. She realized at that point why she had been so miserable all her life: she was not day-born but night-born. She "packed up [her] few rags of clothes" and started out. When her husband—"Jake, the ox," she called him—tried to stop her, she pulled out a Colt .44, announced, "This does my talkin' for me" (270), and headed out through the wilderness. Her odyssey finally led her into the virgin land where Trefethan found her. Of all her remarkable attributes, it was her eyes that most forcibly caught his attention: "That's what took me off my feet—her eyes—blue, not China blue, but deep blue, like the sea and sky all melted into one, and very wise" (265).

And it was London's description of Lucy's eyes that most forcibly caught my own attention, sending me back to *A Dictionary of Symbols*: Blue represents "height and depth (the blue sky above, the blue sea below) . . . darkness made visible . . . truth" (54–55). (Guerin's *Handbook of Critical Approaches to Literature* also contains a useful discussion of Jungian archetypes and their application to literature.) Interpreted in Jungian terms, Lucy (Latin *lucidus*, or "light") is a projection of Trefethan's "anima" or "soul mate" (the feminine element in man's psyche), who promises to provide spiritual enlightenment. But Trefethan confesses that even with her wonderful eyes and womanly beauty, he was compelled to turn down her offer of marriage, lying that he already had a wife and leaving Lucy behind in her Edenic valley. In short, by rejecting his anima, he failed to achieve "individuation," the term Jung uses to describe the process of psychological and spiritual maturing: "It would have been better had I stayed. Look at me now," Trefethan says in a voice "like a funeral bell." The others look and see "the general tiredness and staleness and fatness, all the collapse and ruin of a man who had once been strong but who had lived too easily and too well"—all because he has opted for a fool's gold instead of accepting the richer treasure offered by Lucy (274).

Finally, Trefethan's odd name: in the semester following my Huntington "epiphany," I made copies of "The Night-Born" for my Jack London class at Centenary College. One of my students, familiar with Judaic etymology, told us that, among other interpretations, "tref" means "that which is unclean" and "ethan" means "teller of stories." Again, a perfect fit. Was London fully aware of this when he wrote the story? We know he was thoroughly familiar with the Bible as well as the Greek and Roman classics. On the other hand, perhaps this was another "lucky shot in the dark" like the symbolically rich *Call of the Wild*, which he told Joan London he had written as a good-dog story without intending the allegorical meanings his reviewers found (Joan London 252). Regardless of the answer, this is one of his most teachable works. With its complex structure, its rich lode of archetypal motifs, and its multilayered themes—such as man-made and "man-mean" urban civilization in contrast to salubrious Mother Nature; the eternal quest for romance, Edenic rebirth, and eternal youth; the human "call of the wild"; and the liberation of modern self-directed woman from male dominance—"The Night-Born" has been a hit with every one of my classes for the past four decades.

Since its publication in 1994, *The Portable Jack London* has proved to be my handiest basic text: it contains all the works discussed above (except *White Fang*), plus thirteen short stories representing the extraordinary range of London's creative genius, fifteen nonfiction pieces, twenty-five letters, a substantial introductory essay, chronology, and suggestions for further reading. The nonfiction pieces and letters are related in many cases to the selected fiction. Required readings also include *Martin Eden* and *The Sea-Wolf*, both of which are available in paperback editions. Because of its length, I've been reluctant to add *White Fang* in a fifteen-week course, although I mention it and several other London novels in my lectures. We begin the semester with my introductory lecture—including attention to the dynamic cultural era surrounding London's career—along with the introduction in *The Portable Jack London*. I allow two weeks for *Martin Eden*, comparing the novel with Jack's own career, after which my students read related selections like "The Apostate" and "What Life Means to Me."

During the following four weeks, we study the works that articulate London's "Northland code": "To the Man on Trail," "In a Far Country" (the code is explicitly set forth in the first two paragraphs of this story), both versions of "To Build a Fire," and, of course, "The Night-Born" and *The Call of the Wild*. The class views the film version of *The Call of the Wild* starring Clark Gable and Loretta Young. It is fun—as well as instructive—for my students to see what Hollywood has done in putting a great novel on the screen. Sometimes I show the version Charlton Heston told Joan Rivers was his worst film, after which he quipped, "But the dog was great!"

Weeks 7 and 8 are devoted to London's sociopolitical writings—namely, chapters from *The People of the Abyss*, "How I Became a Socialist," "The Mexican," and "Things Alive" (his 1906 lecture to Yale students, reprinted in the *Portable Jack London* for the first time). During the next three weeks, we discuss *The Sea-Wolf*, noting how London manages to amalgamate the naturalistic novel with the old sentimental romance; we then watch a film based on this novel, either the 1941 classic starring Edward G. Robinson and John Garfield or the 1993 made-for-TV version starring aged Charles Bronson as Wolf Larsen and *Superman* star Christopher Reeve as "Sissy" Van Weyden, arguably the worst casting in Hollywood history. Neither film is true to London's narrative, but both are nonetheless entertaining for my students while enhancing their appreciation for the novel.

The final month covers London's treatment of the South Seas and other cultures in such stories as "Koolau the Leper," "The Chinago," "Mauki," "The Madness of John Harned," and "Nam-Bok the Unveracious" (a Northland version of Plato's allegory of the cave). We wrap up the course with some of his most impressive but lesser-known stories, such as "Told in the Drooling Ward" (a delightful satire drawn from London's personal experience—and the first story of its kind in our literature), "Samuel" (a fascinating portrayal of the archetypal "earth mother"), "War" (a gem comparable to the best in Crane and Hemingway—now more relevant than ever), "The Red One" (a Melanesian "Heart of Darkness" based on the same motif that Stanley Kubrick borrowed from Arthur C. Clarke in *2001: A Space Odyssey*), and "The Water Baby" (the last story London ever wrote, which deftly juxtaposes the two disparate worlds of materialism and myth, thereby revealing a significant "sea-change" in his own philosophical attitude). These and more compose our semester together.

In concluding this brief history from legend to lesson, I should mention one of my greatest pleasures in teaching Jack London: directing four National Endowment for the Humanities summer seminars for teachers. These have brought together not only sixty of the finest teachers in America but also four participants from overseas: from Germany, the Philippines, Albania, and the Congo. The young man from the Congo had a fascinating story: he told our group that he had been born in a jungle village and that after his father had been killed, he migrated to Brazzaville, where he learned French and read *The Call of the Wild*. "That book inspired me to survive," he said. I can think of no testimony more eloquent than his in confirming my belief that Jack London is America's greatest "world author." I have also found Jack London to be our most teachable author.

NOTE

[1] Citations to London's works and correspondence are from *The Portable Jack London*.

The Nature of the Beast in *The Call of the Wild*

Michael Lundblad

In a 1908 article for *Collier's* titled "The Other Animals," Jack London argues that *The Call of the Wild* (1903) and *White Fang* (1906) are "animal stories" that are "in line with the facts of evolution" (199). He is surprised, then, to find himself "bundled neck and crop into the camp of the nature-fakers" by President Roosevelt and John Burroughs, who was one of the best known naturalists at the turn of the twentieth century (200). Burroughs had initiated a critique of what he considered "sham natural history" (128) passed off as the real thing in a burgeoning genre sometimes referred to as the "wild animal story" (see Lutts). His article in the *Atlantic Monthly* in March 1903 took the form of an attack on the novels of writers such as William J. Long, Ernest Thompson Seton, and Charles G. D. Roberts. Burroughs's critique touched off what became known as the nature-fakers controversy, a very public debate that eventually included both Roosevelt and London, with many of the figures involved publishing their views in major national periodicals.[1] London objected to the suggestion that "all animals below man are automatons," which is how he characterized the view of Roosevelt and Burroughs: "They believe that man is the only animal capable of reasoning and that ever does reason. This is a view that makes the twentieth century scientist smile" ("Other Animals" 200). It is also a view that would make theorists and critics in the field of animal studies smile—or perhaps cringe—today.

Much of the recent work in animal studies is directly relevant to representations of animality in *The Call of the Wild* in particular and the nature-fakers controversy more broadly, which can provide a provocative context for exploring London's work. Are his animal characters "realistic," for example, if they are represented with the ability to reason? What if they seem to be capable of ecstatic and even erotic love for their human partners? What are the implications of reading London's nonhuman characters as "real" animals, as opposed to "men in furs"—to borrow Mark Seltzer's influential description (166–72)—or figures that don't fit either of these categories? My aim in this essay is to illustrate how these kinds of questions from both animal studies and animality studies can bring new and important issues into discussions of a text such as *The Call of the Wild*. Animal studies, on the one hand, is a field that opens up questions about how we make philosophical distinctions between human and nonhuman animals, such as the ability to reason, which often lead to considerations of how we treat nonhuman animals in a variety of contexts. Animality studies, on the other hand, is a related field that explores the relation between representations of animality, such as the character of Buck, and the way we think about various human identity categories, such as race and sexuality.

From Animal Studies to the "Real" Buck

What is the nature of the beast in *The Call of the Wild*? This seemingly straightforward question is one that can introduce students to the complexities and implications of recent work in animal studies. Representations of animality—both human and nonhuman—in London's text logically raise questions about what is "realistic" in terms of both behaviors and capabilities of flesh-and-blood dogs like Buck in "real" life. They also raise questions about distinctions between human and nonhuman animals, as well as various frameworks that have been invoked historically either to defend or challenge those distinctions. Donna Haraway's *When Species Meet* is a particularly good example of work in animal studies (and work on dogs in particular) that explores the cultural politics of constructing the human/animal binary and focuses on how animals are treated. Haraway has analyzed constructions of animality for decades, but there are a variety of reasons why animal studies has only recently been recognized as a coherent field within the humanities and social sciences. One reason is the recent work of ethologists and biologists who continue to disprove ongoing claims of biological difference between human and nonhuman animals, including the kinds of reasoning that Roosevelt and Burroughs thought to be impossible "below" the human mind. Another reason is the rise in visibility and influence of the animal welfare movement, broadly conceived, including animal advocacy in a wide range of contexts: from factory farms to laboratories, from zoos to marine "amusement" parks, from companion animals to endangered species. According to some animal studies scholars, the recent turn in the academy to animal issues is simply the next logical social movement to be embraced, following in the footsteps of movements such as feminism, gay rights, civil rights, and environmentalism.

A major reason for the recent growth of animal studies—and perhaps the most important one—is what the late work of Jacques Derrida identifies as "the question of the animal."[2] *The Animal That Therefore I Am* is a 2008 translation of a series of addresses that Derrida gave in 1997 that explores, for example, the problem of reducing all nonhuman animals to *the* animal, as opposed to *the* human. According to Derrida, "Confined within this catch-all concept, within this vast encampment of the animal, in this general signifier, within the strict enclosure of this definite article ('the Animal' and not 'animals'), as in a virgin forest, a zoo, a hunting or fishing ground, a paddock or an abattoir, a space of domestication, are all living things that man does not recognize as his fellows, his neighbors, or his brothers" (34). Reducing the specificity and diversity of all animals to "the animal" is thus, ultimately, a kind of crime: "The confusion of all nonhuman living creatures within the general and common category of the animal is not simply a sin against rigorous thinking, vigilance, lucidity, or empirical authority, it is also a crime. Not a crime against animality, precisely, but a crime of the first order against the animals, against animals" (48). Tracing *the* animal through various continental philosophers in the wake of Descartes, Derrida also explores the "double finitude" that many nonhuman animals share with human beings: a vulnerability of the body and therefore the ability to suffer, as well as the ability to communicate and respond, rather than just react, which would be the case if they were essentially machines or bundles of instincts.[3] For Derrida, responding to an other, whether human or nonhuman, reveals the difference between others, playing out differently between human beings and various nonhuman species. But this recognition need not lead to a hierarchy of human beings over animals. Derrida explores and critiques that kind of hierarchy and human exceptionalism in several influential philosophers, such as Immanuel Kant, Martin Heidegger, Jacques Lacan, and Emmanuel Levinas.[4] Students might be interested in individual research projects relating these philosophers to Jack London's thinking about animality, along with London's reading of other philosophers and social critics.

From the perspective of Derrida, deconstructing the binary of human/animal can also raise the question of how various nonhuman animals should be treated. Cary Wolfe, whose work has been very influential in animal studies, points out that the "question of the animal is linked complexly to the problem of animals' ethical standing as direct or indirect subjects of justice" ("Human" 567). This kind of thinking leads Wolfe to what he calls "posthumanist ethical pluralism," in which subjectivity can no longer be limited to human beings. While Wolfe follows Derrida by distinguishing his work from calls for universal animal rights (and the humanist discourse of rights in particular), he also follows Derrida by drawing attention to the problematic treatment of various nonhuman animals: an emphasis that resonates with much of the recent scholarship in animal studies.

An animal studies approach to the nature of the beast in *The Call of the Wild* might thus consider the extent to which London's representation of a reasoning animal can lead to greater concern for the treatment of dogs like Buck, for example, as a particular kind of animal, rather than a representative of *all* nonhuman animals. Students interested in—or perhaps appalled by—the practice of dog fighting in the United States today, as revealed through the imprisonment of the NFL quarterback Michael Vick, can be pointed to passages in *The Call of the Wild* in which Buck is brutally abused by those wanting him to submit to their agendas. Buck's beating at the hands of the man in the red sweater, for example, is incredibly cruel: "After a particularly fierce blow, he crawled to his feet, too dazed to rush. He staggered limply about, the blood flowing from nose and mouth and ears, his beautiful coat sprayed and flecked with bloody slaver. Then the man advanced and deliberately dealt him a frightful blow on the nose. All the pain he had endured was as nothing compared with the exquisite agony of this" (11).[5] That kind of pain returns, though, in even worse form at the hands of Hal later in the novella: "So greatly had he suffered, and so far gone was he, that the blows did not hurt much. And as they continued to fall upon him, the spark of life within flickered and went down. It was nearly out. He felt strangely numb. As though from a great distance, he was aware that he was being beaten"

(57). If Buck is a real animal with a "double finitude" that is similar to a human being's, then these scenes could be seen as effective ways of drawing attention to abuse otherwise justified by species hierarchies.

Animal Reasoning and Evolution

But how realistic is this representation of an animal? After his beating by the man in the red sweater, Buck, we are told, learns his lesson and generalizes it into a rule: "He saw, once for all, that he stood no chance against a man with a club. He had learned the lesson, and in all his after life he never forgot it. That club was a revelation. It was his introduction to the reign of primitive law, and he met the introduction halfway" (12). If this kind of reasoning seems unrealistic for a dog, should we then see Buck simply as a metaphorical representation of a "primitive" human being or "the animal" within the human? While Burroughs argues that animals "are certainly in any broad generalization our kin" (132), he objects to stories that portray what he calls "simply human beings disguised as animals" (131). Burroughs's primary mark of essential difference, posited as intellect or reason, resonates with similar philosophical distinctions critiqued by Derrida. Burroughs declares, "Of course it is merely guesswork how far our psychology applies to the lower animals. That they experience many of our emotions there can be no doubt, but that they have intellectual and reasoning processes like our own, except in a very rudimentary form, admits of grave doubt" (131). London overstates Burroughs's position as a denial of any form of reasoning in animals, but London's critique of what he calls "homocentrism" in Burroughs is particularly interesting. After extended arguments to prove that animals can, in fact, reason in at least rudimentary ways (often using his own dog as an example), London identifies Burroughs's discomfort with the idea of human beings more closely aligned with animal consciousness. He reveals the "vast gulf" that Burroughs maintains between the human and the animal and argues that despite Burroughs's "well-exploited and patronizing devotion to them, the lower animals are disgustingly low. To him, affinity and kinship with the other animals is a repugnant thing. He will have none of it" ("Other Animals" 207). London, then, appears to be far more open to "kinship" with other animals.

What is "real" in *The Call of the Wild* and London's other work, though, is an evolutionary discourse that ranks all animals—including human beings—hierarchically, even if the gulf between human and nonhuman is not as great as Burroughs would maintain. Human beings and animals are linked in this discourse through the suggestion of what is "natural" for both human and nonhuman animals: violent and aggressive instincts in a survival-of-the-fittest world. London includes this kind of Darwinian logic in his novella as another way of explaining the nature of the beast, in which both human beings and animals are at least partially governed by biological instincts. When the bodies of animals are engaged in what is constructed as biological destiny, what they were "born to do," there is exultant glorification of activities such as hunting. Descriptions of Buck's body tingle with excitement—for example, when he is on the hunt, chasing prey, killing instead of being killed, and so on. His "blood lust, the joy to kill" is "infinitely more intimate" than a human hunter's because he can exult in "running the wild thing down, the living meat, to kill with his own teeth and wash his muzzle to the eyes in warm blood" (33). Another way to read this scene, though, is as a hunting fantasy for white men at the turn of the century who were worried about becoming "overcivilized": men who thought that getting in touch with their "animal instincts" would save them from the "feminizing" influence of culture.

Imagining oneself hunting or running wild, like Buck, can thus be exhilarating for male readers while blurring the line between human beings and animals. The subsequent passage uses the word *ecstasy* three times before it plunges into a joyous description of Buck's body pulsing with life: "He was mastered by the sheer surging of life, the tidal wave of being, the perfect joy of each separate muscle, joint, and sinew in that it was everything that was not death, that it was aglow and rampant, expressing itself in movement, flying exultantly under the stars and over the face of dead matter that did not move" (34). Toward the end of the novella, Buck is once again portrayed as a glorious body in the wild when he becomes a "carnivorous animal, living on a straight meat diet . . . in full flower, at the high tide of his life, overspilling with vigor and virility. . . . Life streamed through him in splendid flood, glad and rampant, until it seemed that it would burst him asunder in sheer ecstasy and pour forth generously over the world" (77–78). Buck's lust for life, particularly in the thrill of the hunt, can thus mark him as a real "wild" beast, on the one hand, or as the fantasized manifestation of a "natural" instinct within a man, on the other hand.

This evolutionary link has the potential to show that some animals are "just like us" in having both instinct and reason. But students might also be interested in thinking about how a survival-of-the-fittest logic can have different consequences: justifying competition and violence, for example, both between and among species. Research projects could focus on the relation between *The Call of the Wild* and the historical development of social Darwinism, perhaps exploring issues such as the difference between Herbert Spencer's phrase "survival of the fittest" and Charles Darwin's original phrase "the struggle for survival" and the implications of both of these phrases for thinking about human aggression and warfare. Other research projects or discussion topics could link London's thinking about animality and social Darwinism with his critiques of capitalism, along with current justifications of economic exploitation that continue to be based on constructions of "animal instincts" in human beings. While animal studies might lead students to think about how various kinds of animals—from pets to work animals—are treated today, animality studies can move students more in the direction of human racial politics and constructions of sexuality, as the remainder of this essay will illustrate.

From Animality Studies to Racial Politics

Exploring evolutionary discourses related to *The Call of the Wild* can reveal significant implications not only for "real" animals but also for constructions of various human identity groups and behaviors at the turn of the twentieth century. In "The Other Animals," for example, London's defense of his own supposedly superior understanding of evolution is based on clear hierarchies, including racial differences among human beings, even if he argues that the gap between "lower humans" and "higher animals" is not as great as Burroughs suggests. He discusses what he calls the "lower humans" of "the tropics" (207) and Tahiti (209), considered to be representative of the "adult savage" (209–10), who can be fooled into thinking that a voice on a telephone must be coming from a man in an adjoining room (209). Whiteness is clearly at the top of the hierarchy, while black "savages" are not so different from "higher animals." London might argue that "We who are so very human are very animal" (210), but his belief in evolutionary theory also both reflects and produces a broader cultural discourse seeking to justify racial boundaries between white and black human beings. If Buck is read as a "higher animal," the nature of the beast in *The Call of the Wild* can also be seen as a site for negotiating anxieties related to race, among other identity categories, at that particular historical and cultural moment.

This kind of analysis can be aligned more with animality studies—rather than animal studies—if the questions raised are not necessarily motivated primarily and explicitly by concern for the treatment of nonhuman animals. Animality studies can help students explore the nature of the beast, in other words, without prioritizing questions of animal ethics. As the introduction to *Species Matters: Humane Advocacy and Cultural Theory* notes:

> This distinction might lead some to conclude that animality studies must be work that ignores "real" animals, but it can also be seen as engaging questions of advocacy in different ways. Animality studies might want to problematize an essentialist human/animal binary, for example, by focusing on that binary's violent history in relation to constructions of what it means to be "human," or how various human groups have been granted or denied "humanity." (Lundblad and DeKoven 3)

London's construction of a racial hierarchy in "The Other Animals" can be linked with a survival-of-the-fittest logic within United States imperialism at the turn of the century, in countries such as Cuba, the Philippines, and Panama, among others, as well as in relation to pervasive racism back home in the United States. President Roosevelt joined writers such as Charlotte Perkins Gilman in worrying about "race suicide," for example, in which the birth of white babies would be outpaced by the birth of nonwhite babies. At the same time, "big stick" policies abroad could be justified in the context of animalized countries fighting each other to survive. "The Problem of the Philippines," by John Barrett, which appeared in the *North American Review* in 1898, crystallizes the link: "The rule of survival of the fittest applies to nations as well as to the animal kingdom. It is a cruel, relentless principle being exercised in a cruel, relentless competition of mighty forces; and these will trample over us without sympathy or remorse unless we are trained to endure and strong enough to stand the pace" (qtd. in Hofstadter [1992] 181). Students can thus be prompted to consider how a text like *The Call of the Wild* can reinforce evolutionary justifications for either conquering or "civilizing" other animalized nations, as well as naturalizing racism in the United States.

There is little doubt that, for Roosevelt, white Americans stood at the top of a hierarchy of nations, even in his criticism of the "nature fakers." In an article titled "'Nature Fakers'" (*Everybody's Magazine*, 1907), in which Roosevelt ridicules the "animal stories" primarily of William J. Long, Roosevelt applies a hierarchical logic to the difference between white and Native Americans. Roosevelt assumes that Native Americans "live in a world of mysticism, and they often ascribe supernatural traits to the animals they know, just as the men of the Middle Ages, with almost the same childlike faith, credited the marvels told of the unicorn, the basilisk, the roc, and the cockatrice" (194). From Roosevelt's perspective, the representation of animals by the "nature fakers" can be linked with this kind of fantasy, even though Roosevelt is more upset with examples of reasoning than survival-of-the-fittest instincts in these animal stories. The problem with writers like Long, Seton, and even London, he argues, is that they claim that their stories are based on fact. Roosevelt sees them instead as obvious allegories for human beings, which would put them closer to the Uncle Remus tales of Joel Chandler Harris: "The wolves and lynxes and other animals which they describe are full brothers of the wild beasts that appear in 'Uncle Remus' and 'Reynard the Fox,' and deserve the same serious consideration from the zoological standpoint" (195). While Roosevelt's suggestion that these representations of animals are really human beings in disguise infuriates writers like London, it also points toward other ways of reading the nature of the beast in a story like *The Call of the Wild*. If these wolves and other animals aren't "real," in other words, what else might they signify at the turn of the century, despite the intentions of these authors?

The Sexual History of the Beast

Students will presumably be very surprised to learn that "wolf" had another very different signification at that historical moment. As George Chauncey has revealed, "wolf," in certain contexts, was used as a term to describe a working-class human male who had anal sex with other human males, who could still be seen as very masculine, without necessarily being seen as "gay." Situating the nature of the beast in relation to shifting constructions of sexuality at the turn of the twentieth century can thus lead to very different ways of reading *The Call of the Wild*, suggesting another framework that animality studies can bring to discussions of this text. The relationship between John Thornton and Buck provides a provocative site for thinking about animality in relation to sexuality, particularly once Thornton is brutally murdered by the "Yeehat" Indians.

Students can be prompted to think further about the nature of this murder and its immediate consequences, focusing on it as a key scene to consider. While the Yeehats are represented as stereotypically superstitious, reminiscent of Roosevelt's racism toward Native Americans, Buck becomes a magical figure once he realizes that Thornton has been killed. The first Yeehat that Buck encounters (the chief) is quickly killed, with Buck "ripping the throat wide open till the rent jugular spouted a fountain of blood" (82). After Buck has destroyed other Yeehats in a fury, "tearing, rending, destroying, in constant and terrific motion which defied the arrows they discharged at him" (82), we are told that "a panic seized the Yeehats, and they fled in terror to the woods, proclaiming as they fled the advent of the Evil Spirit" (82). With an ironic wink, the narrative suggests that the Yeehats do not understand the nature of the beast here, but then we are told that "truly Buck was the Fiend incarnate, raging at their heels and dragging them down like deer as they raced through the trees" (82–83). When he finally goes back and finds the signs of Thornton's death struggle leading to a pond, there is no body to be found: "The pool itself, muddy and discolored from the sluice boxes, effectually hid what it contained, and it contained John Thornton" (83). Focusing on what is hidden in that pool, and why, can raise key questions from the perspective of animality studies.

Why must Thornton be killed in this manner? What does this outcome say about attitudes toward "real" Native Americans, on the one hand, or the relationship between Thornton and Buck, on the other? How does that relationship relate to questions of whether Buck is ultimately, or mostly, a "real" animal as opposed to a metaphor for an idealized human being? These kinds of questions can lead students to explore the significance of the "love" between Buck and Thornton, revealing what can be described as a homoerotic element that would otherwise seem out of place in relation to evolutionary discourses. After being brutalized by the incompetent trio of Hal, Charles, and Mercedes, Buck is saved by Thornton and grows to experience what is described as "[l]ove, genuine passionate love . . . love that was feverish and burning, that was adoration, that was madness, [that] had taken John Thornton to arouse" (59–60). Together they share "love names," and Buck, we are told, "knew no greater joy than that rough embrace and the sound of murmured oaths, and at each jerk back and forth it seemed that his heart would be shaken out of his body so great was his ecstasy" (60). The rough swearing, along with Buck's playful biting of Thornton's hand, seems to be an attempt to lend a "manly" quality to this love play, but it is certainly an intimate ritual, one that makes onlookers uncomfortable. On one occasion, for example, we are told that "[a]s though animated by a common impulse, the onlookers drew back to a respectful distance; nor were they again indiscreet enough to interrupt" (70).

While these portrayals are not inconceivable as part of a relationship between a man and his dog, they can also be read as a displacement of queer desire between men. From this perspective, the text can be seen as ultimately suppressing what we today might call homosexual impulses, after allowing them to surface in ways that resonate with Chauncey's history of the human "wolf." Thornton's death, in other words, can be seen as policing a form of queer desire that had erupted in his relationship with Buck but was ultimately seen as unacceptable. In the end, we are told that Buck makes a pilgrimage to the site of Thornton's murder every year, even after he has finally heeded "the call" and become the leader of a roaming wolf pack.

Students might thus be prompted to consider what the *sexual* history of the beast might be here, in the end. On the one hand, readers can presumably rest assured that Buck is a real heterosexual dog, firmly within an evolutionary discourse, because the narrative suggests he has mated successfully with wolves, resulting in "a change in the breed of timber wolves; for some were seen with splashes of brown on head and muzzle, and with a rift of white centring [sic] down the chest" (85). On the other hand, despite his supposed rejection of all things tame, Buck returns every summer to the same valley to mourn the loss of John Thornton, where he "muses for a time, howling once, long and mournfully, ere he departs" (86). It becomes clear, then, that the "love" between Buck and Thornton is not simply an obstacle to Buck heeding "the call" but rather a passionate and ongoing connection, with a meaning that need not necessarily remain hidden from view in the muddy pool of Thornton's death. To what extent, then, can this text be seen as suggesting progressive possibilities related to queer desire? How progressive is it if the text punishes the queer impulse so brutally? Students could explore this debate either through class discussions or through further research into the history of sexuality at the turn of the twentieth century.

Whether we read London's representation of nonhuman characters as "real" animals or "men in furs," it is difficult to reconcile this kind of erotic relationship with instincts driven by Darwinian reproduction. Jack London might have thought of himself as a Darwinian, but his texts both reinforce and resist broader cultural anxieties and alternatives in relation to sexuality, whether he is conscious of them or not. Asking questions about the nature of the beast in *The Call of the Wild* need not necessarily emphasize the implications of this text in relation to constructions of human identity categories and behaviors. But the frameworks of both animality studies and animal studies can provide provocative new ways of thinking critically about *The Call of the Wild*. These kinds of questions can also give students new ways of relating Jack London's work, along with the nature-fakers controversy, to issues relevant to their lives today, from animal rights and welfare to constructions of human racial and sexual differences, from the way they think about the animals in their lives to the way they think about evolutionary discourses that continue to justify various forms of oppression and exploitation.

NOTES

[1] See Lutts for a very useful collection of these primary source materials. Various pieces from this collection could be engaged productively by students in conjunction with *The Call of the Wild*.

[2] Instructors unfamiliar with Derrida and his general theory of deconstruction can find a useful introduction in Parker's chapter "Deconstruction" (77–100).

[3] Wolfe is a particularly good interlocutor for Derrida in *Animal Rites*. Wolfe also provides a useful and more detailed genealogy of animal studies (as well as Derrida's work on animality) in "Human, All Too Human," in an issue of *PMLA* that highlights twelve essays contributed to a Theories and Methodologies feature on animal studies, including my essay, "From Animal to Animality Studies."

[4] Many of the philosophers that Derrida explores in relation to animality are collected in Calarco and Atterton, a very useful collection that also includes a general introduction to these thinkers.

[5] Quotations to *The Call of the Wild* are from *Jack London: Novels and Stories*.

In a Far Classroom: Using Jack London for an Ecocritical Approach to Teaching Composition

Shannon Cotrell

Recently, I began planning a freshman composition class inspired by two somewhat disparate influences: my curiosity about the seeming ubiquity of reality television programs—particularly those filmed in remote or exotic locations—and my experiences adjusting to the rural setting of a university in northeast Connecticut. I wanted to use shows like *Survivor* and *Lost* in conjunction with several survival-themed literary works to invite students to reflect on how they adapt to new surroundings. Given Jack London's interest in writing about adaptation and travels in unfamiliar, dangerous places, I knew I would be remiss if I didn't include his fiction in the syllabus and had planned on assigning a couple of his short stories to introduce some of the themes we would be discussing throughout the semester. Yet as I thumbed through the pages of London's works, trying to decide which of his stories best suited my goals for the course, I started to see additional possibilities. Consequently, I decided to take the course in a different direction, one that placed less emphasis on reality television and gave London's writings a central role by incorporating fiction and nonfiction from *The Portable Jack London*. This enabled me to expand on my initial concept for the course and generate a wide range of writing topics dealing with the ways environments are perceived and experienced.

Because nearly all my students were first-semester freshmen who were undoubtedly still learning their way around the campus, I saw a unique opportunity to use London's short stories in conjunction with a writing assignment that encouraged them to focus on the mental and physical challenges of adapting to their new surroundings. By combining fiction with firsthand experience, they would (I hoped) develop some of the critical tools needed for other environmentally themed writing assignments and gain a richer understanding of the way they experience place. Although many of London's short stories would have been suitable for this project, I narrowed my choices to four of his Klondike tales: "In a Far Country," "To Build a Fire" (both the 1902 and 1908 versions), and "Love of Life." I was drawn to their emphasis on setting and to the way the places they describe seem utterly foreign, both to readers and the characters. I reasoned that, as readers, my students would experience the landscapes in these stories vicariously and that, like London's protagonists, they would find themselves in an environment that feels so remote and alien that at times it seems to defy imagination. This unfamiliarity would remind them of their status as outsiders and, in doing so, encourage them to reflect on the methods they use to orient themselves in alien environments.

As is often the case, much of the writing that resulted from this first assignment was not what I had anticipated. Students frequently focused on the psychological dimensions of interior spaces, rather than the physical characteristics of an unfamiliar environment. Typically, students used "In a Far Country" to illustrate how terribly wrong things can turn out when people who have "hopelessly fixed habits" and who lack "the protean faculty of adaptability" share an intimate space and limited resources for an extended period of time (11).[1] In some respects, this approach to the assignment was to be expected since, as several students noted, the difficulties and hazards many students encounter during their first semester of college are not nearly as dangerous or menacing as the challenges one might expect to face while trying to survive a winter in the Alaskan wilderness during the 1800s. Despite this disparity, however, students identified several memorable similarities between the struggles of Percy Cuthfert and Carter Weatherbee and their own difficulties—both real and imagined—living with and among strangers. One student, recognizing the darkly humorous dimensions of this cautionary tale, used hyperbole and comic irony to suggest that his frustrations about living on campus were not unlike the conditions that Cuthfert and Weatherbee endure sharing a ten-by-twelve-foot room during the coldest months of the year. He added that, like London's ill-fated and woefully unprepared characters, he and his roommate appeared to have almost nothing in common, but he was confident that they would not resort to squabbling and hoarding food, no matter how bad the campus dining may be.

Some students wrote about other locations on or near campus, and for the most part they too focused on the psychological rather than the physical challenges of adapting to an unfamiliar place. A student who had recently moved from New Haven cited London's concept of "the white silence" to convey his initial impressions of remote sections of the campus and the surrounding area, which is comprised largely of woodlands interrupted by small neighborhoods and scattered houses. After riding his bicycle along some of the winding back roads near campus, he wrote that he found the solitude and stillness of what is often called "the quiet corner" of Connecticut both appealing and unsettling. Similarly, a nontraditional student who had moved to Connecticut from Florida incorporated passages from four different Klondike stories to express her concerns about adjusting to an environment unlike anything she had ever experienced. In what was arguably the strongest essay to come out of this assignment, she likened the confusion she experienced trying to learn her way around the area to the disorientation of the hapless gold prospector in "Love of Life" who barely survives a grueling trek out of Alaska's Coppermine Valley. She observed that the experiences of feeling lost and reading about somebody who becomes lost made her conscious of the degree to which she depends on signs, buildings, and other physical landmarks to construct a mental map of a landscape. Then, turning her attention to the climate of the region, she noted that her lack of firsthand knowledge about cold weather reminded her of the shortcomings of the nameless travelers in "To Build a Fire" and "In a Far Country." Although she knew she wouldn't be facing anything like the brutally cold conditions that London describes in these tales, she doubted that she was truly prepared for her first New England winter—particularly the prospect of spending so much time indoors—and wondered if she, too, might have to pay a price for her lack of imagination and foresight.

Students who did not write about the outdoors in their first essay had another opportunity to do so with their second and third essays, which called for an analysis of contemporary attitudes toward nature. In my efforts to provide a cultural and historical context for this ecocritical analysis, I assigned two more gold-prospecting stories by London, "The Night-Born" and "All Gold Canyon," as well as excerpts from famous nature writers such as William Bartram, Henry David Thoreau, John Muir, Mary Austin, Annie Dillard, and Barry Lopez. At first blush, this may seem to be an unusual combination since, despite his strong interest in the outdoors and literary naturalism, Jack London is not considered a nature writer in the generic sense of the term. Whereas nature writing is usually episodic and consists of firsthand experiences and observations, most of London's writing is fictional, plot-driven, and narrated in the third person. Moreover, nature writing tends to focus on the dynamics of the natural world rather than human actions, which are discussed almost exclusively in terms of their relation to the environment. Finally, unlike most fiction, nature writing is often couched in the language of scientific observation or, at the other end of the spectrum, a transcendental or epiphanic experience. Nevertheless, I found that "The Night-Born" and "All Gold Canyon" can play a useful role in the sort of ecocritical understanding of place that I wanted my students to develop. On a practical level, this is due in part to the accessibility of London's writing style and the general appeal of adventure stories. More important, however, is the extent to which his fiction has influenced the perceptions and representations of nature in American culture. As the humanist geographer Yi Fu Tuan reminds us in his seminal study of environmental perception, *Topophilia*, "the dominant myths of America are nonurban" (193), and much of London's popularity as a writer of adventure stories can be attributed to the way these myths operate in his fiction. As a California writer who had traveled to Alaska during the Klondike gold rush and had his first story, "Typhoon off the Coast of Japan," published the same year (1893) that Frederick Jackson Turner declared that "the frontier has gone" (*Frontier* 38), London was well positioned—both geographically and historically—to convey the complex and often contradictory relation between human beings and nature that constitutes much of the mythology of the frontier experience.

Like much of London's fiction, "The Night-Born" and "All Gold Canyon" illustrate London's ability to weave the mythology of the frontier with his firsthand experiences of it. Yet what sets them apart from much of his Northland fiction is the way they present a markedly different view of nature. Whereas "To Build a Fire," "Love of Life," and "In a Far Country" take place in environments that often seem barren and exceedingly dangerous, the settings of "The Night-Born" and "All Gold Canyon" present us with a peaceful, idealized, almost prelapsarian portrait of nature. Perhaps more important, however, they register the impact human activity can have on such pristine landscapes.

One of the challenges I anticipated in asking college freshman to write critically about the mythology that shapes our perception of nature is that many students appear to lack a clear sense of what these myths are and how they may have originated. The difficulty of this undertaking was compounded by the historical chasm that seemed to lie between my students and a collection of stories that were published nearly a century before they were born. Yet, as we began discussing "The Night-Born" and "All Gold Canyon," I found that because these myths continue to play a significant role in the discourse of popular culture, many of my students already had an intuitive awareness of them (even though they may not have been aware that they did). Moreover, I discovered that focusing on their initial responses to the characters in these stories provided a useful way to begin unpacking some of these myths and writing about how this mythology informs their own attitudes toward nature.

After my students read "The Night-Born" and "All Gold Canyon," I asked them to compare the protagonists in those stories with some of the characters I had assigned at the beginning of the semester and indicate which they preferred. The justifications they gave for their preferences often illustrated the extent to which our values and ideals continue to be shaped by frontier mythology. Perhaps not surprisingly, Cuthfert and Weatherbee generated the most criticism, largely because of their class-related pretensions and general laziness. Conversely, the most popular character from these stories, the prospector in "All Gold Canyon," embodies the sort of qualities one often finds in the hero of the conventional frontier narrative. As students pointed out, he is persistent, hardworking, self-reliant, and apparently good-natured. Moreover, he abides by a code of fairness and common decency, as demonstrated by his outrage that the man who tries to jump his claim shoots him in the back and also by the fact that he takes the time to bury his attacker, despite his belief that "the measly skunk" would not have done the same for him.

When we focused on the relation between the characters and their environment, one criticism was that most of London's characters do not really "see" nature and therefore aren't attuned to their surroundings. As one student noted, the protagonist in the 1908 version of "To Build a Fire" and his literary antecedent in the earlier version, Tom Vincent, view the frozen terrain of the Klondike primarily as a distance to be traversed. She added that in the 1908 version of the story, this inattentiveness to the environment is not just a shortcoming but a tragic flaw. Students maintained also that, like the characters in "To Build a Fire," the protagonists in "Love of Life" and "In a Far Country" seem wholly unaware of the aesthetic dimensions of nature. They qualified this claim, however, by pointing out that, had they been in the same situation as London's characters, they, too, would have found it difficult to focus on anything other than what is necessary to survive. Others argued that these concerns may be a moot point anyway, since there may not have been much natural beauty to admire in such remote and seemingly lifeless landscapes. Their assertion was countered, however, by students who noted that authors such as Thoreau, Dillard, and Lopez complicate conventional assumptions about beauty in nature and where one might expect to find it.

This discussion provided the foundation for two writing assignments, the first of which called for students to take a brief walk or hike in one of the nearby wooded areas open to the public. Working from Lawrence Buell's premise that "environmental literature launches itself from the presumption that we do not think about our surroundings, and our relation to them, as much as we ought to" (261), I instructed students to record their experiences in journal form, using their observations about London's stories and the writings of the aforementioned nature writers as a sort of touchstone. Before they embarked on their adventures, I asked them to consider what nature means to them, both on a practical, experiential level and in a more philosophical sense. I wanted them to examine not only their attitudes toward the outdoors, but their understanding of place-related concepts such as "nature" and "wilderness." Although the tone and substance of the responses generated by this exercise varied widely, most students used the experience to take stock of their environmental knowledge (or lack thereof) and reflect on the cultural influences that inform their perception of nature.

The writing assignment that followed, which was more formal than the journal exercise, called for students to discuss the way nature is represented in "The Night-Born" or "All Gold Canyon" (or both) in relation to contemporary discourse about the environment, particularly with respect to issues of land use and conservation. Although some students made references to both stories in their essays, far more of them made use of "All Gold Canyon." For the most part, this was expected since its narrator gives a significant amount of attention to the natural features of the canyon and the damage done to this Edenic setting by the prospector's efforts to find and unearth "Mr. Pocket." As many students observed, the tranquil, verdant state of the canyon before the prospector's arrival provides a stark contrast to the scarred, pockmarked condition of the hillside at the end of the story. Students disagreed, however, when asked if the story should be read as a criticism of gold prospecting. Some maintained that the affability of the prospector made it easier for them to look beyond the environmental damage he causes (which, some of them insisted, was fairly negligible anyway). Others raised questions about authorial intentionality and audience, arguing that readers who interpret the story as an attack on gold prospecting may be overlooking the probability that neither London nor his readers would have been as attuned to the environment as most people are today. Of the students who argued that the story is a critique of gold prospecting, perhaps the strongest argument came from one who suggested that the environmental destruction caused by the prospector's methods is an act of violence. He added that the impact of this act is underscored by the way nature is not only personified but also feminized, as well as by the violent struggle that ends in the claim jumper's death. The fact that that prospector's attacker is buried in the same hole that the prospector had dug to extract most of the gold, he concluded, reinforces the story's ethos of conservation by connecting these two forms of violence.

On the whole, most of my students seemed far less certain about what sort of environmental message "The Night-Born" conveys. Consequently, only a few of them incorporated the story into their writing, but the few who did produced some of the most insightful responses to the assignment. One of the more memorable essays discussed how contemporary American attitudes about the wilderness are shaped by a complex and often contradictory understanding of what we value most about nature. To illustrate her argument, the student cited Trefethan's account of his encounter with Lucy, the "frontier-born" woman who entreats him to live with her in a valley in the Rocky Mountains that is similar in many respects to the canyon in "All Gold Canyon" before the prospector's arrival. Trefethan's description of this place "where the white man has never set foot" (265) suggests both a virgin wilderness and a picturesque, almost pastoral landscape: "It was a noble valley," he states, "now shut in by high canyon walls, and again opening into beautiful stretches, wide and long, with pasture shoulder-high in the bottoms, meadows dotted with flowers, and with clumps of timber—spruce—virgin and magnificent" (265). He also remarks, however, that "some day the white settlers will be in there and growing wheat down that valley" (265). Whether he is lamenting this eventual transformation of the valley, looking forward to it, or simply pointing out its inevitability is not clear, but what does seem fairly apparent when we juxtapose this description with our reading of "All Gold Canyon" is the presence of several historical influences: a romanticized, pictorial concept of nature that privileges pristine landscapes; a Jeffersonian model; and a deeply rooted tradition of viewing nature as little more than a resource or commodity.

For the final writing assignment, a research paper, we turned our attention to man-made places, such as factories and cities, and used London's writings to facilitate discussion about suitable essay topics. In an effort to focus on some of the social issues often associated with these environments, I assigned several chapters from *The People of the Abyss*, London's firsthand account of the living conditions in the East End of London. Because *The Portable Jack London* does not include reproductions of London's photographs, I also shared images from the edition of the book published in 1995, and from *How the Other Half Lives* (1890), Jacob Riis's exposé of urban squalor in New York City's tenements. Students also read London's short story "The Apostate," which was inspired by his experiences as a child laborer working in canneries and jute mills, and "How I Became a Socialist," an autobiographical essay in which London recounts tramping across thousands of miles of the United States and Canada and being held at the Erie County Penitentiary for vagrancy. Although I did not require students to incorporate London's writing into their essays as I had with previous assignments, this approach generated discussion on a wide range of place-related issues. Much of the writing that came out of these discussions focused on the hazards of working in factories and the seeming ubiquity of sweatshops and child labor, but students also wrote about more visible problems, such as homelessness and the need for public green spaces and parks in urban landscapes.

One feature that all the essays had in common, however, was an implicit recognition that our identity—indeed, our very existence—is bound up with our relation to our environment. Consequently, my teaching of London's works since then has often addressed some of the implications of this relation, particularly with respect to our rapidly increasing dependence on technology and the general population shift toward urban and suburban areas. As Harold Fromm has observed, this has made nature much less immediate to us than it was for our ancestors. He explains that today "a man is much less likely to perish from the heat or cold, to starve for want of food . . . his relation to the other animals and to the vegetable creation appears thickly veiled—by air conditioning, frozen foods, washing machines, detergents, automobiles, electric blankets, and power lawnmowers" (32). That our relation to nature will continue to become increasingly mediated seems inevitable when we consider the amount of time many people now spend "in" cyberspace, which already has begun to replace the traditional classroom at all levels of education. Yet the potential costs of becoming more disconnected from our environment are perhaps greater today than ever. That is why it is vital that we continue looking for opportunities to encourage students to travel beyond their customary boundaries, to heed London's injunction to "put out their hands, and feel the pulse of the world" ("Things Alive" 485). Fortunately, as I discovered by teaching his works, many students still respond to this call.

NOTE

[1] Citations to London's works are from *The Portable Jack London*.

"To Build a Fire" and Questions of Genre

Terry Reilly

After teaching "To Build a Fire" for twenty years in Florida and another eighteen years in Alaska, I have found that interpreting the protagonist's behavior in London's text depends to a great extent on student perspectives about its genre—that is, whether it is read as fiction, nonfiction, creative nonfiction, or metafiction. Calling attention to and questioning the genre of the narrative opens a wide range of research possibilities. Examples of individual and group-oriented student research based on the story range from literary criticism and theory such as naturalism to survival stories and accounts of deaths in Alaskan newspapers to clinical descriptions of the medical condition of hypothermia. Moreover, students learn to be more accepting of different views of the narrative and to be more critical of other genres, including radio and television. This essay first recapitulates my teaching experiences in Florida and the radical alterations I made in my approach to teaching (and my understanding of) "To Build a Fire" after my first full year in Alaska. Then it details teaching techniques that I have developed over the past twelve years and use currently when teaching "To Build a Fire."

From 1976 until 1996, I taught London's "To Build a Fire" at least twice a year in secondary English classes in Palm Beach County, Florida, and from 1988 to 1996 in undergraduate composition classes at the University of Miami in Coral Gables, Florida. When I taught the story in Florida, the students in these classes were ethnically, religiously, and geographically diverse, but they were not what we might refer to as climatically diverse. Most of them had never seen snow, let alone temperatures below freezing. For many of them, London's story, and the concept of extremely cold temperatures, was pure fiction, something as far removed from their personal experience as a selection from Ray Bradbury's *The Illustrated Man* or an excerpt from *The Lord of the Rings*. My experience teaching "To Build a Fire" was thus fairly conventional and straightforward in what may be termed a literary sense: I taught it as a classic piece of short fiction, emphasizing traditional Aristotelian concepts including character, plot, climax, denouement, and so on. We focused on literary themes (man vs. nature, intelligence vs. instinct, etc.) and terms such as metaphor, simile, metonymy, and other literary tropes and forms of descriptive language.

When I moved to Fairbanks, Alaska, in 1996 and began teaching at the University of Alaska, however, I found that my students read and understood "To Build a Fire" in very different ways. Many of these differences can be attributed to two factors. The first is the location of the University of Alaska, Fairbanks (UAF). Situated in interior Alaska, where winter temperatures regularly fall below minus forty degrees Fahrenheit, it is the northernmost Division I research university in the world. Students here are very familiar with the type of weather conditions London describes in the story. The second factor is the diversity of the student population. Students in a "typical" UAF composition class fit into one of five general categories: Native American students, especially Native Alaskan students who belong to one or more of the local indigenous cultures, such as Athabaskan, Yu'pik, Inupiaq, Tlingit, Haida, Aleut; Alaskan "sourdoughs," a name generally given to non–Native Alaskan immigrants (or descendants of immigrants), regardless of ethnicity, who have lived here for at least a generation; "chechaquos"—a term used by Alaskans (and by London) to describe "newcomer(s) in the land" ("To Build a Fire (II)" II, 1302), either from foreign countries or from the Lower 48 (also referred to as "the States"); and military personnel who take the course while stationed at one of the local air force or army bases. Given this diverse population, some of the students in a class at UAF, like those students in Miami, may not have experienced very cold weather. Others have experienced temperatures as cold as those in the story and have known people who suffered frostbite and died of hypothermia. Some of the Native Alaskan students who grew up in rural villages are quite used to hunting and gathering wood and water in conditions similar to those depicted in the story. Some of the military folks in class regularly train outdoors in the winter and have received extensive training for the treatment of hypothermia. Thus, although the students may come from very different backgrounds, it is not unusual for us to be discussing "To Build a Fire" in my class when the temperature outside the classroom is almost as cold as it is in the story.

At UAF, I usually teach "To Build a Fire" in a sophomore-level composition class called Academic Writing about Literature. When I taught the story for the first time at UAF in January of 1997, I decided to teach the text in two one-hour classes near the beginning of the fourteen-week spring semester for two main reasons. First, since I assumed that most of the class would be familiar with London's works from high school, I saw "To Build a Fire" as an easy way to introduce the students to short fiction, to literary criticism, and to the debate usually described as naturalism versus realism. A second, more selfish reason was that as a recently transplanted Floridian, I wanted to learn what I should do if my car broke down at 10:00 p.m. on my way home after class when it was sixty below zero.

I came to the first class at UAF armed with notes, a brief lecture, a list of discussion topics, paper suggestions, and plenty of references to literary criticism that related to London and his works. I began with a brief overview of London's life and works and cautioned the students that in London criticism, biography often overshadows his writing. I began with that old standby—irony. I read the often quoted passage from Jacqueline Tavernier-Courbin's essay "The Many Facets of Jack London's Humor," in which the critic "finds in Jack London's work an ironical view of life and an ironical treatment of fate":

> This ironical view of life is often exemplified by stories in which man pits himself against nature and disregards its basic laws. The punishment then dealt out by nature on the offender may be extreme, but it is always

> ironically suited to the nature of the crime. The classic example of this in London's work is in "To Build a Fire"—the story of the non-survival of a man who disregards the law of the North that says that 'no man must travel alone in the Klondike after fifty below.' (98)

When I asked the students to comment on this passage, several of them took strong exception to it, and one rather eloquently argued:

> Irony is the unexpected, right—like when the firehouse burns down. If a guy walks into a burning house and burns to death, is that ironic? We all drive our cars home alone after class when it's -50 and we don't all die, but if you walk outside in the woods all day when it's -50, you're probably going to freeze to death, whether you're alone or not. There's nothing ironic about that.

I switched tacks by reading more bits of London criticism: James McClintock, I noted, called "To Build a Fire" London's most pessimistic story, arguing that "the Alaskan landscape as a killer . . . is identified with a naturalist logic that denies human significance" (*White Logic* [1975] 50, 44). To emphasize this, I read brief passages from "The White Silence," in which London characterizes the Klondike as "the ghostly wastes of a dead world" and describes its "spirit groping" silence as the most "stupefying" feature of all (143–44). These comments provoked laughter from some of my Alaskan students, and one young woman sarcastically noted that such descriptions reminded her of her job the previous summer working at the information desk at Denali National Park:

> I was right next to a TV where they showed a National Park Service video over and over. The passage you just read sounds just like descriptions in the video—somebody like Vincent Price talking about how Dall sheep "cling precariously to life perched on the edge of an icy oblivion," and so on. It's all so phony and melodramatic. A lot of the tourists who come here from Outside think it's frozen year round, dark for six months, and we all live in Quonset huts.

Once again, I tried to change directions by turning to one student who had helped me out of several such situations; a bright, articulate, and well-read young Athabaskan man from Arctic Village, located about three hundred miles north of Fairbanks in the Brooks Range. "People from your culture have lived here for thousands of years," I said, "What do you do to survive when it's fifty below zero?" With impeccable timing and without missing a beat, he said, "We stay inside." This simple fact, he went on wryly, explains why there are no "Indians" in this particular Jack London story. So much for help.

At the outset of the second class, I asked the students if they had any questions. One of the students quietly asked, "Is this story true?"

"What do you think?" I asked. The discussion soon took off and focused on questions of genre. One student argued that people unfamiliar with central Alaska would regard the story as "true" (and therefore nonfiction), while those of us who live in central Alaska would see it as "unrealistic" and therefore a work of fiction. Another student argued just the opposite: people from outside would see the extreme cold and isolation as "fantastic" and "unbelievable," while we who live here know that just such an event could happen in precisely the way London's narrator describes. Personal anecdotes once again fueled the discussion: in one, a woman was found frozen in a snowdrift less than a hundred feet from the back door of her house. "She got drunk and passed out," concluded the student telling the story. The other story was about a young man whose snow machine broke down in January while he was working a trapline in a remote area a hundred miles or so north of town. After a week or so, the authorities stopped looking for him, but his family didn't seem too concerned. More than a month later, he showed up at a bar in Salcha, supposedly having "lived off the land" with a rifle, some bullets, and a couple of disposable lighters, shooting rabbits and living in snow caves he dug each night. Some of the students didn't seem surprised by this explanation, while others cynically suggested that he had been at the bar in Salcha the whole time. I refrained from telling the students that what they were engaged in while discussing these two stories was the equivalent of literary criticism. Instead, I managed to turn this into a discussion of the relation of fiction, nonfiction, creative nonfiction, and metafiction, which, in turn, led back to questions of life writing and London's doomed protagonist in "To Build a Fire." By the end of the class, the extent to which the discussion of the genre of the narrative and its cultural and literary contexts had become intertwined can perhaps best be expressed by the comments of one student, who noted that the directional lines mapped by the narrator on the first page of the story—from Dyea to Dawson and from Nulato to St. Michael—failed to converge. "I knew the story would end badly right after reading that," he said confidently. "[I]f the narrator is lost, what hope is there for the protagonist?"

Since that first class in 1997, I have taught "To Build a Fire" every few years, and my approach has grown out of that first Alaskan experience. I now teach the story in four one-hour classes near the beginning of the semester as a way to introduce the students to concepts of genre and to initiate individual and group research projects. We begin by reading both the 1902 and 1908 versions of the story and, using Earle Labor and King Hendricks's article "Jack London's Twice-Told Tale," discuss how and perhaps why London revised the story. We then spend the next two classes discussing concepts of genre before the final class, in which they watch the video version of the story narrated by Orson Welles, starring Ian Hogg and a very well-trained husky.

The student papers and research projects that follow are based on each student's interpretation of the genre of the narrative. While some students work on their projects individually, others prefer to work in groups. These group topics are then shared with the rest of the class, and the class projects can then be disseminated to a larger and broader population outside the class.

The research projects that have resulted over the years can be grouped in four main categories. The first are literary studies of the narrative, or what might be described as traditional literary criticism papers that cite prior commentary about the story and build on the corpus of extant criticism. Students who read the story as a type of myth or wild fantasy story tend to focus on the anthropomorphic images of nature in the text, such as the "intangible pall over the face of things," the "hairline" of the trail, the sun described as "that cheerful orb [that] would just peep above the sky line" ("To Build a Fire (II)" 1301, 1303). These commentators tend to see nature in the text as neither evil nor malignant but rather as benign and fragile. After all, they point out, the man gets into trouble first because he breaks through the fragile "ice skin" and second because he disrupts the delicate balance of the snow on the tree limbs. Some see the end of the story as a type of justification for or explanation of an afterlife. In their reading, after the man dies, his spirit continues to journey to Henderson Creek, where it meets the boys and leads them back to his body. In such a reading, the recovery of the body and the transmigration of the soul, fundamental to a number of different religions—including the spiritual beliefs of several indigenous Alaskan groups—provide a redemptive, if not universally affirmative, ending to the story.

Students who read the text as a work of nonfiction often research comparative studies of people who died of hypothermia in Alaska in recent years. Such an approach involves researching newspapers and conducting interviews. The accounts are rather abundant and easy to access in local sources such as the *Fairbanks Daily News-Miner*. These students frequently postulate that the most prevalent and recurring themes in these deaths are alcohol, carelessness, and the disorientation that comes with hypothermia. One group wanted to take a more practical approach and introduce London's text into middle and high school English curricula and to read "To Build a Fire" to preschool- and elementary-aged children at local libraries and schools as a way to inform children about the dangers of hypothermia.

Other groups of students in this category often focus on London's representation of the stages of hypothermia and death in the text and then compare it with medical texts. These students, many of whom are military personnel who have been trained in cold-weather first aid, usually conclude that although London's protagonist knew little or nothing about survival in the cold, London provides clear and knowledgeable representations of the three stages of death by hypothermia. One student extended this analysis and discussed ways that the death of London's protagonist not only recapitulates the stages of hypothermia but also reproduces the five stages of grief that Elisabeth Kübler-Ross identifies in *On Death and Dying*.

Other students tend not to regard "To Build a Fire" as either fiction or nonfiction but as a type of hybrid, as either creative nonfiction or metafiction. Their interests, broadly speaking, are to explore ways that the process of storytelling shapes and reshapes narratives of actual events, either by denying that the narrative has been reshaped or by self-consciously calling attention to that shaping or fictionalization. These students often take comparative approaches to London's text, either by comparing and contrasting the two versions of the story or by discussing it alongside other works such as Stephen Crane's "The Open Boat" or Jon Krakauer's *Into the Wild*, both of which are usually included on the course syllabus. Such students are often helped along by supplementing their research with selections from Lee Gutkind's *The Art of Creative Nonfiction* and Patricia Waugh's *Metafiction*.

The results of this rather scattered teaching approach have been positive in a number of ways. First, students from rural Alaska who are normally rather quiet in class have no qualms about discussing "the man's" actions in the story, since the story is a very familiar one to them. Second, students from warmer climates learn to recognize the symptoms of hypothermia, as well as how to avoid them. Third, students seem to be more eager to write about their findings with regard to the story, in part because their research leads them to write papers that, according to one student, "are more informative and useful than most 'regular' English papers." Finally, as the students interrogate and critique concepts of genre, they learn to be more circumspect and discriminating when presented with representations in other forms—such as news, political speeches, and history—and when experiencing other media, such as television, movies, and radio.

Teaching Jack London's "Koolau the Leper" in a Doctoral Seminar

Jeanne Campbell Reesman

Jack London's powerful short story "Koolau the Leper" created controversy in Hawai'i when it was published in 1908—the elite of Honolulu were angry at London for daring to portray labor abuse in Hawai'i and, even worse for tourism, leprosy. Based on the real Ko'olau's successful defiance of the authorities who came after him on Kauai's Na Pali coast to take him to Molokai or kill him, London's story highlights Ko'olau's tragic recounting of how the whites took over the land in Hawai'i. The story was included in my doctoral seminar called New Texts/New Contexts—Literature of the Postcolonial South Pacific. This course examines the history of various literatures of the Pacific. It analyzes South Pacific works by selected nineteenth- and twentieth-century European American writers against a set of texts by recent and contemporary indigenous Pacific writers from Hawai'i, Samoa, Tonga, and New Zealand in order to examine how different cultural and historical positions and diverse narrative structures and styles reveal authors' cultural assumptions and help create their unique artistic statements.

The various versions of the story of Ko'olau include: the local legend; the version told to London on his sailboat the *Snark* by a crew member who was the son of the sheriff of Kaua'i, whom Ko'olau murdered; the version London wrote; the version by Ko'olau's wife, Piilani Kaluaikoolau's *The True Story of Kaluaikoolau: As Told by His Wife, Piilani*, dictated in Hawaiian in 1906 and translated and published by Frances N. Frazier in 2001; and, most recently, W. S. Merwin's epic poem *The Folding Cliffs: A Narrative* (1998). By comparing and contrasting narrative structures in particular, students were able to examine these versions of the tale for what the storytelling technique tells us about cultural assumptions in the texts. This approach also offered the opportunity to use relevant chapters of London's *The Cruise of the* Snark (1912) and two other stories on leprosy from *The House of Pride* (1912), which also contains "Koolau the Leper": "Good-By, Jack" and "The Sheriff of Kona."

The contemporary outpouring of literary and cultural productions from Pacific Islanders today might be described as examples of cultural decolonization, including an interrogation of previous literary, anthropological, and historical representations of Pacific peoples. Students investigated the narrative structures and styles of each writer, considering such elements as how islander characters are developed and voiced; how settings are portrayed; intended audience; the formal politics of the novel (how the novel creates a normalizing narrative of subjectivity); realistic representations of island history, culture, and resistance to colonization; and the degree of such additional elements as folktale, myth, and religion.

Our texts included

Herman Melville, *Typee: A Peep at Polynesian Life* (1846) and *Omoo* (1847)
Robert Louis Stevenson, *Treasure Island* (1883) and *In the South Seas* (1893)
Jack London, *The Cruise of the* Snark (1911), *Stories of Hawaii* (1908; ed. Day [1984]), *A Son of the Sun: The Adventures of Captain David Grief* (*A Son of the Sun* [1912]; ed. Gary Riedl and Thomas M. Tietze [2001])
Piilani Kaluaikoolau, *The True Story of Kaluaikoolau: As Told by His Wife, Piilani* (1906; trans. Frances N. Frazier [2001])
W. S. Merwin, *The Folding Cliffs: A Narrative* (1998)
Albert Wendt, *Sons for the Return Home* (1973)
Epeli Hau'ofa, *Tales of the Tikongs* (1983)
Witi Tame Ihimaera, *The Whale Rider* (1987)
Lois-Ann Yamanaka, *Wild Meat and the Bully Burgers* (1997)
Maxine Hong Kingston, *The Fifth Book of Peace* (2003)

In addition to literary texts, we also viewed and analyzed visual culture, the films *South Pacific* and *Whale Rider*, and popular culture, with a unit on the tiki phenomenon in the United States. Our goals were to examine critically individual literary works as they reflect the culture and values of Pacific Islanders; to relate the literary works to their general social and cultural context; to develop some basic theories of the narrative characteristics of the literary works to compare and contrast works by mainstream European American writers and contemporary indigenous writers.

Requirements included one research-based original essay (fifteen pages); two written exams (one of which was take-home); three in-class reports of fifteen minutes each, one a preliminary library report on contexts for South Pacific literature, one an annotated bibliography, and one a final report on the required essay. Students were encouraged to do original research, to turn in drafts of their work as they went, and to view the essay as a possible conference presentation and publication. Suggested topics for the contextual report included earliest Europeans in the Pacific, the "discovery" of Tahiti and its aftermath, the voyages of Captain James Cook, the debate between scholars Marshall Sahlins and Gananath Obeyesekere on Captain Cook and the Hawaiians, economic goals of nineteenth-century and early-twentieth-century Europeans and Americans in the Pacific (trading, whaling, agriculture, tourism), racial ideas about the South Pacific held by nineteenth-century and early-twentieth-century Europeans and Americans, Mark Twain's *Roughing It* and *Following the Equator*, missionaries, World War II and images of tropicality brought home by United States servicemen, early forms of resistance to colonization by Pacific Islanders, recent and contemporary resistance by Pacific Islanders, and Paul Theroux's, *The Happy*

Isles of Oceania. Suggested topics for the annotated bibliography reports included Jack London, race, and class in Hawai'i; representations of the tropics in twentieth- and twenty-first-century film; representations of the tropics in American popular culture; names (what to call "the Pacific" and its peoples); a book and film comparison of *The Whale Rider*; Pacific storytelling traditions.

The results of our comparative approach were in several cases quite striking. In *Typee* the students found that the story is told as a series of performances of race and culture: Melville's performances as Tommo and as author, Tommo's comparison of Marquesan and Western life, Tommo's performance in trying to blend in with the Marquesans, Marnoo's performance as taboo, and of course the performance of cannibalism. Tommo's anxious performance of his own American culture and of Marquesan culture simultaneously comes to a climax when the conflict must be answered: the Marquesans want to tattoo Tommo's face, and Tommo must decide to submit or escape. He chooses to escape because the tattooing would locate him firmly in Marquesan culture and thus render him no longer a white or a civilized man at home. Students drew important parallels between this series of performances and Jack London's performances as white man, explorer, artist, and captain in *The Cruise of the* Snark. Closely examining the travel narrative allowed students to view each chapter as a kind of psychological and physical performance by the narrator that aims to place him in or outside a new cultural setting. For example, the London narrator is saddened by the near extinction of Melville's Typeeans fifty years later, overjoyed at the hospitality he receives in Bora Bora, but repelled by the violent and war-like people of the Solomon Islands. Performing Jack London, whiteness, or civilization in the Solomons would be met not with acquiescence but with a hatchet.

There were also important insights into *The Whale Rider* when differences between the popular film of 2003 and the novel were explored, but a comparison of the editions of the novel published in New Zealand and in the United States as a tie-in to the film yielded even more surprising insights into notions of culture. Thanks to a very bright student from New Zealand, we were able to discover how the text was altered for an American audience. He had a copy of the original publication of the novel by Reed Books in Australia, and we were using the Harcourt paperback edition that appeared around the time of the film's release. Comparing the first edition with the Harcourt edition, we found that there were two major ways in which the text was changed. First, the art elements at the beginning of each chapter were unaccountably switched from Maori designs to Southwest Indian designs. But even more disturbing was the excision of all references to Western popular culture from the American edition: the Maori kids talk about "doing a Burt Reynolds" and stealing a car, and they mention numerous Hollywood figures from the films they have seen. We wondered—why take these references out? Wouldn't they help American readers relate more to the Maori youth? In a publishable paper, the student who did the research speculated that Harcourt did not want Americans to relate to Maoris as equals. To the contrary, removing references to Western popular culture from the speech of the Maoris rendered them exotic and distant from Westerners; if they were part of global popular culture, then they would not be so exotically interesting. This student even contacted Ihimaera by e-mail at the University of Fiji to ask why the changes were made. Ihimaera graciously answered him, on the one hand explaining that he could not comment on the terms of his publishing contract with Harcourt but on the other encouraging the student to discuss the discrepancies in class and at professional meetings.

"Koolau the Leper" was the most closely compared text in the course. We read all three versions in order to compare and contrast their narrative focus and style. We found that the main difference among the three versions of Ko'olau's resistance was whether there was any religious significance to it from the narrator's point of view. Piilani focuses not on Ko'olau's resistance to the forces arrayed against him, which at one point included being shelled by the United States Navy but rather on his heroism as a husband and father and his deep Christian faith. Her version does not seem interested in the politics of Ko'olau but rather in the way an innocent man is martyred by the powerful. London heard the tale from Bert Stolz, the son of the sheriff of Kaua'i, Louis Stolz; one might imagine that London would have a hard time making a hero out of someone who killed a crew member's father, but this does not seem to have fazed him. His Ko'olau is a figure of heroic resistance to the white authorities in Honolulu and a symbol of a dying people, overcome with colonial aggression and imported diseases. His Ko'olau is armed and angry and dies with his rifle in his rotting hands. Through Ko'olau's voice, London eloquently criticizes the European Americans who stole Hawai'i from its people:

> They came like lambs, speaking softly. Well might they speak softly, for we were many and strong, and all the islands were ours. As I say, they spoke softly. They were of two kinds. The one kind asked our permission, our gracious permission, to preach to us the word of God. The other kind asked our permission, our gracious permission, to trade with us. That was the beginning. To-day all the islands are theirs, all the land, all the cattle—everything is theirs. They that preached the word of God and they that preached the word of Rum have foregathered and become great chiefs. They live like kings in houses of many rooms, with multitudes of servants to care for them. They who had nothing have everything, and if you, or I, or any Kanaka be hungry, they sneer and say, "Well, why don't you work? There are the plantations." (883)

Piilani and the couple's son are not even mentioned in the story, and religion is something false that is imposed on the Hawaiians by their white masters.

In order to read Merwin's long epic poem, class members were each assigned a section of the poem and were to present it to the class, highlighting key passages, central images, characteristic poetic devices, and the overall "argument" of that section. What we found was that in contrast to London, Merwin tries to preserve Piilani's native voice and her Christian beliefs, but he does this in his own way. Returning the religious dimensions of the story to prominence, Merwin, who knows Hawaiian culture quite well, connects Piilani's spirituality with that of nature. In Hawai'i an all-important metaphor is the *'aina*, or "land"; they speak of those who belong to the land and those newcomers who do not. There is a spiritual kinship between certain springs, mountains, caves, rivers, and Hawaiians, as expressed in numerous legends. Thus Merwin tries to reconnect the original story as closely as possible with the religious traditions and beliefs of ancient Hawai'i. In the end, the class enjoyed an exciting discussion of the narrative forms of the three versions, concluding that Piilani's version is in the form of a traditional Hawaiian chant on the genealogy and actions of a hero, London's is a sort of battle narrative, and Merwin's is a paean to nature using the Ko'olau story as a structure. Students came away with new awareness of comparative textual study of books, of how one legend can be reinterpreted from very different points of view by writers, and, most important, of cultural differences in such tale telling and interpretation.

An Old Favorite in a New Context: Teaching London's *The Call of the Wild* in a Law and Literature Class

Alicia Mischa Renfroe

Of all the classic texts we examine in my undergraduate Law and Literature course, Jack London's *The Call of the Wild* consistently provokes top-notch, wide-ranging class discussion precisely because it resists neat interpretations. Typically quiet students speak confidently about Buck as they reexamine his journey for the ways in which that journey might speak to legal concepts. Law and Literature is an upper-level class in the English department at Middle Tennessee State University, a comprehensive public university serving over twenty-three thousand undergraduates. Given the large and diverse student body, Law and Literature attracts not only English majors but also students from many backgrounds—ranging from prelaw to political science to journalism. With this group in mind, I divide the class into two units. The first unit introduces students to legal themes in literary texts (such as Sophocles's *Antigone*, Shakespeare's *The Merchant of Venice*, Morrison's *The Bluest Eye*, and Kafka's *The Trial*, among others), and the second unit focuses on literary interventions into real-world legal issues such as slavery (Stowe's *Uncle Tom's Cabin* and several slave narratives), working conditions (Sinclair's *The Jungle*), and women's rights (Glaspell, "A Jury of Her Peers"). Students read *The Call of the Wild* near the end of the first unit alongside a short story or two (usually "The Law of Life" or "To Build a Fire"), excerpts from *The People of the Abyss*, and accessible excerpts on the social contract from John Locke, Thomas Hobbes, and Jean-Jacques Rousseau.

In this interdisciplinary context, I suggest that *The Call of the Wild* can be read through the lens of social contract theory as a story of the origins of and justifications for the social contract, as a commentary on our assumptions about law and justice, and as an exemplary illustration of what it means to become a legal subject. We read London after we have finished Sophocles's *Antigone* and Shakespeare's *The Merchant of Venice*, so students come to *The Call of the Wild* with a basic understanding of several legal concepts: positive (man-made) law, natural (higher) law, justice, and equity. In the context of the course as a whole, London's work provides particularly effective ways to complicate the opposition of positive law and natural law so essential to *Antigone*, to illuminate the significance of the social contract and its foundational assumptions about questions about justice and equity in *The Merchant of Venice*, and to highlight concerns about social justice that shape our discussions of slavery, women's rights, and working conditions.

We begin with a general discussion of London's ideas about law and justice. I first ask students to read "The Law of Life" and "To Build a Fire" and to compare

London's treatment of law in these short stories to Sophocles's approach in *Antigone*. In brief, *Antigone* illustrates the clash between the man-made law of Creon's edict forbidding the burial of Polynices and the higher law of the gods that requires certain burial rituals and compels Antigone to comply despite the edict. In this context, natural law reflects the law of the gods, existing above and apart from the world of Thebes. London's short stories suggest an important distinction that can be illuminated by Earle Labor's analysis of London's idea of the god of the White Silence in his "Jack London's Symbolic Wilderness": "the god of the White Silence is a harsh god but a just one: he is an inflexible disciplinarian who brooks no violation of his strict code. He is 'indifferent' in that he neither helps nor actively hinders man in this creature's petty enterprises, nor do these enterprises appreciably alter the wilderness" (32). Jeanne Campbell Reesman makes a similar point about "To Build a Fire": in this story, fire does not equal life; instead, "it consists only of another instance of the man's innate false pride in the face of nature and its inexorable judgment" (*Jack London: A Study* 47). Though London's god of the White Silence certainly owes, as both Labor and Reesman suggest, something to Greek mythology, London's version lacks the personified god figure, transforming it instead into the immediate and indifferent justice situated in nature and thus bringing natural law back to the material realm. To reinforce this point, I also draw students' attention to Jacqueline Tavernier-Courbin's discussion of justice in The Call of the Wild*: A Naturalistic Romance*. In brief, Tavernier-Courbin suggests that justice takes two primary forms in London's work: justice as "the essentially just working out of natural laws" (as in "To Build a Fire" and "In a Far Country") and justice as "random chance, with no particular logic or inevitability" (as in "The White Silence") (105–06). In both cases, natural law does not reflect a higher law associated with a specific religious framework; instead, London's god deals in both inevitability and chance.

With these general ideas in mind, I turn to *The Call of the Wild* and ask students to consider Buck's adventure in the light of accessible excerpts from classic social contract theorists and to think about how London might complicate the idea of a social contract as well as assumptions about many of its key terms—civilization, nature, the rule of law, and justice to name a few. I ask students ahead of time to note references to law and legalistic issues as they read, and I also assign accessible excerpts from John Locke, Thomas Hobbes, and Jean Jacques Rousseau. Taking into account student responses and time constraints, I usually tweak these selections each time I teach the class. Generally speaking, students read representative sections of the following: Thomas Hobbes's *The Leviathan*, "Of the Natural Condition of Mankind" (ch. 13), and "Of the First and Second Natural Laws, and of Contracts" (ch. 14); John Locke's *Second Treatise of Government* (bk. 2, ch. 2), "Of the State of Nature" (ch. 3), "Of the State of War," and "Of Property" (ch. 7); and Jean Jacques Rousseau's *The Social Contract or Principles of Political Right* (bk. 1). Each of these texts is available in an affordable print edition and on the Internet, through *Project Gutenberg*. Electronic versions are particularly useful in a computer-enhanced classroom; if I have not assigned a section that seems relevant to our discussion, I can pull up the appropriate part for students to engage in class. Since I am not teaching a political theory class, I do not expect students to delve deeply into these complex theories, but I do expect that they understand basic definitions of the state of nature and civil society as well as each theorist's general trajectory for the transition from one to the other and the accompanying assumptions about human behavior. Instructors in political theory and philosophy classes could adapt this approach to other theorists and include excerpts on the social contract from Georg Wilhelm Friedrich Hegel, Friedrich Nietzsche, and Karl Marx, among others. As exemplified in David Mike Hamilton's *"The Tools of My Trade": The Annotated Books in Jack London's Library*, London's vast reading lends itself to such an approach, and students are usually interested to learn that London read Rousseau's *The Social Contract* (Hamilton 12; on London and Rousseau, see Fusco).

In a similar vein, I spend time on London's fascinating biography, drawing on Earle Labor and Jeanne Campbell Reesman's accessible *Jack London: Revised Edition*. Most students have heard of London's exploits during the gold rush and of his descent into illness and alcoholism near the end of his life, but few are aware, for instance, that London spent several weeks living in London's East End to prepare to write *The People of the Abyss* or that he wrote *The Star Rover*, a novel arguing for the elimination of straitjackets in prisons.

With this background, we begin our discussion of *The Call of the Wild* by examining Buck's journey from Judge Miller's "great demense" (350) to the Northland with legal issues and social contract theory in mind.[1] To prime class discussion, I use an informal quiz to ask students to consider Buck's experiences in the light of Rousseau's famous declaration: "Man is born free; and everywhere he is in chains" (181). This informal writing helps students engage these complex texts in writing and gain some confidence in their ideas before being asked to contribute to class discussion. After reading a bit of Hobbes, Locke, and Rousseau, most students immediately notice that London reverses the familiar story of the origins of the social contract. Buck's journey begins in civil society and ends in the state of nature. What are we to make of this reversal? Is Buck's adventure simply an atavistic regression to an earlier primitive and perhaps idealized state (as it is often read), or does it tell us something about the assumptions that undergird our ideas about nature, civilization, and law?

English majors often focus on reading the text as an exemplar of Darwinian naturalism. However, while recognizing the merits of such a reading, I do not spend much time on naturalism and instead encourage students, especially those who have read *The Call of the Wild* as a naturalist text in other courses, to reconsider the novel in the light of its exploration of philosophical questions. To flesh out students' understanding of naturalism, I mention Donald Pizer's description of an ethical component of naturalism: "a compensating humanistic value in his characters or their fates which affirms the significance of the individual and his life" (11).

Responses to the informal quiz vary widely based on students' backgrounds and interests. English majors tend to focus on tension between freedom and constraint that runs throughout *The Call of the Wild* while political science majors, particularly those who have completed Middle Tennessee State University's Political Theory course, focus on specific ways that the text might engage social contract theory. Thanks to our preliminary discussion of *Discourse on the Origin and Foundations of Inequality among Men*, students are aware that Rousseau provides a descriptive account of the moral and political development of humankind and suggests that the social contract as we know it is but a construct designed to further the interests of powerful property owners. Indeed, for Rousseau, the invention of private property propels natural man out of an idyllic state of nature and into what becomes a civil society steeped in inequality. Most students note the references to civilization and to law that pepper the first few paragraphs of chapter 1, aptly titled "Into the Primitive." Judge Miller's place has the air of a feudal estate or a southern plantation; Buck is its "king," the "whole realm [is] his," and here he "live[s] the life of a sated aristocrat" (350). However, despite Buck's stature as a "king," he is also the property of his owner, the judge, and as property, he can be stolen and sold. Buck lives in a world that reflects Rousseau's concerns about private property. As London reminds us, Buck comes to the Northland "because men had found a yellow metal in the north, and because Manuel was a gardener's helper whose wages did not lap over the needs of his wife and divers small copies of himself" (364). Students also notice Judge Miller's status not only as property owner but also as a judge—an agent of the state, lawmaker, and arbiter of justice. Judge Miller's world is that of positive law, of the laws made by legislators and interpreted by judges. Thus, Buck's journey can also be viewed as a shift from the realm of positive law to that of natural law.

London's description of Buck's introduction to life in the North illuminates a connection between law, presumably a construct of civil society, and violence. Far removed from Rousseau's idea of a "natural man" who "is restrained by natural compassion from doing injury to others" (Social Contract 91), the men Buck encounters are violent and self-interested. London's description of Buck's arrival sets up several important oppositions and merits quoting in full:

> Buck's first day on the Dyea beach was like a nightmare. Every hour was filled with shock and surprise. He had been suddenly jerked from the heart of civilization and flung into the heart of things primordial. No lazy, sun-kissed life was this, with nothing to do but loaf and be bored. Here was neither peace, nor rest, nor a moment's safety. All was confusion and action, and every moment life and limb were in peril. There was imperative need to be constantly alert; for these dogs and men were not town

> dogs and men. They were savages, all of them, who knew no law but the law of club and fang. (357–58)

Tellingly, London's description echoes Hobbes's famous account of the state of nature. In *The Leviathan*, Hobbes envisions completely self-interested individuals who fight to acquire what they need to survive. Accordingly, he suggests that "the general inclination of all mankind" is "a perpetual and restless desire of power after power, that ceaseth only in death" (66). This inclination typifies man in the state of nature, where the "condition of man . . . is a condition of war of every one against every one" and "every man has a right to every thing; even to one another's body" (86–87). Thrust into an arguably Hobbesian world, Buck learns the "law of club and fang." The man in the red sweater gives Buck "his introduction into the reign of primitive law" and teaches him that "a man with a club [is] a lawgiver, a master to be obeyed, though not necessarily conciliated" (355). This passage makes explicit what is only implied in the description of Judge Miller; in the Northland, the true source of the lawgiver's power is apparent. Judicial authority, law's authority, depends on power, on the potential for violence to undergird its claims.

Often read as a bildungsroman, *The Call of the Wild* not only describes Buck's education as he learns to survive in a new environment but also elucidates the way that legal concepts are internalized and become defining features of the legal subject (Pease). The legal subject refers primarily to a version of subjectivity constructed through law, through its concepts and their normative authority. I ask students to pay close attention to Buck's experiences with each of his owners (Perrault and François; the Scotch half-breed; Hal, Charles, and Mercedes; and finally John Thornton). We spend some time simply listing key events on the board and discerning similarities and differences among the four owners. Interestingly, Buck's first two owners in the north are agents of the Canadian government's mail system and thus representatives of the state (civil society). London's descriptions of François and Perrault echo Locke's conception of rational men who consent to be governed. For Locke, the law of nature transcends empirical experience; it "obliges everyone," and "reason, which is that law, teaches all mankind who will but consult it that, being equal and independent, no one ought to harm another in his life, liberty, or possessions" (264). Similarly, François and Perrault are "fair men, calm and impartial in administering justice" (356); for example, when François punishes another dog who tries to steal Buck's food, Buck determines that he is, first and foremost, "fair" (357). However, even in this situation, Buck's life is characterized by danger and uncertainty.

Through the example of Curly's horrific death, London makes Hobbes's abstraction into a concrete particular, and Buck learns that "that was the way. No fair play. Once down, that was the end of you" (358). Buck's "decivilization" is complete when he steals meat from another dog and transgresses the laws of civil society without "moral consideration" (363). London's description of Buck's first crime of stealing food highlights the violence of this existence: "This first theft marked Buck as fit to survive in the hostile Northland environment. It marked his adaptability, his capacity to adjust himself to changing conditions, the lack of which would have meant swift and terrible death. It marked, further, the decay or going to pieces of his moral nature, a vain thing and a handicap in the ruthless struggle for existence" (363). In describing this change in Buck, London again sets the Northland's law of club and fang against the Southland's law of love and fellowship, calling our attention to the opposition of civil society and the state of nature that undergirds social contract theory and its assumptions about justice. Here, Buck may well participate in a kind of social contract with the Northland's law of club and fang reflecting "a more fundamental and primitive code" (363) inscribed and internalized through violence and justified through the language of rational deliberation. Buck also learns "poise and control" and "a certain deliberateness" in "attitude" (365). Indeed, much like his new masters, Buck is not "prone to rashness and precipitate action" (365) and "could bide his time with a patience that was nothing less than primitive" (370). In these descriptions, Buck sounds more like a judge than a dog who must fight for his very existence, and this characterization foreshadows Buck's eventual position of lawgiver.

Buck becomes a lawgiver only through conquest; to gain control of the team, he must master Spitz once and for all. Described with language reminiscent of forming a government via civil war, Buck leads an "insidious revolt" and encourages the "rebels . . . into all kinds of petty misdemeanors" (372). To counter, Spitz, also "cold and calculating" (373), attempts to quell this insurrection. In this key scene, London's descriptions of both dogs highlight their deliberateness, their ability to act not based on emotion but on a kind of deliberative process. Spitz feels rage without succumbing to "blind rage" and never forgetting "that his enemy was in like passion to rend and destroy" (374). Similarly, Buck fights "by instinct" and "by head as well" (375). When the moment of judgment comes with Buck victorious, Buck follows the law of the Northland: "Buck was inexorable. Mercy was a thing reserved for gentler climes" (375). Exacting the justice of the Northland, Buck operates much like the god of the White Silence.

Buck reflects this law as leader, and following the basic premises of social contract theory Buck claims this position of power "by right" and seems to consent to it on his own terms (376). When François and Perrault offer the leader's position to So-leks, Buck, "in open revolt" (376), refuses to be harnessed and evades François even when he threatens Buck with the dreaded club. After persuading François and Perrault, "Buck [takes] up the duties of leadership" and becomes the lawgiver for the team. Buck outshines Spitz in matters "where judgment was required," and Buck "excel[s] . . . in giving the law and making his mates live up to it" (377). For instance, Buck quickly punishes Joe for not doing his fair share of work. Here, we analyze Buck's role as a lawgiver. Once owned by a judge, Buck now hands down his own verdicts and shows no mercy as he enforces his decisions with the law of the fang.

Even as Buck takes control of the team, he learns again the tenuousness of his position. Although not exactly a slave, Buck is not entirely free. Still the property of the state, Buck and his team are transferred to a Scotch half-breed for the trip back to Dawson. Buck now has "a monotonous life, operating with machine-like regularity" but continues to take pride in his role of "seeing that his mates . . . did their fair share" (378). Worn down by hard work in the service of the state, Buck learns that he can be sold when he is, in effect, worn out. Here London may imply the failure of the state when it surrenders its subjects to the forces of capitalism and private ownership. With his new owners, "two men from the States," Buck's position most closely resembles that of a slave, and through his depiction of Charles, Hal, and Mercedes, London mounts a powerful critique of the ills of civil society (383). Charles's group represents civil society, civilization itself, yet they are arguably the least moral of Buck's owners. Ill prepared for their environment, Charles, Hal, and Mercedes are "callous to the suffering of their animals," and their ignorance of the North harms the team (390). Despite inadequate rest, poor nutrition, and owners who are unprepared and cruel, Buck tries to fulfill his duty as team leader. Pushed to his limits, Buck eventually stops even though force is used to compel him to continue: "Buck refused to move under the rain of heavier blows which now fell upon him. Like his mates, he was barely able to get up, but, unlike them, he had made up his mind not to get up" (393). London's description suggests that Buck chooses not to continue; unable to defend himself, near death, and with a bad feeling about the road ahead, Buck simply quits, and John Thornton must intervene to save his life. However, despite this apparent choice, Buck is property; as Hal asserts, "It's my dog" (393). Threatening to use force if necessary, Thornton, in essence, must steal Buck from Charles and Hal.

Arguably the most "contractual" of his relationships, Buck's tie to Thornton produces provocative class discussion. Students spend some time examining this section and considering the question of Buck's agency, a particularly complicated question for English majors who may be accustomed to reading London as an exemplary practitioner of naturalism. I ask students to consider these questions: Does Buck choose to enter a contract of sorts with Thornton? If so, what are its terms? What does it mean to consent and to use consent as a justification for authority? For social contract theorists such as Locke and Hobbes, consent justifies the outcome of the contract; put another way, when individuals freely choose the terms of the contract, that contract is presumed to be just. On the one hand, Buck's relationship with Thornton seems to reflect the notion of equivalence inherent in contractual exchanges. Thornton saves Buck's life when he takes Buck from Charles so that Buck remains behind while the rest of the team follows Charles onto thin ice to their deaths. In turn, Buck later repays Thornton by saving him from certain death in a powerful river current. Marked by such equivalent actions, their relationship moves beyond contract, in its legal sense, to a kind of "communion": "the strength of Buck's gaze would draw John Thornton's head around, and he would return the gaze, without speech, his heart singing out of his eyes as Buck's heart shone out" (396). Others recognize the depth of their bond. When Buck wins a bet, the two exchange a handshake, of sorts, so intimate that others recognize its significance and move away: "Buck seized Thornton's hand in his teeth. Thornton shook him back and forth. As though animated by a common impulse, the onlookers drew back to a respectful distance; nor were they again discreet enough to interrupt" (404). On the other hand, their relationship also raises questions about the nature of consent and its role as a justification for the justice of an agreement. In one of the most troubling and inexplicable moments in the text, Thornton asks Buck to jump off a cliff as a demonstration of his love. When Buck attempts to comply, Thornton ends up "grappling with Buck on the extreme edge, while Hans and Pete were dragging them back to safety" (398). Once safe, Thornton reacts: "[I]t is splendid, and it is terrible, too. Do you know, it sometimes makes me afraid?" (398). With its strange undercurrent of violence, this scene reveals the extent to which Buck has internalized the concept of consent. He complies with Thornton's dangerous request without pause. Here, consent masks violence and conceals the true nature of Buck's position as a legal subject.

The importance of consent is also suggested by an implied social contract that functions in the Northland. It is also during his time with Thornton that Buck encounters the law in ways that most obviously resonate with law as we know it in civil society. When Thornton attempts to stop a bar fight and gets punched for his trouble, Buck leaps to his defense, goes straight for the antagonist's throat, and has to be "forced back by an array of hostile clubs" (398). This confrontation leads to a "miners' meeting"; much like a grand jury proceeding or trial, the meeting leads to Buck's acquittal since the miners "decided the dog had sufficient provocation, and Buck was discharged" (398). A similar group forms on the spot to rule on the terms of Thornton's bet that Buck can pull a sled loaded with one thousand pounds. Once again, London's description indicates that the conflict is decided through an informal legal proceeding:

> A quibble arose concerning the phrase "break out." O'Brien contended it was Thornton's privilege to knock the runners loose, leaving Buck to "break out" from a dead standstill. Matthewson insisted that the phrase included breaking the runners from the frozen grip of the snow. A majority of the men who had witnessed the making of the bet decided in his favor. (402)

In both of these scenes, the men involved appear to consent not only to the idea of group deliberation but also to the authority of the group's findings and final decision.

A similar kind of authority infuses accounts of the Lost Mine and rumored riches, told in courtroom language: "Dying men had sworn to it, and to the mine the site of which it marked, clinching their testimony with nuggets that were unlike any known grade of gold in the Northland" (405). What is the significance of gold as evidence to buttress the "testimony" of those "dying men" who presumably possess firsthand knowledge? (405). Not only evidence, gold is also a requirement for beginning this quest, and I remind students that Buck provides the means for this quest in the first place: "When Buck earned sixteen hundred dollars in five minutes for John Thornton, he made it possible for his master to pay off certain debts and to journey with his partners into the East after a fabled lost mine" (404). With financial issues behind them, Thornton and his team go "[e]ast on an unknown trail to achieve where men and dogs as good as themselves had failed" and where "the time card was drawn upon the limitless future" (405). It is only in this mythic realm, with its "limitless future" that Buck finally shakes the chains of civil society so aptly critiqued by Rousseau.

In this mythic space, Buck is once again transformed. When the men eventually find a vein in which "the gold showed like yellow butter across the bottom of the washing pan," Buck has nothing to do and spends "long hours musing by the fire" (406). He dreams of the "hairy man" and hears "the call still sounding in the depths of the forest" (407). This call makes him "aware of wild yearning and stirrings for which he knew not what" (407). Unlike his deliberate, careful fight with Spitz, Buck's actions are now rooted in instincts; he does certain things (run with the wolves, sink his nose in the dirt, etc.) because "he [is] impelled to do them, and [does] not reason about them at all" (407). Buck becomes almost supernatural in his reactions. With this heightened awareness, Buck faces yet another major change, the death of John Thornton. Compelled by "his great love for John Thornton," Buck allows "passion to usurp cunning and reason" when he discovers that Thornton has been killed by a group of Yeehats (414). Buck attacks the Yeehats, killing all he can reach, and Buck, the lawgiver, metes out punishment.

Only after Thornton's death can Buck obey the call: "The last tie was broken. Man and the claims of man no longer bound him" (415). London's use of the word "claims" is interesting here since it suggests both individual and communal obligations defined in contractual terms. Here, London's language contains an echo of Rousseau's famous declaration, and Buck shakes off the last of the ties that bind him. We spend some time exploring this scene. Providing a counterpoint to approaches that focus on Buck as just a dog, Jonathan Auerbach claims that "London is *obsessed* with his dog-hero's moral nature and the question of 'justice'" (94). Indeed, questions about law, justice, and authority permeate the text and invite readers to step outside the usual naturalist paradigm to consider a variety of philosophical questions. What does the ending suggest about justice? Is London suggesting that revenge equals justice? That justice is violence? When Buck answers the call, he becomes the subject of myth, the Ghost Dog who avenges his loss by "stealing from their [the Yeehats] camps in fierce winters, robbing their traps, slaying their dogs, and defying their bravest hunters" (417). As an arbiter of justice, Buck becomes the ultimate lawgiver and remains elusive, mythologized through the legends that describe his power.

Read in the light of Rousseau's ideas about the social contract, London's turn to myth makes sense as a critique of assumptions about nature and civilization that undergird social contract theory and suggests that *The Call of the Wild* can be productively read as an examination of how, to paraphrase Rousseau, free men come to be in chains. By reversing the familiar trajectory of social contract theory, London complicates any sense of a clear-cut boundary between civil society and the state of nature. Instead of returning to civilization or to an idyllic state of nature, Buck seems to escape both by ascending to the realm of myth, a move that suggests that, in the real world, the social contract does not automatically provide justice or just social relations. Indeed, true justice, like Buck, becomes the subject of myth.

As we conclude our discussion, I remind students that London wrote *The Call of the Wild* shortly after his visit to London's East End to do research for *The People of the Abyss*. We look at a few passages from *The People of the Abyss* (usually from ch. 22, "Suicide") that illustrate the difficulty in moving from justice as violence or myth to real-world social justice. For instance, in *The People of the Abyss*, London describes "the machine of justice" at work in the Thames Police Court (263). As an observer, London is "half-bewildered by the amazing dispatch with which drunks, disorderlies, vagrants, brawlers, wife-beaters, thieves, fences, gamblers, and women of the street" move through the system, "in a stream as steady as the stream of sentences which fell from the magistrate's lips" (263–64). London also seems troubled by the inconsistencies of real-world justice. He uses the example of a "disgraced woman" who "doses herself and her baby with laudanum" (267). If her baby dies and she lives, she "is charged with murder, convicted, and sentenced to ten years' penal servitude" (267). In his analysis of this powerful example, London points to an interesting contradiction in the law's treatment of intentional acts. He notes that "recovering, the Law holds her responsible for her actions; yet had she died, the same Law would have rendered a verdict of temporary insanity" (267). London powerfully concludes that "such verdicts are crimes against truth. The Law is a lie, and through it men lie most shamelessly" (267). For London, real-world justice performs a kind of rhetorical violence that justifies the all too literal violence of incarceration and punishment.

Attentive to the question of justice throughout his career, London is a perfect choice for a class on law and literature, and I hope that he will eventually join Sophocles, Shakespeare, Kafka, and others as a staple of such classes. Situating *The Call of the Wild* in this rich interdisciplinary context, whether in a class on law and literature or elsewhere, will certainly lead to new insights about the text as well as to an enriched understanding of London's vast reading and its myriad influences on his work.

NOTE

[1] Citations to *The Call of the Wild* are from *The Portable Jack London*.

Teaching Jack London across the Years and around the World

Sam S. Baskett

I have variously engaged with Jack London for much of my life. I first became aware of him when my father recommended *The Call of the Wild* to me around 1935. There was a copy in our Missouri home, although he remembered reading it in *The Saturday Evening Post* in 1903. This teenage encounter fixed my attitude toward London for a long while: he wrote exciting, untaxing adventure stories for boys. *White Fang* was also at hand, and I next devoured that book. Others have been impressed by it as well, including a fatuous British aristocrat, Lord Somebody, who told Nancy Mitford that he had read only one novel in his life, *White Fang*, and it was so good he had never bothered to read another. I did pick up two or three more Alaska stories, but I began to think of myself as going beyond "boys' books." My level of reading, obviously, my intellectual/literary perceptivity, was not up to that of Simone de Beauvoir, who wrote Nelson Algren in 1947—he had recommended London—"Yes, I know Jack London. I read nearly all his books when I was a young girl and afterwards—some of them, and chiefly *Martin Eden*, I was very fond of" (de Beauvoir 54). Strange, I might have thought once, but by the time I saw her letter I had already taught *The Sea-Wolf* at a Japanese college for women.

In my college, it would not have been possible to teach London in any depth, for the Norman Foerster anthology (and, I have learned, it was typical) used in the American literature survey included only "All Gold Canyon," that wonderfully woven story with mythic dimensions, although I doubt they would have been noted even if the story was assigned. My undergraduate teachers were hardly to blame for not mentioning London. They were merely organizing the relevant course in accordance with the accepted view that London was marginal, so marginal that none of the novels were easily available. Even the groundbreaking critic Alfred Kazin, who in 1942 devoted a section of *On Native Grounds* to London, had reservations: "The greatest story he ever wrote was the story he lived" (111). Was he one of those subartists who out of the very richness of their personal experience only seem to suggest the presence of art in their work?

This was my take on Jack London, if I had one, when I began graduate study at the University of California, Berkeley, in 1946 after the war. How far London was below my literary horizon is suggested by the fact that I think he never once had come to mind during the years I had spent on the Pacific Ocean. (Actually, in 1943 I had navigated a subchaser in the wake of the *Snark* almost island by island to the Solomons without being aware of London.) I did then read *On Native Grounds* at Berkeley, thus reinforcing my understanding that in the press of all the things I *must* read, London was expendable. For Kazin is not easily dismissed as a critic. London patently does have artistic failings as well as troubling inconsistencies and contradictions; despite his shortcomings, however, he also can command the reader's attention and excite his or her sensibilities, a double point to be emphasized as the teacher introduces his work to undergraduates, a "balance," as I discuss below.

My experiences as a graduate student with Jack London, will, I believe, be of some interest to the readers of *Approaches to Teaching the Works of Jack London*, whether graduate students themselves or their professors. London was thus still almost unknown territory to me when in 1948 I began looking for a dissertation topic. A tutorial under Professor James D. Hart failed to produce one, but my exploratory papers must have indicated to him that my interests then tended toward the area that was to become American studies rather than belles lettres. For, some months later, he suggested Jack London's social fiction. Hart's impression was that London had exaggerated and distorted the California society in his supposedly realistic fiction. My elation at his unexpected aid and my relief at having a project on which to focus were immediately countered with a sinking feeling. If I knew anything about London, it was that he was beyond the academic pale. Even my mentor, in introducing his idea, had referred to London somewhat slightingly, both as a writer and as an ideologue. Still, one, given my circumstances, did not reject lightly a suggestion from the respected editor of the *Oxford Companion to American Literature*. So I said I would look into the idea.

I did know enough about London to turn first to *Martin Eden*. I related immediately to the young sailor, and, energized by the enthusiasm of the style, I raced through the story of Martin's "rise" and "fall." A year in the merchant marine on a Pacific oil tanker as an "ordinary seaman" helped, but my response was on a deeper level. T. S. Eliot once remarked of a writer he only half admired that "he enters me, but I cannot enter him." The novel worked both ways with me on that first reading, and I looked forward to plunging into the other fiction and the project I had approached so tentatively.

But immediately my enthusiasm was dampened. The American literature seminar for the term coming up was being offered by George R. Stewart, the senior Americanist. I submitted a proposal on *Martin Eden*, but, saying he thought he knew what I would find there, Stewart directed me to *John Barleycorn*. It had its vivid moments in the early chapters, but the obvious flaws were harder for me to pass over than those in *Martin Eden*. I have long since come to admire the book. Anyway, I took on the book and was later able to mine my seminar paper for "Jack London on the Oakland Waterfront" in *American Literature*, my first publication and in a sense one of the first "modern" articles to be published on London. Thus my initial approach to him, as directed by Stewart, was "biographical," although I dealt with a limited phase of London's life, and that, alas, somewhat superficially.

It would be exciting to examine this "fictive" autobiography, more thoroughly than I did even much later, in the tradition of philosophic pessimism, of William

James's ideas about the "self," whom London was reading just prior to writing the book. It could be a fascinating aspect of a course in American autobiography (read perhaps with *Martin Eden*—both are and are not autobiographies: a genre approach) along with others—a "cultural/historical" approach, perhaps in an American studies program.

The approach suggested by Hart might be termed "sociological"—as a basis for aesthetic evaluation. I suspected that my assumptions about the relation between Jack London's fictional world and the "real" world might be considered naive, an uneasiness that stayed with me as I collected all the material I could from both areas preparatory to "wiring the circuit" between them. If my assumptions were faulty, neither of my advisers ever said so—and I found nothing in critical theory to support or help me define what I was trying to do. In fact, the "New Criticism" then coming into vogue insisted on the sharp distinction between life and "art." But since I thought—and still to a degree think—of literature as reflecting life, as well as being a comment on it, I went ahead as best I could.

Decades later I have discovered two insightful studies that would have been to the point then, books that are helpful in approaching London either as a critic or as a teacher. Both are by Morris Dickstein and both affirm "semi-sociological" criticism. *The Double Agent: The Critic and Society* ensued from Dickstein's reaction in the early sixties to what he saw as a practice of deadening routine the New Critics promoted with their line-by-line explication and his belief that the critic in approaching literature must take society into account. *Mirror in the Roadway: Literature and the Real World*, a collection of essays, explores and largely accepts the assumption that literature, especially fiction, is "unapologetically about the life we live outside of literature," referring in particular to early-twentieth-century American writers that modernism "put out of fashion" (1).

One of the essays, "Damaged Literacy," is especially valuable for its wide applicability to teaching *any* fiction. Dickstein calls for a "better balance" between the professional's "hermeneutics of suspicion" and the "ordinary reader's" first reaction of "wonder and surprise" that fiction may elicit (227). If we set aside the question of just how "ordinary" the undergraduate is, we can agree that his or her level is presumably below that of the professional. And considering London's weaknesses, manifest at times to even the most dedicated of readers, and the undoubted "wonder and surprise" he has afforded so many readers of different degrees of literary sophistication, Dickstein's admonition—and he is a distinguished "professional" himself—would seem to have particular relevance to approaching London with undergraduates.

And indeed it is well to be aware of this problem in teaching London's "social" writings, either fiction (*The Iron Heel*, "The Mexican," "Strength of the Strong") or nonfiction (his essays of social protest, *The People of the Abyss*). Let me cite two recent experiences with that book. Now in academic retirement and living part-time in the city of London, I was interviewed in my home for over two hours about London generally and that book especially, the scathing sympathetic report on early-twentieth-century conditions in the East End. Having apparently just developed an enthusiasm for *The People of the Abyss*, my interviewer wanted material to use in introducing London to the "ordinary" BBC Radio 4 audience. I thought I gave the author's favorite of his works its balanced due, which included noting Robert Peluso's "suspicions" that London's undoubted sympathy for the poor so affectingly presented in the book is countered by an underlying note of American exceptionalism. None of this was used on the broadcast, perhaps wisely, considering its mission. But the audience was given a heartwarming rather than a balanced view of the book and its author. Likewise, a few years ago *Socialism Today*, the organ of the Old Labour Party, requested an article that became my "Jack London's Call of Socialism," but, again, no "hermeneutics of suspicion" were wanted. The classroom teacher, who might well be presenting some of the works mentioned above (there are many other possibilities) in an American studies or popular culture program, is ideally in a position to maintain a better "balance."

I'll turn now more specifically to my classroom experiences with London, except that for years after I began teaching there was *no* experience. He was not included in the anthology used in the college where I first taught, nor in any anthologies of the time, as Paul Lauter has noted. As for the novels, none were included in the department reading lists for the relevant courses—indeed, there was not much in print to list. To that end—and, of course, to make further use of the work I had done—I wrote some fifty English departments asking what of London, if anything, they taught or would like to teach; and out of a range of answers I was able to craft a letter to Rinehart that led, in 1956, to *Martin Eden* as number 80 in that series, with my general introduction.

With the edition available, and now teaching at Michigan State, where I could choose the texts for my section of the American Realism and Naturalism course, I assigned it. I found *Martin Eden* the best introduction to London even after other texts, such as *The Sea-Wolf*, were available, although I did refer to the other works I considered significant in giving London as full treatment as the time allowed, as I did all the realistic and naturalistic writers included.

This pretty much constituted my teaching London on the undergraduate level. In my graduate course dealing with the same literary period, which I taught frequently over the years, I came to use *The Education of Henry Adams* as a base from which to consider a range of novels, allowing the students to choose their own text to work on for class reports and an extensive final paper discussing their particular novels—I arranged for all to be covered—in relation to Adams's "education." I always included a work (or works) by London. I lectured on *The Education* in depth, also considering it as "autobiography," and brought *Martin Eden* and *John Barleycorn* to bear on this aspect. In the reports and in the class discussions stemming from them, and, especially from the term papers, I learned a great deal from students, particularly James McClintock, whose *White Logic* was a development of work begun in the course and continued in a tutorial. He was soon his own best director, however.

By the time Earle Labor, whose contribution to the revived interest in Jack London studies cannot be overestimated (along with that of Jeanne Reesman), asked me for a paper for the Jack London issue of *Modern Fiction Studies* in 1976, my approach was beginning to include more emphasis on close reading roughly at the time Dickstein was finding it "deadening." But London, as he claimed, did "weave" his works.

Although my teaching for the reasons I have indicated mainly focused on *Martin Eden*, I continued to rethink various other works more carefully than before, and I was drawn to connections between London and other major writers, comparisons that enhanced my appreciation of his grappling with profound questions, the motifs of his fiction. As a result of my graduate course I found it not just possible but illuminating to compare Martin and the Henry Adams persona in *The Education* with another aspect of Martin's characterization that evokes Fitzgerald's Gatsby. Despite Martin and Henry's profound differences, they both make parallel attempts at "running order through chaos," as Adams described the purpose of his "education." Joseph Conrad's "Youth" and *The Heart of Darkness* took me further into Martin and the Jack London of *John Barleycorn* than I had managed before. It took courage—some might suggest a different word—to present an MLA paper, "The Drunken Boat: Jack London's Romantic Imagination," but I found that the "wild" juxtaposition of London and Rimbaud stimulated me to think about London's "Romanticism." There are obvious connections with Herman Melville on a superficial level, but more profoundly there are suggestions in London of the elusive complications of the Romantic self, noted by Andrew Delbanco in his recent study of Melville, in the Romantic duality of Martin and his author and in the early and late personae of *John Barleycorn*—the Adamic quality coupled with the awareness of "the power of blackness" (Melville 243; Levin). Youth and age? Possibly more than that. I am not necessarily suggesting such courses for undergraduates, but, for me, developing these perhaps eccentric and unequal comparisons had led to a deeper consideration of London's scope and artistry and informed my treatment in the classes I did teach.

In the process of all this, I began to consider London more in terms of aesthetics, his wavering in different works (although I remain more interested in his ideas) and even in the same works between what Frank Lentricchia termed the nineteenth-century "idealistic" (romantic) and "secretarial" (naturalistic) imaginations with London taking sometimes optimistic, sometimes pessimistic stances in each mode (8, 20). Using such texts as *Martin Eden*, *The Call of the Wild*, "Bâtard," and one of the South Seas stories might be a rewarding way of getting at his aesthetic suppositions as he attempts to see into an ideal beauty and also into a universe of evil, grappling as always with the nature and value of life.

In partial retirement by the late eighties, I taught on a Semester at Sea program tied in with the University of Pittsburgh on a round-the-world voyage from Vancouver to Florida. My course was Novels of the World. As we traversed the North Pacific on the way to Japan, *The Sea-Wolf* indeed seemed appropriate. In a rough sea, I conducted class with an arm around a stanchion for support. My surprise was that women in the class disagreed with the usual view of the Maud Brewster aspect as a mawkish distraction. I challenged them to write a paper defending it, and I was convinced enough to try the book the next year in a womens' college in Kobe, Japan, and they were even more taken with that aspect of the story. This led to my brief foray into gender criticism in "Sea Change in *The Sea-Wolf*."

During the course of my career, I have taught London not only in Japan but also in Mexico, Turkey, and Great Britain, teaching short stories as well as *Martin Eden*, *The Sea-Wolf*, and *The Call of the Wild*, invariably finding the students receptive. Geographically, in my experience, Jack London knows no bounds.

These were not American students, of course, but teaching London abroad gave me another related idea for a somewhat different approach that might work well at home: a "geographic" approach to teaching London. A few years ago I attended a conference in Svedberg, Denmark, on the use of "place" in contemporary literature. Thus I was unable to give a paper on London, but the papers were very provocative, as was the study by Frederick Turner I then learned of, discussing the relation of various American writers to their geographic places.

Remembering London's travels and his fictional use of his knowledge of so many places in different parts of the world—and, of course, my own experience of different "geographies"— I would find it exciting and, I think, illuminating to take such an approach in a specific study involved in a course, or leading perhaps to one. Place in London's works has been examined before, but I'm thinking of a sharper focus in an undergraduate class (perhaps in American studies?). To what extent does London evoke the spirit of the place, as D. H. Lawrence does so tellingly in his *Studies in Classic American Literature*? A reviewer of Delbanco's Melville book that I mention above comments that the author relates Melville's biography with the occasions imagined in his writings (Grimes). For "occasion," read—or perhaps add—"place." Instead, he concentrates on placing the fiction in historical and political context, and, through a series of imaginative leaps, on making connections between Melville's works and the circumstances surrounding their creation.

NOTES ON CONTRIBUTORS

The late **Sam S. Baskett** who died in 2013, was the former longtime chair of the English department at Michigan State University and a prolific scholar and critic. Baskett's dissertation at the University of California, Berkeley, on Jack London in 1960 was among the first ever, and his 1956 edition of *Martin Eden* from Rinehart, with its brilliant introduction, brought London newly into focus among readers in general and the literary critics in particular. Sam was the first president of the Jack London Society when it was founded in 1990. He later contributed leading work in London's themes of androgyny.

Kenneth K. Brandt is professor of English at the Savannah College of Art and Design. He is the executive coordinator of the Jack London Society, the editor of *The Call: The Magazine of the Jack London Society*, and has published articles on Charles Bukowski, Ernest Hemingway, Robinson Jeffers, Jack London, Cormac McCarthy, and Joyce Carol Oates. His forthcoming book is *Jack London: Writers and Their Work*.

Donna M. Campbell is associate professor of English at Washington State University. She is the author of *Resisting Regionalism: Gender and Naturalism in American Fiction, 1885–1915*, and her articles on Jack London have appeared in *Studies in American Naturalism*, *Literature and Belief*, *Jack London: One Hundred Years a Writer*, *The Call*, and *Jack London: Critical Insights*. Her recent work on naturalism and regionalism has appeared in *The Cambridge History of the American Novel*, *The Oxford Handbook of American Literary Naturalism*, *A Companion to Regional Literatures of the United States*, and *American Literary Realism*. Her current book project is called "*Bitter Tastes: Naturalism, Early Film, and American Women's Writing*."

Shannon Cotrell teaches English and writing at Juniata College. He is primarily interested in literary naturalism, travel narratives, and other literature that calls attention to the experience of place.

María DeGuzmán is professor of English and comparative literature and founding director of Latina/o Studies at the University of North Carolina, Chapel Hill. She is the author of two books: *Spain's Long Shadow: The Black Legend, Off-Whiteness, and Anglo-American Empire* and *Buenas Noches, American Culture: Latina/o Aesthetics of Night*. She has published articles on Latina/o cultural production, and she writes and teaches about relationships between literature and various kinds of photographic practice. She is also a conceptual photographer who has published essays and photo stories involving her photography. Most recently she has teamed up with the visual artist Janet Cooling and is composing original music.

Robert M. Dowling is professor of English at Central Connecticut State University and serves on the editorial board of *The Eugene O'Neill Review* and the board of directors of the Eugene O'Neill Society. His previous books include *Slumming in New York: From the Waterfront to Mythic Harlem*, the two-volume *Critical Companion to Eugene O'Neill*, and *Eugene O'Neill and His Early Contemporaries: Bohemians, Radicals, Progressives, and the Avant Garde* (coedited with Eileen Herrmann). Dowling is the author of "'Sad Endings and Negative Heroes': The Naturalist Tradition in American Drama"

(*The Oxford Handbook to American Literary Naturalism*, 2011), and his latest projects include a compendium of O'Neill's opening night reviews, *Eugene O'Neill: The Contemporary Reviews* (coedited with Jackson R. Bryer), and his biography *Eugene O'Neill: A Life in Four Acts*.

Anita Duneer is associate professor of English at Rhode Island College, where she teaches American and postcolonial literatures. She is at work on a book about Jack London and the sea, which merges interests in maritime literature and literary naturalism. Her recent publications include the essay "Jack London's Seafaring Women" in *Studies in American Naturalism* and an article forthcoming in *American Literary Realism* entitled "Crafting the Sea," which reads London's *Martin Eden* as a novel of the sea.

The late **Andrew J. Furer** received his PhD from Harvard University and taught there and at Fordham University for many years, presenting exciting seminars on naturalism, Jack London, and the American "new woman." He is the author of numerous significant publications on Jack London, including essays on London and race. His obituary appeared in the *New York Times* on November 3, 2010. He introduced Earle Labor to Anna Walling Hamburger, the daughter of Anna Strunsky, and they interviewed her together on Cape Cod on 11 July 1995.

Sara S. Hodson is the curator of literary manuscripts for the Huntington Library. She has spoken and published widely on literary and archival topics, especially privacy and confidentiality in modern manuscript collections. She received the Lifetime Achievement Award from the Society of California Archivists, and in 2004 she was elected a Fellow of the Society of American Archivists. She was named Woman of the Year in 2012 by the Jack London Foundation. She has edited *Jack London: One Hundred Years a Writer* with Jeanne Campbell Reesman. Their book, *Jack London, Photographer* was edited with Philip Adam. Her recent essay, "The People of the Abyss: Tensions and Tenements in the Capital of Poverty," will appear in *The Oxford Handbook to Jack London*.

Jeff Jaeckle is the editor of *Film Dialogue* and the coeditor of *ReFocus: The Films of Preston Sturges*. His scholarship on cinema and literature has also appeared in *Film Quarterly*, *New Review of Film and Television Studies*, *Quarterly Review of Film and Video*, and *The Oxford Handbook of American Literary Naturalism*. He teaches at Portland Community College.

Earle Labor, emeritus professor of American literature and director of the Jack London Research Center at Centenary College of Louisiana, has been called "the internationally recognized maestro of Jack London studies." During the past half century he has published more than one hundred articles, reviews, and short pieces as well as nine books on London, including the three-volume Stanford Editions of *The Letters of Jack London* and *The Complete Short Stories of Jack London*, edited by Robert C. Leitz and I. Milo Shepard. In 1966, as a visiting professor at Utah State University, he taught the first course on Jack London ever offered in the United States; in 1974, as a Fulbright Professor at the University of Aarhus, Denmark, he presented the first Jack London course in Western Europe. His *Jack London* in the Twayne United States Authors Series (1974), revised with Jeanne Campbell Reesman as coauthor (1994), was the first book-length critical biography of London's career. His *Jack London: An American Life in Letters* won the Western Writers of America's 2014 Spur Award for Best Western Nonfiction Biography.

Paul Lauter is Allan K. and Gwendolyn Miles Smith Professor of Literature (emeritus) at Trinity College (Hartford). He remains general editor of the groundbreaking *Heath Anthology of American Literature*, now in its seventh edition. Lauter is also coeditor of the *Oxford On-Line Bibliography of American Literature*. His most recent book is *From Walden Pond to Jurassic Park*. He is working on a study of the impact of sixties activism on current culture and education.

The late **Debbie López** was associate professor of English at the University of Texas, San Antonio, where she was MA in English Graduate Advisor of Record and a much-beloved teacher until her death on 14 October 2011. She received her PhD from Harvard University under the direction of Sacvan Bercovitch. She also taught at the University of Alabama. She was the author of numerous essays on Jack London, and at her death was at work on her book on Anglo-American literature, covering Keats, Melville, and Hawthorne.

Michael Lundblad is associate professor in the Department of Literature, Area Studies, and European Languages (ILOS) at the University of Oslo in Norway. He is the author of *The Birth of a Jungle: Animality in Progressive-Era U.S. Literature and Culture*, the coeditor of *Species Matters: Humane Advocacy and Cultural Theory*, and the editor of the forthcoming "Animalities: Literary and Cultural Studies Beyond the Human."

Barry Menikoff is professor emeritus of English and American literature at the University of Hawai'i. A book on Robert Louis Stevenson is forthcoming from the Huntington Library Press. He is currently writing a memoir of his Brooklyn years.

Keith Newlin is professor of English at the University of North Carolina, Wilmington. The author or editor of fifteen books, recent volumes include *Hamlin Garland, A Life* and, as editor, *Garland in His Own Time*, *The Oxford Handbook of American Literary Naturalism*, *A Summer to Be: A Memoir by the Daughter of Hamlin Garland*, and *A Theodore Dreiser Encyclopedia*. At present he is the coeditor of *Studies in American Naturalism*, distributed by the University of Nebraska Press.

Jeanne Campbell Reesman is professor of English and Jack and Laura Richmond Endowed Fellow in American Literature at the University of Texas, San Antonio. She has served there as graduate director of the PhD in English; division director of English, classics, philosophy, and communication; and graduate dean. She is the author of numerous books and articles on Jack London, including most recently *Jack London's Racial Lives* and, with Sara. S. Hodson, *Jack London, Photographer*. She is at work on her latest book, "Mark Twain vs. God: The Story of a Relationship." She has served as a Fulbright Professor in Greece (2007) and France (2010).

Terry Reilly is professor of English at the University of Alaska, Fairbanks, where he teaches Shakespeare, early modern English and European literature, surveys of modern world literature, and composition. He has published a number of articles on early modern English literature and law, as well as on the works of Chaucer, Conrad, Joyce, Goethe, T. E. Lawrence, Thomas Pynchon, and Doris Lessing. He is currently working on a book-length project titled "Lobotomy and Postmodern Discourse: The Interplay of Neuroscience and Literature in American and British Cultures, 1935–1962."

Alicia Mischa Renfroe is an associate professor of English at Middle Tennessee State University, where she teaches courses in law and literature and American literature.

She has published work on Davis, Alcott, Wharton, Sinclair, Howells, Hemingway, and others.

Gina M. Rossetti is an associate professor of English at Saint Xavier University in Chicago, Illinois. Her pedagogical and scholarly interests center on antebellum American literature through the 1920s, with particular focus on American literary naturalism and Jack London's fiction. Her recent scholarly work has appeared in *Studies in American Naturalism*, *The Journal of the Short Story in English / Les Cahiers de la Nouvelle*, *The Oxford Handbook to American Literary Naturalism*, as well as in her own book, *Imagining the Primitive in Naturalist and Modernist Literature*. At present, she is at work on a book project that examines London's selected fiction in terms of race and class.

Aaron Shaheen is UC Foundation Associate Professor of English at the University of Tennessee, Chattanooga, where he teaches courses in American literature of the late nineteenth and early twentieth centuries. He has published articles in numerous journals, including *PMLA*, *Texas Studies in Literature and Language*, and *American Literary Realism*. He is also the author of the monograph *Androgynous Democracy: Modern American Literature and the Dual-Sexed Body Politic*. At present he is working on a book-length study on the role of prosthesis in American literature and culture of the post–World War I era.

Jay Williams is senior managing editor of *Critical Inquiry*. He published and edited the *Jack London Journal* (1994–2001), edited *Signature Derrida*, and published essays on Jack London, Sinclair Lewis, and the Grateful Dead. *Author under Sail: The Imagination of Jack London, 1893–1902*, the first of two volumes, came out in 2014.

SURVEY PARTICIPANTS

Sam S. Baskett, *Michigan State University*
Lawrence I. Berkove, *University of Michigan, Dearborn*
Hal Blythe, *Eastern Kentucky University*
Kenneth K. Brandt, *Savannah College of Art and Design*
Donna M. Campbell, *Washington State University*
Patrick Chura, *University of Akron*
Shannon Cotrell, *University of Connecticut*
María DeGuzmán, *University of North Carolina, Chapel Hill*
Patrick Dooley, *St. Bonaventure University*
Robert M. Dowling, *Central Connecticut State University*
Anita Duneer, *Rhode Island College*
Andrew J. Furer, *Fordham University*
G. Galbayar, *National University of Mongolia*
Sara S. Hodson, *Huntington Library*
Jeff Jaeckle, *Michigan State University*
Holger Kersten, *University of Magdeburg, Germany*
Earle Labor, *Centenary College of Louisiana*
Paul Lauter, *Trinity College*
Debbie López, *University of Texas at San Antonio*
Jessica Greening Loudermilk, *University of California, Davis*
Michael Lundblad, *Colorado State University*
Takaharu Mori, *International University of Kagoshima, Japan*
Yumjir Munkh-Amgalan, *National University of Mongolia*
Keith Newlin, *University of North Carolina, Wilmington*
Susan Nuernberg, *University of Wisconsin, Oshkosh*
Jeanne Campbell Reesman, *University of Texas, San Antonio*
Terry Reilly, *University of Alaska, Fairbanks*
Alicia Mischa Renfroe, *Middle Tennessee State University*
Gary Riedl, *Wayzata High School*
Marinelle Ringer, *Philander Smith College*
Gina M. Rossetti, *Saint Xavier University*
Aaron Shaheen, *University of Tennessee, Chattanooga*
Reinaldo Francisco Silva, *University of Aveiro, Portugal*
Charlie Sweet, *Eastern Kentucky University*
Thomas Tietze, *Wayzata High School*
Eiji Tsujii, *Ritsumeikan University, Japan*
Jeff Turpin, *University of Texas, San Antonio*
Charles N. Watson, Jr., *Syracuse University*
Jay Williams, *Critical Inquiry*

WORKS CITED

Acosta, Oscar "Zeta." "Teleplay: The Catalina Papers." *Oscar "Zeta" Acosta: The Uncollected Works*. Ed. Ilan Stavans. Houston: Arte Público, 1996. 255. Print.

Alger, Horatio, Jr. *Ragged Dick and Struggling Upward*. Rpt. Penguin: New York, 1985. Print.

Auerbach, Jonathan. Introduction. *Northland Stories by Jack London*. Ed. Auerbach. Harmondsworth: Penguin, 1997. vii–xxiii.

———. *Male Call: Becoming Jack London*. Durham: Duke UP, 1996. Print.

Bacon, Francis. *Essays*. *Project Gutenburg*. Project Gutenburg, 2013. Web. 21 Oct. 2014.

Baskett, Sam S. "Jack London's Call of Socialism." *Socialism Today* 10 (1996): 25–28. Print.

———. "Jack London's Heart of Darkness." *American Quarterly* 10.1 (1958): 66–77. Rpt. in Berkove, *Critical Insights* 151–66.

———. "Jack London 'in the Midst of It All.'" Hodson and Reesman 123–46.

———. "Sea Change in *The Sea-Wolf*." Cassuto and Reesman 92–109.

Bate, W. Jackson. *John Keats*. Cambridge: Belknap–Harvard UP, 1963. Print.

Baym, Nina, Jeanne Campbell Reesman, and Arnold Krupat, eds. *The Norton Anthology of American Literature*. 7th ed. Vol. C. New York: Norton, 2007. Print.

Beauvoir, Simone de, and Nelson Algren. *A Transatlantic Love Affair: Letters to Nelson Algren*. New York: New, 1998. Print.

Bedwell, Laura. "Jack London's 'Samuel' and the Abstract Shrine of Truth." *Studies in American Naturalism* 2.2 (2007): 150–65. Print.

Bender, Bert. *The Descent of Love: Darwin and the Theory of Sexual Selection in American Fiction, 1871–1926*. Philadelphia: U of Pennsylvania P, 1996. Print.

———. *Evolution and 'the Sex Problem': American Narratives During the Eclipse of Darwinism*. Kent: Kent State UP, 2004. Print.

———. "Jack London and 'the Sex Problem." Hodson and Reesman 147–188.

Berkove, Lawrence I. "*Before Adam* and *The Scarlet Plague*: Two Novels of Evolution by Jack London." *ALN: The American Literary Naturalism Newsletter* 2.1 (2007): 13–16. Print.

———, ed. *Critical Insights: Jack London*. Pasadena: Salem, 2011. Print.

———. "Jack London and Evolution: From Spencer to Huxley." *American Literary Realism* 36 (2004): 243–55. Print.

———. "Jack London's 'Second Thoughts': The Short Fiction of His Late Period." Hodson and Reesman 60–76.

———. "On Jack London: Darwinism and the Evolution of Jack London." Berkove, *Critical Insights* 3–24.

———. "Thomas Stevens: London's Comic Agent of Evolutionary Criticism." *Thalia* 12.1–2 (1992): 61–68. Print.

Best of Jack London: Short Stories. Dir. Larry Albert. Topics, 2001. CD.

Bird, Isabella L. *The Hawaiian Archipelago: Six Months among the Palm Groves, Coral Reefs, and Volcanoes of the Sandwich Islands*. London: J. Murray, 1875. Print.

Black, Joseph, et al., eds. "Algernon Charles Swinburne." *The Broadview Anthology of British Literature: The Victorian Era*. 2nd ed. Peterborough: Broadview, 2012. 614–15. Print.

"The Boy Socialist." *The* San Francisco Chronicle *Reader*. Ed. William Hogan and William German. Boston: Little, 1962. 171–72. Print.

Brandt, Kenneth K. "Love in the Time of Darwinism: Dialectical Approximations in Jack London's *Martin Eden*." Berkove, *Critical Insights* 41–57.

Braudy, Leo. *The Frenzy of Renown: Fame and Its History*. 1986. New York: Vintage, 1997. Print.

Brooks, Cleanth. "Jack London (1876–1916.)" Brooks, Lewis, and Warren 2: 1632–34.

Brooks, Cleanth, R. W. B. Lewis, and Robert Penn Warren, eds. *American Literature: The Makers and the Making*. 2 vols. New York: St. Martin's, 1973. Print.

Buell, Lawrence. *The Environmental Imagination: Thoreau Nature Writing, and the Formation of American Culture*. Cambridge: Belknap–Harvard UP, 1995. Print.

Burroughs, John. "Real and Sham Natural History." *Atlantic Monthly* 91 (March 1903): 298–309. Rpt. in *The Wild Animal Story*. Ed. Ralph H. Lutts. Philadelphia: Temple UP, 1998. 129–43. Print.

Butler, Judith. *Bodies That Matter: On the Discursive Limits of Sex*. New York: Routledge, 1993. Print.

———. "Performative Acts and Gender Constitution: An Essay in Phenomenology and Feminist Theory." *Theatre Journal* 40.4 (1988): 519–31. *JSTOR*. Web. 3 Sept. 2010.

Calarco, Matthew, and Peter Atterton, eds. *Animal Philosophy: Essential Readings in Continental Thought*. London: Continuum, 2004. Print.

The Call of the Wild. Dir. Ken Annakin. Perf. Charlton Heston and Michèle Mercier. 1972. Metro-Goldwyn Mayer, 1997. DVD.

The Call of the Wild. Dir. Peter Svatek. Perf. Rutger Hauer, Richard Dreyfuss. Hallmark Home Entertainment, 1997. VHS.

The Call of the Wild. Dir. William Wellman. Perf. Clark Gable, Loretta Young. 1935. Twentieth-Century Fox, 2006. DVD.

Campbell, Donna M. "'The (American) Muse's Tragedy': Jack London, Edith Wharton, and *The Little Lady of the Big House*." Hodson and Reesman 189–216.

———. "The Critical Reception of Jack London." Berkove, *Critical Insights* 96–115.

———, ed. *Literary Movements*. Washington State U, n.d. Web. 20 July 2014.

Campbell, Jeanne. "'Falling Stars': Myth in 'The Red One.'" *Jack London Newsletter* 11.2–3 (1978): 87–101. Print.

Campbell, Joseph. *The Hero with a Thousand Faces*. 2nd ed. Princeton: Princeton UP, 1968. Print. Bollingen Ser.

———. *The Power of Myth*. With Bill Moyers. Ed. Betty Sue Flowers. New York: Doubleday, 1988. Print.

Cassuto, Leonard, and Jeanne Campbell Reesman, eds. *Rereading Jack London*. Stanford: Stanford UP, 1996. Print.

Chauncey, George. *Gay New York: Gender, Urban Culture, and the Makings of the Gay Male World, 1890–1940*. New York: Basic, 1994. Print.

Chesnutt, Charles W. *"The Wife of His Youth" and Other Stories of the Color Line*. 1899. Introd. Earl Schenck Miers. Ann Arbor: U of Michigan P, 1998. Print.

Cirlot, J. E. *A Dictionary of Symbols*. Trans. Jack Sage. Fwd. Herbert Read. 2nd ed. New York: Philosophical Lib., 1971. Print.

Conrad, Joseph. "To Ernst Bendz [Letter of March 7, 1923]." *Joseph Conrad: Life and Letters*. Vol. 2. Garden City: Doubleday, 1927. 295–96. Print.

Crane, Stephen. *The Open Boat and Other Tales of Adventure*. New York: Doubleday, 1898. 1–64. Print.

Crow, Charles. "Homecoming in the California Visionary Romance." *Western American Literature* 24.1 (1989): 1–19. Print.

———. "Jack London's 'Samuel' as Gothic Tale: The Terrible and Tragic Involved with Love." *Litteraria Pragensia: Studies in Literature and Culture* 11.21 (2001): 81–87. Print.

Curtis, Gary N. "Appeal to Nature." *Fallacy Files*. N.p., 2001. Web. 15 July 2009. <http://www.fallacyfiles.org/adnature.html>.

Davidson, Cathy N., and Jessamyn Hatcher, eds. *No More Separate Spheres! A Next Wave American Studies Reader*. Durham: Duke UP, 2002. Print.

DeGuzmán, María, and Debbie López. "Algebra of Twisted Figures: Transvaluation in *Martin Eden*." Hodson and Reesman 98–122.

Delbanco, Andrew. *Melville: His World and Work*. New York: Knopf, 2005. Print.

Dennett, Daniel C. *Darwin's Dangerous Idea*. New York: Simon, 1996. Print.

Derrida, Jacques. *The Animal That Therefore I Am*. Ed. Marie-Louise Mallet. Trans. David Wills. New York: Fordham UP, 2008. Print.

———. *Specters of Marx: The State of the Debt, the Work of Mourning, and the New International*. Trans. Peggy Kamuf. New York: Routledge, 1994.

Desmond, Adrian, and James Moore. *Darwin*. London: Penguin, 1991. Print.

Dickstein, Morris. *Mirror in the Roadway: Literature and the Real World*. Princeton: Princeton UP, 2007. Print.

Dillingham, William B. *Frank Norris: Instinct and Art*. Lincoln: U of Nebraska P, 1969. Print.

Dooley, Patrick K. *A Community of Inquiry: Conversations between Classical American Philosophy and American Literature*. Kent: Kent State UP, 2008. Print.

Dowling, Robert M. *Slumming in New York: From the Waterfront to Mythic Harlem*. Champaign: U of Illinois P, 2007. Print.

Duntley, Joshua D., and Todd K. Shackelford. "Introduction and Overview." *Evolutionary Forensic Psychology: Darwinian Foundations of Crime and Law*. Ed. Duntley and Shackelford. New York: Oxford UP, 2008. 3–19. Print.

Dyer, Daniel. *Jack London: A Biography*. New York: Scholastic, 1997. Print.

———. *Jack London's* The Call of the Wild *for Teachers*. Norman: U of Oklahoma P, 1997. Print.

Eco, Umberto. *The Role of the Reader: Explorations in the Semiotics of Texts*. Bloomington: U of Indiana P, 1979. Advances in Semiotics Ser.

Education in the Balance: A Report on the Academic Workforce in English. *Modern Language Association*. MLA, 2008. Web. 21 Jan. 2014.

Edmond, Rod. *Representing the South Pacific: Colonial Discourse from Cook to Gauguin*. Cambridge: Cambridge UP, 1997. Print.

"An Elemental Maid." 1903. Nuernberg, *Critical Response* 40–41.

Emerson, Ralph Waldo. "Self-Reliance." *Essays: First Series*. New York: Crowell, 1891. 32–68. Print.

Fanon, Frantz. *The Wretched of the Earth*. Pref. Jean-Paul Sartre. Trans. Constance Farrington. New York: Grove, 1963. Print.

Far, Sui Sin (Edith Maude Eaton). "Mrs. Spring Fragrance." 1910/1912. *"Mrs. Spring Fragrance" and Other Writings*. Ed. Amy Ling and Annette White-Parks. Urbana: U of Illinois P, 1995. 17–41. Print.

Farmer, Philip José, ed. *Mother Was a Lovely Beast*. Radnor: Chilton, 1974. Print.

Ferguson, Lillian. "California Girl's Wild Ghost Dance." *Sunday* [San Francisco] *Examiner* 15 July 1900. Print. Huntington Lib. JL 1306.

Fiedler, Leslie. *Love and Death in the American Novel*. 1960. New York: Stein, 1966. Print.

Foner, Philip. *Jack London: American Rebel—A Collection of His Social Writings Together with an Extensive Study of the Man and His Times*. New York: Citadel P, 1947.

———. ed. "Jack London: American Rebel." *The Social Writings of Jack London*. Ed. Foner. Secaucus: Citadel P, 1964. 26. Print.

Fromm, Harold. "From Transcendence to Obsolescence: A Route Map." *The Ecocriticism Reader*. Ed. Cheryll Glotfelty and Fromm. Athens: U of Georgia P, 1996. 30–39. Print.

Furer, Andrew J. "Jack London's New Woman: A Little Lady with a Big Stick." *Studies in American Fiction* 22.2 (1994): 185–214. Print.

Fusco, Richard. "On Primitivism in *The Call of the Wild*." *American Literary Realism* 20.1 (1987): 76–80. Print.

Gair, Christopher. *Complicity and Resistance in Jack London's Novels: From Naturalism to Nature*. Lewiston: Mellen, 1997. Print.

———. "Hegemony, Metaphor, and Structural Difference: The 'Strange Dualism' of 'South of the Slot.'" *Arizona Quarterly* 49 (1993): 73–97. Print.

Geismar, Maxwell. *Rebels and Ancestors: The American Novel, 1890–1915*. Boston: Houghton, 1953. Print.

Giles, David. "The Quest for Fame." *The Celebrity Culture Reader*. Ed. P. David Marshall. New York: Routledge, 2006. 470–86. Print.

Gilman, Charlotte Perkins. *Women and Economics: A Study of the Relation between Women and Men*. Ed. Carl N. Degler. New York: Harper, 1966. Print.

Gissing, George. *New Grub Street*. 1891. *Project Gutenberg*. Project Gutenberg, 2013. Web. 21 Oct. 2014.

Gould, Charles. *America: A Family Matter*. New York: Scribner's, 1922. Print.

Great Writers: Jack London. Kultur Films, 2001.

Grimes, William. "Melville: His World and Work." *The New York Times*. New York Times, 5 Oct. 2005. Web. 8 Sept. 2014.

Guerin, Wilfred L., et al. *A Handbook of Critical Approaches to Literature*. 5th ed. New York: Oxford UP, 2005. Print.

Gutkind, Lee. *The Art of Creative Nonfiction: Writing and Selling the Literature of Reality*. New York: Wiley, 1997. Print.

Haley, James M. *Wolf: The Lives of Jack London*. New York: Basic, 2010. Print.

Hamilton, David Mike. *"The Tools of My Trade": The Annotated Books in Jack London's Library*. Seattle: U of Washington P, 1986. Print.

Haraway, Donna J. *When Species Meet*. Minneapolis: U of Minnesota P, 2008. Print.

Haughey, Homer L., and Connie Kale Johnson. *Jack London Homes Album*. Stockton: Heritage, 1987. Print.

———. *Jack London Ranch Album*. Stockton: Heritage, 1985. Print.

Hayes, Gregory W., and Matt Atkinson. *Jack London's Wolf House*. Glen Ellen: Valley of the Moon Natural History Assn., 2010. Print.

Hedrick, Joan D. *Solitary Comrade: Jack London and His Work*. Chapel Hill: U of North Carolina P, 1982. Print.

Hendricks, King. Letter to Earle Labor. 25 Sept. 1965. TS.

Hensley, Dennis E. "Jack London's Use of the Linguistic Style of the King James Bible." *Jack London Echoes* 3 (1983): 4–11. Print.

Heston, Charlton. Interview by Joan Rivers. *The Late Show Starring Joan Rivers*. 3 Nov. 1986. Television.

Hobbes, Thomas. *The Leviathan*. 1651. Ed. and introd. J. C. A. Gaskin. Oxford: Oxford UP, 1996. Print.

Hodson, Sara S. Message to Kenneth K. Brandt. 6 Feb. 2015. E-mail.

Hodson, Sara S., and Jeanne Campbell Reesman, eds. *Jack London: One Hundred Years a Writer*. San Marino: Huntington, 2002. Print.

Hofstadter, Richard. *Social Darwinism in American Thought*. 1944. Boston: Beacon, 1992. Print.

———. *Social Darwinism in American Thought*. Rev. ed. Boston: Beacon, 1955. Print.

Homberger, Eric. *American Writers and Radical Politics, 1900–39: Equivocal Commitments*. New York: St. Martin's, 1986. Print.

Horkheimer, Max, and Theodor Adorno. *The Dialectic of Enlightenment: Philosophical Fragments*. Ed. Gunzelin Schmid Noerr. Trans. Edmund Jephcott. Stanford: Stanford UP, 2002. Print.

Howard, June. *Form and History in American Literary Naturalism*. Chapel Hill: U of North Carolina P, 1985. Print.

Huxley, Thomas Henry. "Evolution and Ethics." Appleman 501–03.

Jack London. Dir. Alfred Santell. Perf. Michael O'Shea, Susan Hayward. United American Video, 1943. VHS.

Jack London. Introd. John McKenna. Spec issue of *Eureka Studies in Teaching Short Fiction* 5.1 (2004): 3–88. Print.

James, William. *Psychology: Briefer Course*. 1892. Ed. Fredson Bowers and Ignas Skrupskelis. Cambridge: Harvard UP, 1984. Print.

Johnson, Martin. *Through the South Seas with Jack London*. New York: Dodd, 1913. Rpt. Cedar Springs: Wolf House Books, 1967. Print.

Johnston, Carolyn. *Jack London: An American Radical?* Westport: Greenwood, 1984. Print.

Kaplan, Amy. *The Social Construction of American Realism*. 1988. Chicago: U of Chicago P, 1992. Print.

Kaufman, Alan. "'We're Saxons . . . and Not Dagoes': The Role of Racism in Jack London's Late Novels." *Jack London Newsletter* 16.3 (1983): 96–103. Print.

Kazin, Alfred. *On Native Grounds: An Interpretation of Modern American Prose Literature*. 1942. Mariner Books, 2005. Print.

Kershaw, Alex. *Jack London: A Life*. New York: St. Martin's, 1999. Print.

Kingman, Russ. *Jack London: A Definitive Chronology*. Middletown: Rejl, 1992. Print.

———. *A Pictorial Life of Jack London*. New York: Crown, 1979. Print.

Kipnis, Ira, *The American Socialist Movement, 1897–1912*. New York: Columbia UP, 1952. Print.

Klondike Fever. Dir. Peter Carter. Perf. Rod Steiger and Angie Dickinson. Trinity Home Entertainment, 1980. DVD.

Kolodny, Annette. *The Lay of the Land: Metaphor as Experience and History in American Life and Letters*. Chapel Hill: U of North Carolina P, 1984 Print.

Krakauer, Jon. *Into the Wild*. New York: Anchor, 1997. Print.

Kübler-Ross, Elisabeth. *On Death and Dying*. New York: Scribner, 1997. Print.

Labor, Earle. "The Archetypal Woman as 'Martyr to Truth': Jack London's 'Samuel.'" *American Literary Realism* 24.2 (1992): 23–32. Print.

———. "Biography of Jack London." Berkove, *Critical Insights* 25–33.

———. "From 'All Gold Canyon' to *The Acorn-Planter*: Jack London's Agrarian Vision." *Western American Literature* 11.2 (1976): 83–102. Rpt. in Berkove, *Critical Insights* 196–217.

———. *Jack London: An American Life*. New York: Farrar, 2013. Print.

———. *Jack London*. New York: Twayne, 1974. Print. Twayne's United States Authors Ser. Print.

———. "Jack London's Symbolic Wilderness: Four Versions." *Nineteenth-Century Fiction* 17 (1962): 149–61. Rpt. in *Jack London: Essays in Criticism*. Ed. Ray Ownby. Santa Barbara: Peregrine, 1978: 31–42.

Labor, Earle, and King Hendricks. "Jack London's Twice-Told Tale." *Studies in Short Fiction* 4 (1967): 334–47. Print.

Labor, Earle, with Jeanne Campbell Reesman. *Jack London: Revised Edition*. New York: Twayne, 1994. Print.

Lasartemay, Eugene P., and Mary Rudge. *For Love of Jack London: His Life with Jennie Prentiss—A True Love Story*. New York: Vantage, 1991. Print.

Lauter, Paul. "London's Place in American Studies." *The Call: The Magazine of the Jack London Society* 14.1 (2003): 11–17. Print.

Lawlor, Mary. *Recalling the Wild: Naturalism and the Closing of the American West*. New Brunswick: Rutgers UP, 2000. Print.

Lentricchia, Frank. *The Gaiety of Language: An Essay on the Radical Poetics of W. B. Yeats and Wallace Stevens*. Berkeley: U of California, 1968. Print.

Levin, Harry. *The Power of Blackness: Hawthorne, Poe, Melville*. New York: Knopf, 1958. Print.

Lewis, Sinclair. *It Can't Happen Here*. Garden City: Sun Dial, 1935. Print.

Link, Eric Carl. *The Vast and Terrible Drama*. Tuscaloosa: U of Alabama P, 2004. Print.

Locke, John. *The Second Treatise of Government*. 1690. *Political Writings of John Locke*. Ed. and introd. David Wootton. New York: Penguin, 1993. 261–387. Print.

London, Charmian Kittredge. *The Book of Jack London*. 2 vols. New York: Century, 1921. Print.

———. *The Log of the* Snark. New York: Macmillan, 1915. Print.

London, Jack. *The Abysmal Brute*. Lincoln: U of Nebraska P, 2000. Print.

———. "Again the Literary Aspirant." *No Mentor but Myself*. Ed. Dale L. Walker. Port Washington: Kennikat, 1979. Print.

———. "All Gold Canyon." London, *Portable Jack London* 100–17.

———. "Amplification of Synopsis of the Last Half of Sea Novel." N.d. MS. Special Collections. U of Virginia Lib., Charlottesville.

———. *The Asian Writings of Jack London: Essays, Letters, Newspaper Dispatches, and Short Fiction*. Ed. Daniel A. Métraux. Lewiston: Mellen, 2009. Print.

———. *Before Adam*. Lincoln: U of Nebraska P, 2000. Print.

———. *Burning Daylight*. N.p.: Echo, n.d. Print.

———. *The Call of the Wild*. London, *Jack London: Novels and Stories* 1–86.

———. *The Call of the Wild*. London, *Portable Jack London* 347–417.

———. *The Call of the Wild*. Ed. Daniel Dyer. Norman: U of Oklahoma P, 1995. Print.

———. *The Call of the Wild*. Ed. Earl J. Wilcox and Elizabeth Wilcox. Boston: Houghton, 2003. Print. New Riverside Eds. Paul Lauter, gen. ed.

———. *The Call of the Wild*. New York: Lib. of Amer., 2009. Print. Paperback Classics.

———. *The Call of the Wild*. Ed. Nicholas Ruddick. Peterborough, Ont.: Broadview, 2010. Print.

———. The Call of the Wild *and "Bâtard."* New York: Simon, 2005. Print. Enriched Classics.

———. The Call of the Wild, White Fang, *and Other Stories*. Oxford: Oxford UP, 1990. Oxford World's Classics.

———. The Call of the Wild, White Fang, *and "To Build a Fire."* New York: Mod. Lib., 1998. Print. Mod. Lib. Classics.

———. *Complete Poetry of Jack London*. Ed. Daniel J. Wichlan. Waterford: Little Red Tree, 2007. Print.

———. *Complete Short Stories of Jack London*. Ed. Earle Labor, Robert C. Leitz III, and I. Milo Shepard. 3 vols. Stanford: Stanford UP, 1993. Print.

———. *Cruise of the* Snark. Introd. Anthony Brandt. Washington: Natl. Geographic Soc., 2003. Print.

———. *Cruise of the* Snark. N.p.: Narrative, n.d. Print.

———. *Cruise of the* Snark. New York: Penguin, 2004. Print.

———. *A Daughter of the Snows*. N.p.: Tutis, n.d. Print.

———. "The Economics of the Klondike." *American Monthly Review of Reviews* 21 Jan. 1900: 72–74. Print.

———. *Fantastic Tales: Jack London's Tales of Fantasy Fiction*. Ed. Dale Walker. Lincoln: U of Nebraska P, 1999. Print.

———. *The Game*. Lincoln: U of Nebraska P, 2001. Print.

———. "In a Far Country." London, *Portable Jack London* 11–25.

———. Interview with Jack London. By Sophie Treadwell. *San Francisco Bulletin* 28 Feb. 1914. *Materials: Interview II*. N.p., n.d. Web. 11 Nov. 2014. <http://www.jack-london.org/05-mat-interview2_e.htm>. 7 Nov. 2014.

———. *The Iron Heel*. Ed. John Auerbach. New York: Penguin, 2006. Print.

———. *The Iron Heel*. London, *Jack London: Novels and Social Writings* 315–554.

———. *Jack London: Novels and Social Writings*. Ed. Donald Pizer. New York: Lib. of Amer., 1982. Print.

———. *Jack London: Novels and Stories*. Ed. Donald Pizer. New York: Lib. of Amer., 1982. Print.

———. *Jack London on the Road*. Ed. Richard Etulain. Logan: Utah State UP, 1979. Print.

———. *Jack London on the Road: The Tramp Diary and Other Hobo Writings*. Ed. Richard Etulain. Logan: Utah State UP, 1979. Print.

———. *Jack London Reports: War Correspondence, Sports Articles, and Miscellaneous Writings*. Ed. King Hendricks and Irving Shepard. Garden City: Doubleday, 1970. Print.

———. *Jack London: San Francisco Stories*. Ed. Matthew Asprey. Sydney: Samizdat, 2011. Print.

———. *Jack London's Tales of Cannibals and Headhunters: Nine South Seas Stories by America's Master of Adventure*. Ed. Gary Riedl and Thomas R. Tietze. Albuquerque: U of New Mexico P, 2006. Print.

———. *Jack London: The Unpublished and Uncollected Articles and Essays*. Ed. Daniel J. Wichlan. Bloomington: AuthorHouse, 2007. Print.

———. *John Barleycorn: Alcoholic Memoirs*. New York: Oxford UP, 1989. Print. Oxford World's Classics.

———. *John Barleycorn*. London, *Jack London: Novels and Social Writings* 933–1112.

———. *John Barleycorn*. New York: Mod. Lib., 2001. Print. Mod. Lib. Classics.

———. *Klondike Tales*. New York: Mod. Lib., 2001. Print. Mod. Lib. Classics.

———. "Koolau the Leper." London, *Jack London: Novels and Stories* 883–98.

———. *Letters of Jack London*. Ed. Earle Labor, Robert C. Leitz III, and I. Milo Shepard. 3 vols. Stanford: Stanford UP, 1988. Print.

———. *Martin Eden*. Ed. Sam S. Baskett. New York: Rinehart, 1956. Print.

———. *Martin Eden*. London, *Jack London: Novels and Social Writings* 556–931.

———. *Martin Eden*. [New York]: Macmillan, 1913. *Project Gutenberg*. Project Gutenberg, n.d. Web. 21 Oct. 2014.

———. *Martin Eden*. New York: Mod. Lib., 2002. Print. Mod. Lib. Classics.

———. *Martin Eden*. New York: Penguin, 1993. Print. Penguin Classics.

———. *Martin Eden*. New York: Penguin, 1984. Print.

———. "Mexico's Army and Ours." *Collier's* 53 (30 May 1914): 5–7.

———. "The Night-Born." London, *Portable Jack London* 263–75.

———. *No Mentor but Myself: A Collection of Articles, Essays, Reviews, and Letters by Jack London, on Writing and Writers*. Ed. Dale Walker and Jeanne Reesman. Stanford: Stanford UP, 1999. Print.

———. *Northland Stories*. Introd. Jonathan Auerbach. New York: Penguin, 1997. Print. Penguin Twentieth-Century Classics.

———. "The Other Animals." *Collier's* 41 (5 Sept. 1908): 10+. Rpt. in Lutts 199–210.

———. *The People of the Abyss*. New York: Hill, 1995. Print.

———. "Pessimism, Optimism, and Patriotism." *Jack London Collector*, p. 18.

———. "A Piece of Steak." London, *Complete Short Stories* 2: 1629–45.

———. *The Portable Jack London*. Ed. Earle Labor. New York: Penguin, 1994. Print.

———. *Radical Jack London: Writings on War and Revolution*. Ed. Jonah Raskin. Berkeley: U of California P, 2008. Print.

———. *"Revolution" and Other Essays*. New York: Macmillan, 1909. Print.

———. *The Road*. Ed. Todd DePastino. New Brunswick: Rutgers UP, 2006. Print. Subterranean Lives.

———. *The Road*. LaVergne: Nabu, 2011. Print.

———. "Samuel." London, *Complete Short Stories* 2: 1611–28.

———. *The Scarlet Plague*. New York: Nuvision, 2008. Print.

———. *The Sea-Wolf*. London, *Jack London: Novels and Stories* 479–772.

———. *The Sea-Wolf*. New York: Mod. Lib., 2000. Print. Mod. Lib. Classics.

———. *The Sea-Wolf*. New York: Oxford UP, 1992. Print. Oxford World's Classics.

———. The Sea-Wolf *and Other Stories*. New York: Penguin, 1989. Print. Penguin Twentieth-Century Classics.

———. The Sea-Wolf *and Selected Stories*. New York: Signet, 2004. Print. Hundredth Anniversary ed.

———. *A Son of the Sun: The Adventures of Captain David Grief*. Introd. and notes by Gary Riedl and Thomas R. Tietze. Norman: U of Oklahoma P, 2001. Print.

———. "South of the Slot." London, *Complete Short Stories* 2: 1580–94.

———. "South of the Slot." 1909. *The Heath Anthology of American Literature*. 7th ed. Vol. C. Boston: Wadsworth, 2014. 1287–98. Print. 5 vols.

———. *South Sea Tales*. New York: Mod. Lib., 2002. Print. Mod. Lib. Classics.

———. *The Star Rover*. N.p.: Create Space, 2005. Print.

———. *The Star Rover*. New York: Mod. Lib., 2003. Print. Mod. Lib. Classics.

———. *Stories of Hawaii*. Ed. A. Grove Day. New York: Appleton-Century, 1965. Print.

———. "The Story of an Eyewitness." *Collier's* 36 (5 May 1906): 22–23. Print.

———. "The Strength of the Strong." London, *Complete Short Stories* 2: 1566–79.

———. "Synopsis of Sea Novel." N.d. MS. Special Collections. U of Virginia Lib., Charlottesville.

———. "Things Alive." London, *Portable Jack London* 483–85.

———. "To Build a Fire (11)." London, *Complete Short Stories* 2: 1301–15.

———. "To Build a Fire (1902)." London, *Portable Jack London* 56–62.

———. "To Build a Fire (1908)." London, *Portable Jack London* 136–50.

———. *"To Build a Fire" and Other Stories*. Ed. Donald Pizer. New York: Bantam, 2007. Print.

———. "To Cloudesley Johns." London, *Portable Jack London* 530–32.

———. "To Richard W. Gilder." 22 Dec. 1908. London, *Portable Jack London* 544–45.

———. *The Valley of the Moon*. New York: Macmillan, 1913. Print.

———. *The Valley of the Moon*. N.p.: Aegypan, n.d. Print.

———. "Wanted: A New Law of Development." *War of the Classes*. London: Mills, 1905. 173–208. Print.

———. *The War of the Classes*. New York: Macmillan, 1905. Print.

———. "What Socialism Is." 1895. *Jack London: The Unpublished and Uncollected Articles* 13–15.

———. "The White Silence." London, *Complete Short Stories* 1: 141–49.

London, Joan. *Jack London and His Times*. New York: Doubleday, 1939. Rpt. Seattle: U of Washington P, 1968. Print.

Lundblad, Michael. "From Animal to Animality Studies." *PMLA* 124.2 (2009): 496–502. Print.

Lundblad, Michael, and Marianne DeKoven. "Introduction: Animality and Advocacy." *Species Matters: Humane Advocacy and Cultural Theory*. Ed. DeKoven and Lundblad. New York: Columbia UP, 2012. 1–16. Print.

Lutts, Ralph H., ed. *The Wild Animal Story*. Philadelphia: Temple UP, 1998. Print.

Lynn, Kenneth S. "Jack London: The Brain Merchant." *The Dream of Success: A Study of the Modern American Imagination*. Boston: Little, 1955. 139–216. Print

Martin, Ronald E. *American Literature and the Universe of Force*. Durham: Duke UP, 1981. Print.

Martin, Stoddard. *California Writers: Jack London, John Steinbeck: The Tough Guys*. New York: St. Martin's, 1983. Print.

Marx, Karl. "Contribution to the Critique of Hegel's *Philosophy of the Right*: Introduction." Excerpt. *The Portable Karl Marx*. Ed. Eugene Kamenka. New York: Penguin, 1983. 115–24. Print.

Marx, Karl, and Friedrich Engels. *The Communist Manifesto*. 1848. Ed. Martin Malia. New York: Signet, 1998. Print.

———. *Manifesto of the Communist Party*. *The Marx-Engels Reader*. Ed. Robert C. Tucker. 2nd ed. New York: Norton, 1978. 473–500. Print.

McClintock, James I. "Jack London's Use of Carl Jung's Psychology of the Unconscious." *American Literature* 42.3 (1970): 336–47. Rpt. in Berkove, *Critical Insights* 167–79.

———. *White Logic: Jack London's Short Stories*. Cedar Rapids: Wolf House, 1975. Rpt. as *Jack London's Strong Truths: A Study of the Short Stories*. East Lansing: Michigan State UP, 1997.

McElrath, Joseph R., Jr. "Jack London's *Martin Eden*: the Multiple Dimensions of a Literary Masterpiece." Hodson and Reesman 77–97.

McKenna, John J. "Jack London's 'The Law of Life': A Twenty-First Century Prophesy." *Eureka Studies in Teaching Short Fiction* 5.1 (2004): 20–25. Print.

McLaughlin, Joseph. *Writing the Urban Jungle: Reading Empire in London from Doyle to Eliot*. Charlottesville: UP of Virginia, 2000. Print.

Melville, Herman. "Hawthorne and His Mosses." *The Piazza Tales and Other Prose Pieces 1839–1860*. Ed. Harrison Hayford, Alma A. MacDougall, and G. Thomas Tanselle. Evanston: Northwestern UP–Newberry Lib., 1987. 239–53. Print.

Mencken, H. L. "Jack London." Prejudices, *First Series*. New York: Knopf, 1919. 236–39. Print.

Merwin, W. S. *The Folding Cliffs: A Narrative*. New York: Random House, 1998. Print.

Mitchell, Lee Clark. "'And Rescue Us from Ourselves': Becoming Someone in Jack London's *The Sea-Wolf*." *American Literature* 70.2 (1998): 317–35. Print.

Moore, R. Laurence. *European Socialists and the American Promised Land*. Oxford: Oxford UP, 1970. Print.

Newlin, Keith, ed. *The Oxford Handbook of American Literary Naturalism*. Oxford: Oxford UP, 2011. Print.

Norris, Frank. "Novelists of the Future: The Training They Need." *The Literary Criticism of Frank Norris*. Ed. Donald Pizer. Austin: U of Texas P, 1964. 13–14. Print.

Note to "Samuel." *Bookman* May 1913: 285. Print.

Nuernberg, Susan, ed. *The Critical Response to Jack London*. Westport: Greenwood, 1995. Print.

———. Introduction. Nuernberg, *Critical Response* xxiii–xxxvi.

———. "New York City, Social Progress, and the Crowd: Jack London's 'Telic Action & Collective Stupidity.'" *American Literary Realism* 40.1 (2007): 83–88. Rpt. in Berkove, *Critical Insights* 314–20.

O'Connor, Richard. *Jack London: A Biography*. New York: Little, 1964. Print.

O'Donnell Arosteguy, Katie. "Things Men Must Do': Negotiating American Masculinity in Jack London's *The Valley of the Moon*." *Atenea* 28.1 (2008): 37–54. Print.

Oliveri, Vinnie. "Sex, Gender, and Death in *The Sea-Wolf*." *Pacific Coast Philology* 38 (2003): 99–115. Print.

Orgeron, Marsha. "Rethinking Authorship: Jack London and the Motion Picture Industry." *American Literature* 75.1 (2003): 91–117. Print.

Orwell, George. "Introduction to *Love of Life and Other Stories*, by Jack London." *In Front of Your Nose*. Ed. Sonia Orwell and Jan Angus. New York: Harcourt, 1968. 23–29. Print. Vol. 4 of *The Collected Essays, Journalism and Letters of George Orwell*.

Ownbey, Ray Wilson, ed. *Jack London: Essays in Criticism*. Santa Barbara: Peregrine Smith, 1978. Print.

Parker, Robert Dale. *How to Interpret Literature: Critical Theory for Literary and Cultural Studies*. New York: Oxford UP, 2008. Print.

Pease, Donald E. "Psychoanalyzing the Narrative Logics of Naturalism: *The Call of the Wild*." *Journal of Modern Literature*. 25.3–4 (2002): 14–39. Print.

Peluso, Robert. "Gazing at Royalty: Jack London's *The People of the Abyss* and the Emergence of American Imperialism." Cassuto and Reesman 55–74.

Petry, Ann. *The Street*. 1946. New York: Mariner, 1998. Print.

Piilani Kaluaikoolau, *The True Story of Kaluaikoolau: As Told by His Wife, Piilani*. 1906. Trans. Frances N. Frazier. Honolulu: U of Hawai'i P, 2001. Print.

Pizer, Donald. *Realism and Naturalism in Nineteenth-Century American Literature*. 1966. Rev. ed. Carbondale: Southern Illinois UP, 1984. Print.

Portelli, Alessandro. "Jack London's Missing Revolution: Notes on *The Iron Heel*." *Science Fictions Studies* 9 (1982): 180–94. Print.

Propp, V. *Morphology of the Folk Tale*. 2nd. ed. Trans. Louis A. Wagner. Austin: U of Texas P, 1968. Print.

Raskin, Jonah, ed. *The Radical Jack London: Writings on War and Revolution*. Berkeley: U of California P, 2008. Print.

Reesman, Jeanne Campbell. *Critical Companion to Jack London: A Literary Reference to His Life and Work*. New York: Facts on File, 2011. Print.

———. *Jack London: A Study of the Short Fiction*. New York: Twayne, 1998. Print.

———. "Jack London." *Oxford Bibliographies*. Oxford UP, 29 August 2012. Web. 1 Apr. 2015.

———. "Jack London, Jack Johnson, and the 'Great White Hope.'" Berkove, *Critical Insights* 321–62.

———. *Jack London's Racial Lives*. Athens: U of Georgia P, 2009. Print.

———. "The Literary Careers of Mark Twain and Jack London." Berkove, *Critical Insights* 76–95.

———. "Prospects for the Study of Jack London." *Resources for American Literary Study* 25.2 (1999): 133–58. Rpt. and rev. in *Prospects II*. Ed. Jackson Bryer and Richard Kopley. New York: AMS, 2009. Print.

Reesman, Jeanne Campbell, Sara S. Hodson, and Philip Adam. *Jack London, Photographer*. Athens: U of Georgia P, 2010. Print.

Renza, Louis A. "Edgar Allan Poe, Henry James, and Jack London: A Private Correspondence." *Boundary 2* 27.2 (2000): 83–111. Print.

Rideout, Walter B., *The Radical Novel in the United States, 1900–1954: Some Interrelations of Literature and Society*. New York, 1992. Print.

Riedl, Gary, and Thomas Tietze. "Introduction to *Jack London's Tales of Cannibals and Headhunters*." Berkove, *Critical Insights* 280–313.

———, eds. *Jack London's Tales of Cannibals and Headhunters: Nine South Seas Stories by America's Master of Adventure*. Albuquerque: U of New Mexico P, 2006. Print.

Riis, Jacob A. *How the Other Half Lives*. New York: Dover, 1971. Print.

Robillard, Douglas. "Anna Strunsky and Jack London." *Essays in Arts and Sciences* 30 (2001): 17–31. Print.

Roosevelt, Theodore. Excerpt from *The Strenuous Life*. Baym, Reesman, and Krupat 1156–59.

———. "'Nature Fakers.'" *Everybody's Magazine* 17 (Sept. 1907): 427–30. Rpt. in *The Wild Animal Story*. Ed. Ralph H. Lutts. Philadelphia: Temple UP, 1998. 192–98. Print.

Roper, Robert. "The *Paris Review* Perspective." Berkove, *Critical Insights* 34–38.

Rosenberg, Alex. "Darwinism in Moral Philosophy and Social Theory." *The Cambridge Companion to Darwin*. Ed. Jonathan Hodge and Gregory Radick. Cambridge UP, 2003, 310–32. Print.

Rossetti, Gina M. *Imagining the Primitive in Naturalist and Modernist Literature*. Columbia: U of Missouri P, 2006. Print.

Roth, Philip. *The Plot against America*. Boston: Houghton Mifflin, 2004. Print.

Rothberg, Abraham. "Old Stock: Jack London and His Valley of the Moon." *Southwest Review* 62 (1977): 361–68. Print.

Rousseau, Jean-Jacques. The Social Contract *and* Discourses. Trans. G. D. H. Cole. London: Everyman, 1993. Print.

Ruh, Adam, and Gary Scharnhorst. "'Fifteen Minutes on Socialism with Jack London': A Recovered Interview." *Studies in American Naturalism* 2 (2007): 66–77. Print.

Runyon, Damon. "A Nice Price." *Damon Runyon Omnibus*. *Project Gutenberg Australia*. Project Gutenberg, May 2014. Web. 21 Oct. 2014.

Sandburg, Carl. "Jack London: A Common Man." *Tomorrow* 2.4 (1906): 35–39. Print.

Schocket, Eric. "Undercover Explorations of the 'Other Half,' or the Writer as Class Transvestite." *Representations* 64 (1998): 109–33. Print.

The Sea-Wolf. Dir. Michael Curtiz. Perf. Edward G. Robinson and Ida Lupino. 1941. Warner Bros., 1998. VHS.

Sedgwick, Eve Kosofsky. *The Coherence of Gothic Conventions*. North Stratford: Ayer, 1999. Print.

———. *Epistemology of the Closet*. Berkeley: U of California P, 1990. Print.

Seltzer, Mark. *Bodies and Machines*. New York: Routledge, 1992. Print.

Shaheen, Aaron. "The Competing Narratives of Modernity in Jack London's *The Iron Heel*." *American Literary Realism, 1870–1910* 41.1 (2008): 35–51. Print.

Sherman, Joan. *Jack London: A Reference Guide*. Boston: Hall, 1977. Print.

Showalter, Elaine. *Sexual Anarchy: Gender and Culture at the Fin de Siecle*. New York: Bloomsbury, 1992. Print.

Sinclair, Andrew. *Jack: A Biography of Jack London*. New York: Harper, 1977. Print.

Sophocles. *The Theban Plays*; King Oedipus, Oedipus at Colonus, Antigone. London: Penguin, 1947. Print.

Sorrentino, Paul. "A Biographical Connection between Jack London and Kate Douglas Wiggin." *American Literary Realism* 32. (1999): 82–84. Print.

Spencer, Herbert. *First Principles*. 1862. New York: Appleton, 1930. Print.

———. *Principles of Sociology*. 3 vols. New York: Appleton, 1916. *HathiTrust Digital Library*. Web. 20 Oct. 2014.

———. *Social Statistics*. 1851. New York: Appleton, 1890. Print.

Speranza, Gino. *Race or Nation: A Conflict of Divided Loyalties*. Indianapolis: Bobbs, 1923. Print.

Stasz, Clarice. *American Dreamers: Charmian and Jack London*. New York: St. Martin's, 1988. Print.

———. "Androgyny in the Novels of Jack London." *Western American Literature* 11.2 (1976): 121–33. Rpt. in Berkove, *Critical Insights* 218–32.

———. "Charmian London, Eliza Shepard, and the Jack London Biographers: Misjudgments, Misunderstandings, and Malice." *Jack London Journal* 5 (1998): 219–40. Print.

———. *Jack London's Women*. Amherst: U of Massachusetts P, 2001. Print.

———. "Social Darwinism, Gender, and Humor in *Adventure*." Cassuto and Reesman 130–140.

Stoddard, Charles Warren. "The Lepers of Molokai." *Overland Monthly and Out West Magazine* 11.1 (1873): 89. Print.

Stone, Irving. *Sailor on Horseback: The Biography of Jack London*. Cambridge: Houghton, 1938. Print.

Streissguth, Thomas. *The Roaring Twenties*. New York: Infobase, 2009.

Swift, Jonathan. *Gulliver's Travels*. Rpt. New York: Heritage, 1910. Print.

Swinburne, Algernon Charles. *Poems and Ballads and Atalanta in Calydon*. Ed. Kenneth Haynes. London: Penguin, 2000. Print.

Szalay, Michael. *New Deal Modernism: American Literature and the Invention of the Welfare State*. Durham: Duke UP, 2000. Print.

Tabili, Laura. "'A Maritime Race': Masculinity and the Racial Division of Labor in British Merchant Ships, 1900–1939." *Iron Men, Wooden Women: Gender and Seafaring in the Atlantic World, 1700–1920*. Ed. Margaret S. Creighton and Lisa Norling. Baltimore: Johns Hopkins UP, 1996. 169–188. Print.

Tales of the Klondike. Perf. Orson Welles, Eva Gabor. Canadian Broadcasting Corporation, 16 May 1981. Television.

Tavernier-Courbin, Jacqueline. "Bessie: The First Mrs. Jack London." *Jack London Journal* 5 (1998): 168–218. Print.

———. The Call of the Wild*: A Naturalistic Romance*. New York: Twayne, 1994.

———, ed. *Critical Essays on Jack London*. Boston: Hall, 1983. Print.

———. "Jack London and Anna Strunsky: Lovers at Cross-Purposes." Hodson and Reesman 21–43.

———. "Jack London in Context." Berkove, *Critical Insights* 58–75.

———. "The Many Facets of Jack London's Humor." Tavernier-Courbin, *Critical Essays* 89–101.

———. "A Romantic Novel." *Jack London Journal* 1 (1994): 215–30. Rpt. in Berkove, *Critical Insights* 233–48.

Theisen, Kay M. "Realism as Represented in 'South of the Slot,' Naturalism as Represented in 'To Build a Fire': Critical Thinking and Pedagogy." *Eureka Studies in Teaching Short Fiction* 5.2 (2005): 99–107. Print.

Thoreau, Henry David. "Thoreau's Cry of the Human." *A Week on the Concord and Merrimac Rivers*. 1849. New York: Holt, Rinehart, 1963. 43. Print. Rpt. from *[San Francisco] Sunday Examiner Magazine* 15 July 1900.

To Build a Fire. Dir. David Cobham. Perf. Ian Hogg. Narr. Orson Welles. 1969. VCI, 1999. DVD.

Tolkien, J. R. R. *The Lord of the Rings*. 3 vols. Rpt. Boston: Houghton, 1994. Print.

Tsujii, Eiji. "Jack London and the Yellow Peril." *Jack London Newsletter* 9.2 (1976): 96–98. Print.

Tuan, Yi Fu. *Topophilia*. Englewood Cliffs: Prentice-Hall, 1974. Print.

Turner, Frederick Jackson. Excerpt from "The Significance of the Frontier in American History." Baym, Reesman, and Krupat 1149–53.

———. *The Frontier in American History*. New York: Holt, 1920. Print.

Van Vorst, Mrs. John, and Marie. *The Woman Who Toils, Being the Experience of Two Ladies as Factory Girls*. 1903. New York: BiblioBazaar, 2006. Print.

Viotte, Michel. *Jack London: L'enfant secret du rêve californien*. Gedeon Programmes France 3, 1995. VHS.

Walcutt, Charles Child. *American Literary Naturalism: A Divided Stream*. Minneapolis: U of Minnesota P, 1956. Print.

———. *Jack London*. Minneapolis: U of Minnesota P, 1967. Print.

———. "Jack London: Blond Beasts and Supermen." Berkove, *Critical Insights* 119–50. Rpt. from Walcutt, *American Literary Naturalism* 87–113.

Walker, Dale L., and James E. Sisson III. *The Fiction of Jack London: A Chronological Bibliography*. El Paso: Texas Western, 1972. Print.

Walker, Franklin. *Jack London and the Klondike: The Genesis of an American Writer*. San Marino: Huntington Lib., 1966. Print.

Walkout. Dir. Edward James Olmos. Home Box Office, 2006.

Wall Street. Dir. Oliver Stone. Perf. Michael Douglas and Charlie Sheen. 1987. Twentieth-Century Fox, 2007. DVD.

Ward, Susan. "Jack London's Women: Civilization vs. The Frontier." *Jack London Newsletter* 9 (1976): 81–85. Print.

Watson, Charles N., Jr. *The Novels of Jack London: A Reappraisal*. Madison: U of Wisconsin P, 1983. Print.

Waugh, Patricia. *Metafiction: The Theory and Practice of Self-Conscious Fiction*. New York: Routledge, 1988. Print.

Whalen-Bridge, John. *Political Fiction and the American Self*. Urbana: U of Illinois P, 1998. Print.

White Fang. Dir. Randal Kleiser. Per. Klaus Maria Brandauer, Ethan Hawke. Walt Disney Home Video, 1991. DVD.

Whitman, Walt. "Out of the Cradle Endlessly Rocking." *Leaves of Grass: Authoritative Texts, Prefaces, Whitman on His Art, Criticism*. Ed. Sculley Bradley and Harold William Blodgett. New York: Norton, 1973. 246–53. Print.

Wilcox, Earl J., ed. The Call of the Wild *by Jack London: A Casebook with Text, Background Sources, Reviews, Critical Essays, and Bibliography*. Chicago: Nelson, 1980. Print.

———. "'The Kipling of the Klondike': Naturalism in London's Early Fiction." *Jack London Newsletter* 6.1 (1973): 1–12. Rpt. in Berkove, *Critical Insights* 180–95.

Williams, Jay. *Author Under Sail: The Imagination of Jack London, 1893–1902*. Lincoln: U of Nebraska P, 2014. Print.

———. "The Cell." *Jack London Journal* 2 (1995): 133–55. Rpt. in Berkove, *Critical Insights* 249–79.

———. "Introduction to Sarah Orne Jewett, 'Human Documents: An Introduction.'" *Jack London Journal* 1 (1994): 268. Print.

———. "Jack London's Works by Date of Composition." *The Jack London Online Collection*. N.p., n.d. Web. <http://london.sonoma.edu/Bibliographies/comp_date.html>.

Williams, Jeffrey J. "Student Debt and the Spirit of Indenture." *Dissent* 55.4 (2008): 73–78. *Project Muse*. Web. 27 Jan. 2014.

Williams, Raymond. *Culture and Society, 1780–1950*. New York: Columbia UP, 1983. Print.

———. *Keywords: A Vocabulary of Culture and Society*. Rev. ed. Oxford: Oxford UP, 2014. Print.

Williams, Tony. "From Novel to Film." *Jack London's* The Sea-Wolf*: A Screenplay*. Ed. Rocco Fumento and Tony Williams. Carbondale: Southern Illinois UP, 1998. xvii–xxvi. Print.

———. "Hollywood and *The Sea-Wolf*." *Nineteenth-Century American Fiction on Screen*. Ed. R. Barton Palmer. Cambridge: Cambridge UP, 2007. 206–18. Print.

———. *Jack London: The Movies*. Middletown: Rejl, 1992. Print.

Wilson, Christopher P. "The Brain Worker: Jack London." *The Labor of Words: Literary Professionalism in the Progressive Era*. Athens: U of Georgia P, 1985. 92–112. Print.

Wilson, E. O. *On Human Nature*. Cambridge: Harvard UP–Bantam, 1978. Print.

Wolfe, Cary. *Animal Rites: American Culture, the Discourse of Species, and Posthumanist Theory*. Chicago: U of Chicago P, 2003. Print.

———. "Human, All Too Human: 'Animal Studies' and the Humanities." *PMLA* 124.2 (2009): 564–75. Print.

Zamen, Mark E. *Standing Room Only: Jack London's Controversial Career as a Public Speaker*. Fwd. Earle Labor. New York: Lang, 1990. Print.

Zitkala-Ša (Gertrude Simmons Bonnin). "A Warrior's Daughter" (1902). *Zitkala-Ša: American Indian Stories, Legends, and Other Writings*. New York: Penguin, 2003. 130–142. Print.

INDEX

Modern Language Association of America

Approaches to Teaching World Literature

To purchase MLA publications, visit www.mla.org/bookstore.

Achebe's Things Fall Apart. Ed. Bernth Lindfors. 1991.
Arthurian Tradition. Ed. Maureen Fries and Jeanie Watson. 1992.
Atwood's The Handmaid's Tale *and Other Works*. Ed. Sharon R. Wilson, Thomas B. Friedman, and Shannon Hengen. 1996.
Austen's Emma. Ed. Marcia McClintock Folsom. 2004.
Austen's Mansfield Park. Ed. Marcia McClintock Folsom and John Wiltshire. 2014.
Austen's Pride and Prejudice. Ed. Marcia McClintock Folsom. 1993.
Balzac's Old Goriot. Ed. Michal Peled Ginsburg. 2000.
Baudelaire's Flowers of Evil. Ed. Laurence M. Porter. 2000.
Beckett's Waiting for Godot. Ed. June Schlueter and Enoch Brater. 1991.
Behn's Oroonoko. Ed. Cynthia Richards and Mary Ann O'Donnell. 2014.
Beowulf. Ed. Jess B. Bessinger, Jr., and Robert F. Yeager. 1984.
Blake's Songs of Innocence and of Experience. Ed. Robert F. Gleckner and Mark L. Greenberg. 1989.
Boccaccio's Decameron. Ed. James H. McGregor. 2000.
British Women Poets of the Romantic Period. Ed. Stephen C. Behrendt and Harriet Kramer Linkin. 1997.
Charlotte Brontë's Jane Eyre. Ed. Diane Long Hoeveler and Beth Lau. 1993.
Emily Brontë's Wuthering Heights. Ed. Sue Lonoff and Terri A. Hasseler. 2006.
Byron's Poetry. Ed. Frederick W. Shilstone. 1991.
Works of Italo Calvino. Ed. Franco Ricci. 2013.
Camus's The Plague. Ed. Steven G. Kellman. 1985.
Cather's My Ántonia. Ed. Susan J. Rosowski. 1989.
Cervantes' Don Quixote. First edition. Ed. Richard Bjornson. 1984.
Cervantes' Don Quixote. Second edition. Ed. James A. Parr and Lisa Vollendorf. 2015.
Chaucer's Canterbury Tales. First edition Ed. Joseph Gibaldi. 1980.
Chaucer's Canterbury Tales. Second edition. Ed. Peter W. Travis and Frank Grady. 2014.
Chaucer's Troilus and Criseyde *and the Shorter Poems*. Ed. Tison Pugh and Angela Jane Weisl. 2006.
Chopin's The Awakening. Ed. Bernard Koloski. 1988.
Coetzee's Disgrace *and Other Works*. Ed. Laura Wright, Jane Poyner, and Elleke Boehmer. 2014.
Coleridge's Poetry and Prose. Ed. Richard E. Matlak. 1991.
Collodi's Pinocchio *and Its Adaptations*. Ed. Michael Sherberg. 2006.
Conrad's "Heart of Darkness" and "The Secret Sharer." Ed. Hunt Hawkins and Brian W. Shaffer. 2002.
Dante's Divine Comedy. Ed. Carole Slade. 1982.

Defoe's Robinson Crusoe. Ed. Maximillian E. Novak and Carl Fisher. 2005.
DeLillo's White Noise. Ed. Tim Engles and John N. Duvall. 2006.
Dickens's Bleak House. Ed. John O. Jordan and Gordon Bigelow. 2009.
Dickens's David Copperfield. Ed. Richard J. Dunn. 1984.
Dickinson's Poetry. Ed. Robin Riley Fast and Christine Mack Gordon. 1989.
Narrative of the Life of Frederick Douglass. Ed. James C. Hall. 1999.
Works of John Dryden. Ed. Jayne Lewis and Lisa Zunshine. 2013.
Duras's Ourika. Ed. Mary Ellen Birkett and Christopher Rivers. 2009.
Early Modern Spanish Drama. Ed. Laura R. Bass and Margaret R. Greer. 2006.
Eliot's Middlemarch. Ed. Kathleen Blake. 1990.
Eliot's Poetry and Plays. Ed. Jewel Spears Brooker. 1988.
Shorter Elizabethan Poetry. Ed. Patrick Cheney and Anne Lake Prescott. 2000.
Ellison's Invisible Man. Ed. Susan Resneck Parr and Pancho Savery. 1989.
English Renaissance Drama. Ed. Karen Bamford and Alexander Leggatt. 2002.
Works of Louise Erdrich. Ed. Gregg Sarris, Connie A. Jacobs, and James R. Giles. 2004.
Dramas of Euripides. Ed. Robin Mitchell-Boyask. 2002.
Faulkner's As I Lay Dying. Ed. Patrick O'Donnell and Lynda Zwinger. 2011.
Faulkner's The Sound and the Fury. Ed. Stephen Hahn and Arthur F. Kinney. 1996.
Fitzgerald's The Great Gatsby. Ed. Jackson R. Bryer and Nancy P. VanArsdale. 2009.
Flaubert's Madame Bovary. Ed. Laurence M. Porter and Eugene F. Gray. 1995.
García Márquez's One Hundred Years of Solitude. Ed. María Elena de Valdés and Mario J. Valdés. 1990.
Gilman's "The Yellow Wall-Paper" and Herland. Ed. Denise D. Knight and Cynthia J. Davis. 2003.
Goethe's Faust. Ed. Douglas J. McMillan. 1987.
Gothic Fiction: The British and American Traditions. Ed. Diane Long Hoeveler and Tamar Heller. 2003.
Poetry of John Gower. Ed. R. F. Yeager and Brian W. Gastle. 2011.
Grass's The Tin Drum. Ed. Monika Shafi. 2008.
H.D.'s Poetry and Prose. Ed. Annette Debo and Lara Vetter. 2011.
Hebrew Bible as Literature in Translation. Ed. Barry N. Olshen and Yael S. Feldman. 1989.
Homer's Iliad *and* Odyssey. Ed. Kostas Myrsiades. 1987.
Hurston's Their Eyes Were Watching God *and Other Works*. Ed. John Lowe. 2009.
Ibsen's A Doll House. Ed. Yvonne Shafer. 1985.
Henry James's Daisy Miller *and* The Turn of the Screw. Ed. Kimberly C. Reed and Peter G. Beidler. 2005.
Works of Samuel Johnson. Ed. David R. Anderson and Gwin J. Kolb. 1993.
Joyce's Ulysses. Ed. Kathleen McCormick and Erwin R. Steinberg. 1993.
Works of Sor Juana Inés de la Cruz. Ed. Emilie L. Bergmann and Stacey Schlau. 2007.
Kafka's Short Fiction. Ed. Richard T. Gray. 1995.

Keats's Poetry. Ed. Walter H. Evert and Jack W. Rhodes. 1991.
Kingston's The Woman Warrior. Ed. Shirley Geok-lin Lim. 1991.
Lafayette's The Princess of Clèves. Ed. Faith E. Beasley and Katharine Ann Jensen. 1998.
Writings of Bartolomé de Las Casas. Ed. Santa Arias and Eyda M. Merediz. 2008.
Works of D. H. Lawrence. Ed. M. Elizabeth Sargent and Garry Watson. 2001.
Lazarillo de Tormes *and the Picaresque Tradition*. Ed. Anne J. Cruz. 2009.
Lessing's The Golden Notebook. Ed. Carey Kaplan and Ellen Cronan Rose. 1989.
Works of Primo Levi. Ed. Nicholas Patruno and Roberta Ricci. 2014.
Works of Jack London. Ed. Kenneth K. Brandt and Jeanne Campbell Reesman. 2015.
Works of Naguib Mahfouz. Ed. Waïl S. Hassan and Susan Muaddi Darraj. 2011.
Mann's Death in Venice *and Other Short Fiction*. Ed. Jeffrey B. Berlin. 1992.
Marguerite de Navarre's Heptameron. Ed. Colette H. Winn. 2007.
Works of Carmen Martín Gaite. Ed. Joan L. Brown. 2013.
Medieval English Drama. Ed. Richard K. Emmerson. 1990.
Melville's Moby-Dick. Ed. Martin Bickman. 1985.
Metaphysical Poets. Ed. Sidney Gottlieb. 1990.
Miller's Death of a Salesman. Ed. Matthew C. Roudané. 1995.
Milton's Paradise Lost. First edition. Ed. Galbraith M. Crump. 1986.
Milton's Paradise Lost. Second edition. Ed. Peter C. Herman. 2012.
Milton's Shorter Poetry and Prose. Ed. Peter C. Herman. 2007.
Molière's Tartuffe *and Other Plays*. Ed. James F. Gaines and Michael S. Koppisch. 1995.
Momaday's The Way to Rainy Mountain. Ed. Kenneth M. Roemer. 1988.
Montaigne's Essays. Ed. Patrick Henry. 1994.
Novels of Toni Morrison. Ed. Nellie Y. McKay and Kathryn Earle. 1997.
Murasaki Shikibu's The Tale of Genji. Ed. Edward Kamens. 1993.
Nabokov's Lolita. Ed. Zoran Kuzmanovich and Galya Diment. 2008.
Works of Ngũgĩ wa Thiong'o. Ed. Oliver Lovesey. 2012.
Works of Tim O'Brien. Ed. Alex Vernon and Catherine Calloway. 2010.
Works of Ovid and the Ovidian Tradition. Ed. Barbara Weiden Boyd and Cora Fox. 2010.
Petrarch's Canzoniere *and the Petrarchan Tradition*. Ed. Christopher Kleinhenz and Andrea Dini. 2014.
Poe's Prose and Poetry. Ed. Jeffrey Andrew Weinstock and Tony Magistrale. 2008.
Pope's Poetry. Ed. Wallace Jackson and R. Paul Yoder. 1993.
Proust's Fiction and Criticism. Ed. Elyane Dezon-Jones and Inge Crosman Wimmers. 2003.
Puig's Kiss of the Spider Woman. Ed. Daniel Balderston and Francine Masiello. 2007.
Pynchon's The Crying of Lot 49 *and Other Works*. Ed. Thomas H. Schaub. 2008.
Works of François Rabelais. Ed. Todd W. Reeser and Floyd Gray. 2011.
Novels of Samuel Richardson. Ed. Lisa Zunshine and Jocelyn Harris. 2006.

Rousseau's Confessions *and* Reveries of the Solitary Walker. Ed. John C. O'Neal and Ourida Mostefai. 2003.
Scott's Waverley Novels. Ed. Evan Gottlieb and Ian Duncan. 2009.
Shakespeare's Hamlet. Ed. Bernice W. Kliman. 2001.
Shakespeare's King Lear. Ed. Robert H. Ray. 1986.
Shakespeare's Othello. Ed. Peter Erickson and Maurice Hunt. 2005.
Shakespeare's Romeo and Juliet. Ed. Maurice Hunt. 2000.
Shakespeare's The Taming of the Shrew. Ed. Margaret Dupuis and Grace Tiffany. 2013.
Shakespeare's The Tempest *and Other Late Romances*. Ed. Maurice Hunt. 1992.
Shelley's Frankenstein. Ed. Stephen C. Behrendt. 1990.
Shelley's Poetry. Ed. Spencer Hall. 1990.
Sir Gawain and the Green Knight. Ed. Miriam Youngerman Miller and Jane Chance. 1986.
Song of Roland. Ed. William W. Kibler and Leslie Zarker Morgan. 2006.
Spenser's Faerie Queene. Ed. David Lee Miller and Alexander Dunlop. 1994.
Stendhal's The Red and the Black. Ed. Dean de la Motte and Stirling Haig. 1999.
Sterne's Tristram Shandy. Ed. Melvyn New. 1989.
Works of Robert Louis Stevenson. Ed. Caroline McCracken-Flesher. 2013.
The Story of the Stone (Dream of the Red Chamber). Ed. Andrew Schonebaum and Tina Lu. 2012.
Stowe's Uncle Tom's Cabin. Ed. Elizabeth Ammons and Susan Belasco. 2000.
Swift's Gulliver's Travels. Ed. Edward J. Rielly. 1988.
Teresa of Ávila and the Spanish Mystics. Ed. Alison Weber. 2009.
Thoreau's Walden *and Other Works*. Ed. Richard J. Schneider. 1996.
Tolkien's The Lord of the Rings *and Other Works*. Ed. Leslie A. Donovan. 2015.
Tolstoy's Anna Karenina. Ed. Liza Knapp and Amy Mandelker. 2003.
Vergil's Aeneid. Ed. William S. Anderson and Lorina N. Quartarone. 2002.
Voltaire's Candide. Ed. Renée Waldinger. 1987.
Whitman's Leaves of Grass. Ed. Donald D. Kummings. 1990.
Wiesel's Night. Ed. Alan Rosen. 2007.
Works of Oscar Wilde. Ed. Philip E. Smith II. 2008.
Woolf's Mrs. Dalloway. Ed. Eileen Barrett and Ruth O. Saxton. 2009.
Woolf's To the Lighthouse. Ed. Beth Rigel Daugherty and Mary Beth Pringle. 2001.
Wordsworth's Poetry. Ed. Spencer Hall, with Jonathan Ramsey. 1986.
Wright's Native Son. Ed. James A. Miller. 1997.